CELEBRITY IN THE 21ST CENTURY

Selected Titles in ABC-CLIO's
CONTEMPORARY
WORLD ISSUES
Series

For a complete list of titles in this series, please visit
www.abc-clio.com.

Books in the Contemporary World Issues series address vital issues in today's society, such as genetic engineering, pollution, and biodiversity. Written by professional writers, scholars, and nonacademic experts, these books are authoritative, clearly written, up-to-date, and objective. They provide a good starting point for research by high school and college students, scholars, and general readers as well as by legislators, businesspeople, activists, and others.

Each book, carefully organized and easy to use, contains an overview of the subject, a detailed chronology, biographical sketches, facts and data and/or documents and other primary-source material, a directory of organizations and agencies, annotated lists of print and nonprint resources, and an index.

Readers of books in the Contemporary World Issues series will find the information they need to have a better understanding of the social, political, environmental, and economic issues facing the world today.

CELEBRITY IN THE 21ST CENTURY

A Reference Handbook

Larry Z. Leslie

CONTEMPORARY WORLD ISSUES

 ABC-CLIO

Santa Barbara, California • Denver, Colorado • Oxford, England

Library of Congress Cataloging-in-Publication Data

Leslie, Larry Z.
   Celebrity in the 21st century : a reference handbook / Larry Z. Leslie.
      p. cm.—(Contemporary world issues)
   Includes bibliographical references and index.
ISBN 978-1-59884-484-9 (hard copy : alk. paper)—ISBN 978-1-59884-485-6 (ebook)
1. Celebrities—United States—History—21st century. 2. Popular culture—United States—History—21st century. 3. United States—Civilization—21st century. 4. United States—Social life and customs—21st century. 5. Fame—Social aspects—United States—History—21st century. 6. Mass media—Social aspects—United States—History—21st century. 7. Celebrities—United States—Biography. I. Title.

E169.12.L454   2011
920.073—dc22   2010039842

ISBN: 978-1-59884-484-9
EISBN: 978-1-59884-485-6

15 14 13 12 11   1 2 3 4 5

This book is also available on the World Wide Web as an eBook.
Visit www.abc-clio.com for details.

ABC-CLIO, LLC
130 Cremona Drive, P.O. Box 1911
Santa Barbara, California 93116-1911

This book is printed on acid-free paper ∞

Manufactured in the United States of America

Contents

List of Tables

Preface

One of the popular features on *The Tonight Show with Jay Leno* is a segment called "Jaywalking." Leno, microphone in hand, stops individuals on the street and asks them simple questions: "Who gave America the Statue of Liberty?" "How many lungs do you have?" "What are the three branches of the federal government?" "Which weighs more: a pound of muscle or a pound of fat?" Naturally, the audience laughs when they give the wrong answers. Still, we are inclined to forgive these poorly informed folks for their lack of specific knowledge. After all, most people work hard just to get by; those questions have little to do with everyday life and are therefore not important to them. It might be interesting, however, if Leno were to ask these people on the street to name two or three celebrities. Chances are everyone could come up with a correct answer. We may not know our history, our physiology, or our weights and measures, but we know our celebrities. This says something about contemporary culture.

Contemporary culture is, for all practical purposes, popular culture. Media—that is, radio, television, magazines, music, video games, the Internet, film, and all the rest—are what we are most interested in and pay the most attention to. Celebrities are one of popular culture's most important products. There are many other pop culture products, of course: YouTube, Facebook, Hip-Hop music, the movies, and *American Idol*, to name a few. Celebrities owe their recognition to these and other aspects of popular culture that provide the means for them to implant themselves firmly in the minds and hearts of the public. Because celebrities are important to many of us, understanding what celebrity is all about can be useful in helping us understand ourselves.

While the notion of celebrity may seem insignificant to some people, the fact that celebrities play an important role in contemporary culture makes them subjects worthy of serious study. Is celebrity a broad category into which we can place anyone who has achieved any sort of recognition? If so, how much and what kind of recognition are required for one to be a celebrity? Is celebrity a narrow category into which we can place only those who have accomplishments and qualities beyond simple recognition? In some cases, this book will provide answers to those questions and raise new ones. In other cases, the book will allow readers to exercise their judgment or apply their opinions in answering a question.

Chapter 1 provides an historical context for understanding celebrity. Who were the first celebrities? The chapter explores celebrity in the early Egyptian, Greek, and Roman cultures. It follows the development of celebrity across time, from Europe to America, emphasizing media as the most important factor in modern celebrity. The public's role in celebrity is examined in this chapter, which concludes with a presentation of the different types of celebrity apparent in contemporary culture.

Chapter 2 addresses problems and issues, some of them controversial, relating to celebrities. Solutions to problems are often suggested. The chapter discusses what happens when celebrities behave in ways that violate society's social or moral standards. Profiles of magazines and television programs that feature news and gossip about celebrities reveal a great deal about these information outlets as well as about fans who follow their favorite celebrities. The role of electronic media in celebrity is explored, and the chapter concludes with an examination of several misconceptions about celebrity.

Because the world is essentially a global village, celebrities are no longer restricted to work or recognition in a single country. Worldwide celebrities are introduced in Chapter 3. Many worldwide celebrities work in either entertainment or politics. However, celebrities may become internationally recognized for their accomplishments in one (or more) of several other fields: the arts, science, medicine, and business, among others.

Readers who are interested in the historical development of celebrity in more detail than found in Chapter 1 will enjoy the chronology presented in Chapter 4. Beginning with the classical civilizations, the notion of celebrity is traced in its various developmental stages up to the present time. Celebrity is presented alongside other significant events. Chapter 5 shows the range of celebrity across many occupations by presenting biographical profiles of more than two dozen individuals who are currently celebrities and who will continue to be celebrities well into the second and third decades of the 21st century.

Chapter 6 presents data and documents relating to a variety of celebrity activities and situations. Readers will find information on celebrity families, earnings, and religious beliefs as well as data about celebrities who died young and celebrities who do not use their real names. Celebrity writers, celebrity chefs, celebrity criminals, celebrity musicians, and more provide additional insights into the role of celebrities in contemporary culture. Readers may be especially interested in the section detailing some of the letters (and objects) celebrities have received from their fans.

Many celebrities take an interest in the world beyond their own spheres of influence and contribute both time and money to worthy causes. Chapter 7 profiles celebrity charities and then looks at professional and business organizations popular with celebrities. Some readers will enjoy the list of celebrity news and gossip Web sites that concludes the chapter. For those who wish to read more about celebrities or study some aspect of celebrity in depth, Chapter 8 provides print and non-print resources. The annotated list of books, journals, articles, magazines, videos, audio CDs, and Internet sites shows the broad range of information available.

I wish to express my sincere appreciation to those who assisted in the preparation of this book. Special thanks to Bob Batchelor, a friend, colleague, and fellow golfer who first recommended me for the project and whose advice was extremely valuable. The gang at ABC-CLIO, particularly Robin Tutt, Mim Vasan, Cathleen Casey, and Jane Messah, as well as the production and marketing departments, provided guidance and support throughout. Thank you all. It was fun!

1

Background and History

A Modern Celebrity

Word of his death spread quickly. It raced first through the emergency room in a California hospital, spilled out into the street, then across the country, and around the world. Pop music icon Michael Jackson was dead. Many of his fans were hysterical. Some were sobbing; others dressed up as Michael and danced in tribute (Corliss 2009). In the days that followed, millions of people around the world—from England (where he was soon to begin a new concert tour) to Europe, China, and Japan—mourned the passing of one of the all-time great musical artists. Memorial services were held; fans flocked to record stores to buy his music.

It is not surprising that the death of a world-renowned celebrity would be widely acknowledged. However, at the time of his death in June 2009, Jackson had not had a hit record in years. There were other issues in Jackson's life: plastic surgery had altered his face almost beyond recognition; charges of child molestation in 1993 (settled out of court for a reported $20 million) and more molestation charges in 2003; that embarrassing incident in Germany in 2002 where he showed off his baby son to gathered fans by dangling the youngster over a hotel balcony (Corliss 2009). A jeweled glove on one hand, worn for no apparent reason? No problem. None of these things made any difference to his fans. They remembered him as a talented singer and a gifted dancer. They loved his music, his style, and his eccentricities. Why did this 50-year-old man remain a celebrity when his best years were clearly behind him?

Most of us could identify several people whom we consider to be celebrities. We would likely have a variety of reasons for selecting them. But the celebrity label may be applied to individuals too often these days. Not everyone is a celebrity. Some people are merely well known. Some people are famous. Is there a difference in being well known, being famous, and being a celebrity? What qualifies one as a celebrity? Where did the notion of celebrity begin? Who was the first celebrity? To understand the concept of celebrity and the use of the term in the 21st century, we need to look at how the word *celebrity* developed. It would be helpful to know its meaning and how that meaning changed over the years as the term was applied to noteworthy individuals.

Early Uses and Meanings

During the early days of civilization, primitive tribes probably celebrated often. We don't know much about how these early tribes communicated. Did they have languages? Perhaps. We do know they communicated something of their lives in drawings and paintings on cave walls. The cave paintings of Lascaux, France, and Altamira, Spain, are well known.

Paintings have also been discovered in Mexico, Peru, and other Central and South American countries. Some of the paintings seem to depict celebrations. A good day hunting, victory over a competing tribe for food or territory, the elevation of a tribe member to chief, or perhaps even the birth of a child were appropriate occasions for celebration. It is unlikely, however, that the tribes called their gatherings celebrations. They probably just all got together, had something to eat and drink, maybe smiled a lot, and then retired for the evening. It may not have been all that significant to them. Survival, however, was important to these early tribes, and celebrating their continued survival may have brought a temporary sense of relief, but little else. More hard work awaited them the next day. Today, of course, we celebrate all sorts of things: births, weddings, accomplishments at work, the achievement of a long-sought goal, a large pay increase, a winning sports team, and national holidays. Someone is always celebrating something. It has not always been this way.

One of the earliest uses of the word *celebration* in English was in a work by Sir Philip Sidney. In 1580, Sidney used the word to describe a performance or solemn ceremony, such as a ceremony of marriage. In 1600, Richard Hooker used *celebrity* to refer to "the condition of being much extolled or talked about" (Simpson and Weiner 1989, 1018–1019). The term can be found in the work of Samuel Johnson in 1751 to mean a feast or ceremony as well as publically praising or extolling an individual. In 1838, the poet Matthew Arnold further developed the term by noting that a celebrity was a public person, a celebrated character. Of course, no one really knows when or where the terms *celebration* and *celebrity* were first used.

The word *famous* can be found as early as the 1400s in Sir Thomas Malory's *Le Morte D'Arthur* (The Death of Arthur). Both John Milton and John Dryden used the word; for them, its meaning was rather straightforward: "celebrated in fame or public report; much talked about." The word also had negative meanings. It is safe to say that our current use of these terms derives mainly from their early usage in English literature. Furthermore, it is clear that for an individual to be famous, to be talked about or celebrated, a minimum set of conditions must apply: a role in public life; important or interesting accomplishments that are communicated to the general public; and recognition by the public that the individual's activities are significant enough to merit continued attention.

Is a famous person automatically a celebrity? One might infer that from the early uses described previously, but that judgment would be incorrect. Some scholars believe that "celebrities have been around for as long as human beings have lived together in groups" (McCutcheon, Maltby, Houran, and Ashe 2004, 60). This book rejects that view as simplistic. Celebrity, as the term is used in contemporary culture, is a concept that was not present in earlier civilizations but developed over time and depended, among other things, on the quality and flow of information to the general public. As new methods were developed to communicate with the public, the concept of celebrity evolved and became more complex. Obviously, the words *famous* and *celebrity* are closely related, but there is a marked difference among individuals to whom these terms are applied. That difference will be explained in the upcoming pages in this chapter. Some historical perspective is needed to provide context before we attempt to discuss celebrity in today's (and tomorrow's) culture. Why the history lesson? You can't have a complete understanding of anything unless you know the interrelated circumstances and conditions that enable it to occur. Celebrity is no exception (Cashmore 2006).

The Classical Civilizations

Three early civilizations are often called classical because of the excellent contributions they made, not only to their own time, but also to ours. The Egyptians (ca. 3100 BCE–200 BCE) were great builders. The Sphinx and the pyramids remain a testament to their construction skills. Remarkably well-preserved mummies show that the Egyptians were excellent embalmers. Egyptian farmers developed important irrigation techniques (Roberts 1993). For all their accomplishments, however, it is unlikely there were any celebrities in ancient Egypt, at least none that fits our modern notion of celebrity. Egypt's rulers are legendary: Ramses, Cleopatra, King Tutankhamen, and Hatshepsut. They led interesting and sometimes exciting lives. But the typical Egyptian probably did not think much about them. Aside from the hieroglyphics that were often part of Egyptian temples and monuments, and pictograms on clay tablets that few people other than Egyptian priests could read or interpret, communication was primarily oral (Fang 2008); stories about rulers and warriors were circulated, but life for most Egyptians was hard. Agriculture was extremely important, so many Egyptians worked the land. The success or failure of a crop depended on the Nile River overflowing its banks and depositing a rich layer of soil. Farmers, together with builders and tradesmen, were often drafted to work as slaves on the ruler's monuments or pyramid (Roberts 1993). While most slaves probably knew the name of the ruler for whom they worked, it is unlikely they held that person in high esteem. We in modern times know the names and accomplishments of many Egyptian rulers. We might even call Cleopatra, for example, a celebrity. But our judgment is based on historical perspective and a description of her life in art and literature over time. Cleopatra's Egyptians had no such perspective. She was their queen for awhile, well known among some, and of little interest to many. In short, there is no evidence that Egyptians recognized anyone as a celebrity.

The Greeks (ca. 1200 BCE–320 BCE), like the Egyptians, were skilled builders. The Parthenon still stands, and many buildings around the world use the Doric, Ionic, or Corinthian columns that were so much a part of Greek architecture. Cities became important in Greek civilization, particularly Athens and Sparta, although some Greeks still lived in rural areas. A few were landowners, but most rural residents worked the land as farmers and led pretty humble lives (Roberts 1993). Traders, craftsmen, shippers, and—above all—warriors were also major influences on Greek life. Communication about people and events was primarily oral. However, the culture made great advances in literature and philosophy: the plays of Sophocles; Homer's *Iliad and Odyssey*; and the philosophies of Socrates, Plato, and Aristotle. Plato's Academy was established, as were other schools, and education became important. Pythagoras was active in the field of mathematics. Powerful military figures, like Alexander the Great, led massive armies and eventually conquered the entire Persian Empire (Woolf 2008). Many Greeks lived in or near the cities, making it much easier to talk about major figures in the culture. No doubt some who attended the plays of Sophocles or read the work of Homer considered them famous. Socrates was something of a public figure, too, having committed suicide after being condemned to death by the government for his controversial views. While there was much talk about and recognition of these and other well-known individuals among the Greeks, there is no indication that these men rose to the level of celebrity. However, Alexander the Great probably came the closest to being a celebrity. He was widely known for his military and leadership skills, and because his armies acquired almost 3,000 miles of territory, there was much celebration upon his return from the various wars (Woolf 2008; Roberts 1993).

It should be noted that oral communication was not the only way to transmit information in the Egyptian and Greek cultures. Some information was written on papyrus or parchment, in addition to clay tablets. This information was not widely available to members of the general public, most of whom could not read anyway. Although some citizens listened to debates in the Greek Assembly (Thomas 1992), the typical Greek, like the Egyptian, had to depend on hearing the latest news from a friend or neighbor. The news might not have been accurate. Word-of-mouth communication is often unreliable; rumors become truth; stories are enhanced. Nevertheless, we can see some progress from the Egyptian to the Greek culture. The Greeks were more likely to have known about the major figures in their culture and were much closer to identifying a celebrity than were the Egyptians. Most Greek literature was written to be heard or sung (Thomas 1992). Those in attendance at such performances most likely knew, for example, who wrote the play they were watching. We must take care, however, not to force our 21st-century perspective on the historical record of these early civilizations. By our modern standards, Socrates, Sophocles, Plato, and Aristotle would indeed all be celebrities. But there is no evidence that they were considered such by the Greeks. They were well known, but—as we shall see—being well known is not enough to make one a celebrity, particularly in the 21st century, and almost certainly not in the early civilizations where the concept of celebrity did not exist.

The third classical civilization belongs to the Romans (ca. 753 BCE–410 CE) who changed life in several ways. The Roman Empire extended over much of the known world, thanks to a large and aggressive army. Although some men were full-time, professional soldiers, every male citizen who owned property was required to serve in the military, if needed. Other Roman citizens were shopkeepers, tradesmen, or farmers (Roberts 1993). The Romans made important contributions to engineering, art, and literature. Christianity developed during this period and later became the official religion of the empire (Woolf 2008). Were there celebrities in Roman culture? Many individuals were famous or well known: Julius Caesar, Nero, Caligula, Marcus Aurelius, Mark Antony, Horace, Ovid, and Virgil, among others. These men fit precisely the definition of famous presented earlier in this chapter. They were in public life, their accomplishments were important and interesting, information about them was communicated to the public, and the public judged their actions to be worthy of continued attention. We have seen that communication was primarily oral in the Egyptian and Greek civilizations. The Romans added an important component to oral communication. News and announcements were read aloud to crowds in the forum or other public places, but the information was mostly limited to items approved by the government—most likely the emperor. Nevertheless, this practice enabled the general public to become better acquainted with the culture's influential individuals. The public did not always approve of what it heard, but hearing about the exploits of the army or the latest proclamation by the emperor focused attention on those individuals and actions likely to impact public life. To be sure, some communication was written, probably on parchment or papyrus; documents containing announcements or proclamations were often posted after being read aloud, but few of these documents have survived. It is doubtful Roman citizens had much access to them; most Romans could neither read nor write.

To answer an earlier question, were there celebrities in Roman culture? No major figures in Roman life were famous or well known, and while there were plenty of celebrations during Roman times, there is no evidence that any famous or well-known individuals were called celebrities.

The World in Transition

The collapse of the Roman Empire marked the end of the classical period and the beginning of the medieval era in world history (Woolf 2008). Many aspects of the classical era faded away and were replaced by new practices and new traditions. Civilizations began to grow in other parts of the world: the Celts were active in Western Europe and Northern Spain; the Germanic people prospered in Northern Europe; cultures developed in India, China, and Japan; across the Atlantic, the Mayan civilization held sway in Central America. These were important and influential additions to the culture of the world. Nevertheless, we will continue to concentrate on the development of culture in Europe as the leading influence on many aspects of contemporary American life.

Religion and the church were the major influences on life during the medieval era, sometimes called the Middle Ages (ca. 400 CE–1400 CE). This historical period saw much political and social activity; important contributions were made to music, literature, and art; moreover, Christianity survived the fall of Rome and became a powerful force during this period. The pope became a major political figure as well as the most important religious leader. The Crusades occurred during this period, the Vikings expanded their culture, and the Black Death swept across Europe (Woolf 2008). Clearly, the Middle Ages were years of change. A few individuals became well known during this time, but their fame was not widespread. It was more difficult to communicate with increasingly larger populations and expanding territories. Communication was primarily oral, but transportation was improving, and information flowed more easily from one area to another than was the case with previous civilizations. Still, by one estimate, a typical man in the 10th century may have encountered fewer than 200 people during his whole life (Menache 1990). Monks, living in monasteries, worked on manuscripts, but most people still could not read. Thus, fewer people were famous because the public was larger and spread over many developing territories. If you were famous, you were likely well known primarily in your own limited geographical area. The exception, of course, was the pope who was widely known because of his influence on religious and political life. Well-known individuals during this historical period included the Italian poet Dante, explorer Marco Polo, Charlemagne, and Thomas Becket, the Archbishop of Canterbury.

Important Progress in Europe

Communication improved significantly during the Renaissance/ Reformation period (ca. 1400 CE–1650 CE). A clear shift occurred from handwritten parchment documents to printed material. This major development was the result of the invention of moveable type by Johannes Gutenberg in the mid-15th century. Although paper had been invented by the Chinese much earlier, its movement into Western culture was slow. Copies of manuscripts were still being written by hand and woodblock printing was still in fashion (Kleinschmidt 2000). Nevertheless, with both paper and the printing press now available, all sorts of documents could be produced and distributed (Rodman 2006). Although some historians believe the invention of the printing press did not have an immediate impact and was therefore not much of a revolution (Eisenstein 2005), there can be little doubt that it was important in bringing about change. Use of the printing press spread rapidly throughout Europe (Fussel 2005). More people learned to read. It became easier for individuals in public life to become well known for their accomplishments. Today, we are well acquainted with the famous people of this era: Chaucer, Michelangelo, Copernicus, Galileo, Henry VIII, Martin Luther, El Greco, Rembrandt, and Shakespeare. The actions and accomplishments of many of these individuals surely came to the attention of the general public. Were they celebrities? By this time, the word *celebrity* had sprung from the more general *celebration* in some of the literature of the time, although there is no evidence that this term was regularly applied to the famous in public life. It is important to note that oral communication was not replaced by the printed word during this time. Most communication required direct contact between communicator and audience in guild meetings, community assemblies, religious gatherings, and the like (Menache 1990).

Change came more rapidly during the Enlightenment (ca. 1650 CE–1850 CE). The arrival of this important historical period signaled dramatic progress in all areas of life (Roberts 1993). The human spirit and mind were awakened; the ability to reason led science to become a major influence in understanding the physical world; significant contributions were made in art, music, philosophy, and religion. There was no mass communication in this era, in the sense that we use the term today. Written communication included letters, diaries, literature, and other material, but usually only members of the upper class could read and write; those who were well-off could often be found in salons, academies, and coffee shops. On the other hand, shopkeepers, semi-skilled workers, servants, even some skilled laborers often got their information in conversations with neighbors, friends, or those they met at festivals or fairs. Market days in rural areas were popular settings for exchanging information. Books were popular during the Enlightenment, but they were expensive and beyond the means of all but the most affluent (Munck 2000). Still, the list of famous people during this time reads like a *Who's Who* of history: philosophers Descartes, Voltaire, and Rousseau; musicians Handel, Hayden, Mozart, Bach, and Beethoven; French rulers Louis XIV, Louis XVI, and Marie Antoinette; English painter William Hogarth; scholar and mathematician Isaac Newton; and English poet Alexander Pope.

The entire world was now well acquainted with written communication. Although oral communication did not disappear, of course, many people felt the written word had a power the spoken word lacked. Even today, we say, "Get it in writing." As people became educated, they were more likely to read. Newspapers were common in 18th-century Europe; it was easier to follow the lives and actions of important people in public life.

We should pause for a moment here, having just completed a whirlwind trip through the history of Western civilization, and recall what we know. We know early civilizations had important, noteworthy people in public life and that some information about their actions and accomplishments was available to the public primarily through oral communication. Written communication existed, but its usefulness to the general public was limited. We found there were no celebrities in these early cultures, but that there were people who were well known or famous. Such people played an important role in public life, had their actions or accomplishments communicated to the public, and were significant enough to merit continued public attention.

Additionally, we noted that the invention of the printing press and paper enabled the public to receive all sorts of printed or written information.

America Stirs

Across the Atlantic, a new nation was growing. The New England colonies were established around 1620. The Declaration of Independence was signed in 1776. Anyone who has studied American history knows the challenges faced by Colonial America, particularly in dealing with Native Americans and with the influence of foreign nations. We also know who was famous during 18th-century America: Benjamin Franklin, Thomas Jefferson, George Washington, and a host of others typically called the Founding Fathers. We also recognize Nathaniel Hawthorne, Edgar Allan Poe, Ralph Waldo Emerson, and Henry David Thoreau, among others, as making significant contributions to early American literature. Artists were busy in early America, too: John J. Audubon, Frederic Remington, Nathaniel Currier, James Ives, and James Whistler. The first regularly published newspaper in America was the *Boston News-Letter* in 1704. It printed political documents and opinion pieces; gossip and rumors, neither very accurate, were also part of the paper. The *Boston Gazette* came along in 1719 (Rodman 2006).

The Rise of Media in 19th-Century America

The arrival of the 19th century in America signaled the beginning of a new age: the era of mass media. The public was no longer dependent only on oral communication and simple printed documents for news and information. When the penny press arrived in 1833, America had its first mass medium (Campbell, Martin, and Fabos 2007). Newspapers were now within the reach of many Americans. For just one cent, readers could get gossip, crime news, and advertising messages. Although magazines appeared a few years before the penny press, their development was slow. *The Saturday Evening Post* was the first magazine to have a large public following (Biagi 2005). By the beginning of the 20th century, more than six thousand magazines were being published, although most of them were intended for local or regional audiences (Campbell et al. 2007).

One new technology is noteworthy here, although it did not lead to another mass medium. The first electric telegraph line, in 1844, made communication across long distances almost instantaneous. Where newspapers and magazines had to be transported from where they were printed to where they would be sold, the "lightning lines" of the telegraph had no such problem (Czitrom 1982). However, only brief messages could be sent by telegraph; therefore, we must consider it a personal medium, not a mass medium.

Progress came rapidly as America moved toward the end of the 19th century. The book industry flourished; mass market paperbacks became available in the 1870s. Newspapers increased their circulation. Engravings and illustrations were added to magazines, making them more appealing to the public. Early steps were taken in developing sound recordings and film images. Experiments with radio waves were being conducted and work was underway on a cathode ray tube, the forerunner of the television picture tube (Campbell et al. 2007). Even as media were appearing on the American landscape, there was much political and social change elsewhere in the country. America's population was growing, oil was discovered in Pennsylvania, steel plants were established, and the telephone was invented. Americans went to war three times during these years: the Mexican-American War, the Civil War, and the Spanish-American War (Miller and Thompson 2006). The new mass media, primarily newspapers and magazines at this point, enabled the American public to follow social, political, and technological developments, and to become well acquainted with individuals who were making contributions to public life.

Were there celebrities in 19th-century America? Up to this point, we've been saying that individuals who were active in public life often became famous or well known because their actions or accomplishments were communicated to the public and were significant enough to merit continued attention, but that they did not qualify as celebrities. Here's another important question, the answer to which will guide our discussion for the remainder of this chapter. How does one go from being famous or well known to being a celebrity? It is really quite simple: *celebrity depends on regular media exposure.* Moreover, an individual must, in some way, *seek fame and recognition.* In other words, one's activities must be reported by the media, or, in some cases, be made available to the public as media. Here's an example. English novelist

Charles Dickens wrote more than 30 novels as well as numerous short stories and nonfiction articles. Charles Dickens was a celebrity. His novels were usually serialized in magazines before being collected as books. He sought fame and recognition by touring England and America, reading his work to audiences in formal, lecture-like settings. In both England and America, the public read about him in the newspapers, read his work in magazines or books, and perhaps attended or heard talk about his performance at a reading. Clearly, the media most responsible for Dickens's celebrity were magazines and books, but he solidified his place as a celebrity by seeking fame and recognition.

During the 19th century, a great many Americans were famous or well known: President Abraham Lincoln; Civil War generals Robert E. Lee and Ulysses S. Grant; architect Frank Lloyd Wright; inventor Thomas Edison; industrialists Andrew Carnegie and John D. Rockefeller; newspaper publisher William Randolph Hearst; poet Walt Whitman; writer and satirist Mark Twain, and a host of others in many areas of American life. Do these individuals qualify as celebrities? Yes, some of them do. It could be argued that Lincoln, Lee, and Grant were not fame seekers, but merely men thrust into the public consciousness by the difficulty and scope of their work. But the others in this list were indeed celebrities. They sought to be recognized and honored for their accomplishments. Americans not only read about these individuals in newspapers and magazines, but also connected personally with them. Whitman's poetry and Hearst's newspapers were available to the public, for example. Edison's telephone, light bulb, and primitive motion pictures were stunning additions to American life (Miller and Thompson 2006). In other words, the work of the famous and well known became an important part of the lives of many Americans who welcomed these advances, were anxious to see what was to come next, and depended on media to keep them informed.

Media Gain Strength in the Early 20th Century

In his book *Intimate Strangers: The Culture of Celebrity*, Richard Schickel (1985) makes this bold statement: "there was no such thing as celebrity prior to the beginning of the 20th century."

He notes that in the 1940s, the word *celebrity* was almost never used in print or conversation. If one read about people in the papers or in magazine profiles, or heard about them on the air, they were called "successful" or "famous" (23).

That changed in 1959 with the publication of Blackwell and Amory's *International Celebrity Register*, a book containing brief, biographical summaries of more than 2,000 public figures. The book covered "a multitude of fields" and contained profiles of sports figures, businessmen, scientists, comedians, young actresses, and even Supreme Court justices (Ponce de Leon 2002, 11). The book was immediately controversial. Individuals had apparently been selected for the book based not on their accomplishments, but on their visibility. The historian Daniel J. Boorstin roundly criticized the book, suggesting it embraced "the vacuous and the ephemeral" and that those listed were merely famous for being well known. To Boorstin, this sort of celebrity was a "pseudo-human event," with little relationship to reality (12). Nevertheless, visibility is what distinguishes celebrities from the masses; moreover, visibility is made possible by the media's shaping of celebrities as extraordinary, complex, and interesting individuals with unique talents and gifts (Ponce de Leon 2002). Visibility was made possible by an expanding media. Newspapers reported on important political, social, and business issues. The magazine industry advanced with the publication of the *Ladies Home Journal*, *Reader's Digest*, *Time*, and *Life*. Book publishing prospered; book clubs were introduced. Many American homes had phonographs. Early movie theaters, called nickelodeons, brought film to many cities. Radio, already beginning to form broadcasting networks, became an influential mass medium, reaching what some call its golden age in the 1930s (Campbell et al. 2007). By the time World War II began in 1939 (America officially entered the war in 1941), print, radio, recording, and film were well established as integral parts of American life; television was in its infancy, having been introduced to the public by President Franklin D. Roosevelt at the 1939 World's Fair (Biagi 2005). With the coming of television and the end of World War II, 20th-century media were poised to become an even more powerful and influential force in American life. One thing is clear: becoming a celebrity was fairly easy in the 20th century. Individuals in public life, or the public sphere as it is sometimes called, could not avoid media attention. Many of them did not want to avoid it, but depended on it, in fact, to lift them to celebrity status.

From the end of World War II until the early 1980s, it is not enough to say that media grew. The word that best describes the tremendous advances in media technology and content is the verb *exploded*. Look at what happened during those years:

- cassette tapes became popular
- rock-and-roll music and then hip-hop captured the attention of young and old alike
- cable television provided diverse programming to many American homes
- FM radio surpassed AM radio in popularity
- the Corporation for Public Broadcasting was authorized
- the Internet was established, followed soon by the development of e-mail
- video cassette recorders (VCRs) allowed Americans to see movies at home on VHS-formatted videocassettes
- *USA Today*, America's first national newspaper, began publication
- compact discs (CDs) replaced cassette tapes as personal sources of recorded music
- Cable News Network (CNN) became the first full-time cable news outlet
- fiber optic cable and hypertext enabled information to be transmitted and linked rapidly (Campbell et al. 2007).

This rich media environment made it possible for individuals in public life—and even some in private life—to become celebrities. Still, "the emergence of celebrity depended to a large extent on the social, economic, and political transformations that have remade the world since the 16th century, and by new values and beliefs" that have resulted in modernization. Thus, *celebrity can be seen as fame modernized* (Ponce de Leon 2002, 13).

Media Become Powerful in the Late 20th Century

When you think about it, progress is a remarkable thing. So much can happen in a culture in a very short time. Sometimes the word *progress* does not do justice to the breadth and depth of change. This is certainly true if one considers media progress in the late 20th century. Media growth is steady and considerable attention is given to improving some of the products and services developed in the first part of the century. Talk becomes a popular radio format. Multiple-screen theaters open. Web browsers make Internet use easy; the Internet becomes a mass medium. Online shopping is common. Some big-city newspapers begin to fail as consumers turn to the Internet for news and information. Digital video discs (DVDs) replace videocassettes for viewing movies at home. Cable news outlets expand. High definition broadcasting begins using digital rather than analog signals (Campbell et al. 2007; Biagi 2005). In effect, at century's end, "the bar had been lowered: in previous decades famous figures . . . had to work harder to achieve fame or notoriety" (Cashmore 2006, p. 4). Celebrities now find it easy to reach, capture, and sustain the interest of the general public in their lives and activities.

The Public's Role in Celebrity

It might appear that celebrity is all media's doing, that media exposure alone can make an obscure individual famous. While it is true that media play an important part in celebrity, the general public plays a significant role, too. As Braudy (1986) writes, "in a society committed to progress, the seeking of fame, the climbing of the ladder of renown expresses something essential in that society's nature" (5).

We think we know celebrities; we think we know what motivates and inspires them. We believe ourselves to be much closer to them than we are to individuals with whom we might have regular, professional contact—doctors, pharmacists, hair stylists, retail clerks, mechanics, and the like. We know celebrities better than we know those who provide us routine services, or think we do. However, in reality our relationship with celebrities is based not on real intimacy but on the illusion of intimacy. We really don't know celebrities, and they really don't want to know us. A famous movie star put it this way: when you are faced with a crowd, "walk fast. Don't stop and shake hands. You touch them, they don't touch you" (Schickel 1985, 5). We know celebrities are not normal members of society, but they are extensions of what is normal, extensions of our desires. Their fame allows them to stand apart from us, but with our approval. We give them this power because they appear to be the personification of individuality, to be themselves in a way no one else can afford to be. We don't mind if they are occasionally socially irresponsible (Braudy 1986; Schickel 1985). In short, we want to be like them, but we know we can't. We can, however, live a little vicariously through them.

Sociologist Francesco Alberoni suggests that certain conditions must exist for individuals to become famous, to become stars or celebrities, among which are the following: an economic environment conducive to the production of media texts such as films, television programs, music recordings, books, and the like; the ability of celebrities or their representatives to publicize or market celebrity talent; the ability of celebrities to connect with the collective unconscious, to speak to the inner wants and needs of the public (Dyer 1998). The term *collective unconscious* was described by psychiatrist Carl Jung as "a form of the unconscious (that part of the mind containing memories and impulses of which the individual is not aware) common to mankind as a whole and originating in the inherited structure of the brain. According to Jung, the collective unconscious contains archetypes, or universal primordial images and ideas" (*Encyclopedia Britannica*). Stated simply, celebrities appeal to "the public's primal fantasies and basic emotions, lifting people from their everyday lives and making them believe anything's possible" (Steele 2009). Celebrities play to our innate tendencies, tricking us into believing that they are our "intimate daily companions." They "summon our most human yearnings: to love, admire, copy, and, of course, to gossip and to jeer" (Flora 2004). The lives of celebrities "create a sort of psychic energy field that surrounds us and penetrates us, binding our universe together" (Schickel 1985, 275). To the typical member of the general public, a celebrity appears "to fulfill both a dream of autonomy and, at the same time, a dream of intimate, almost familial connection among figures of glamour and authority" (255).

As times change, media become more influential, and the number of people who are famous and well known increases, our current definition of celebrity may soon be inadequate to define the complex nature of the phenomenon, particularly as we move deeper into the 21st century. Before going forward, let's pause again and review our current definition. At the end of the 20th century, a celebrity can be said to have each of the following characteristics:

1. leads a public life; is involved in work or activity in some area of the public sphere
2. has accomplishments of interest and importance to the general public
3. is well known or famous, usually because of those accomplishments
4. seeks to become a celebrity by finding ways to be regularly seen and heard, thus maintaining status as a well-known, famous individual
5. is highly visible on or in media
6. connects with the public on a subconscious level, embodying its dreams and desires.

Celebrities as Stars

Are celebrities also stars? Maybe, but not necessarily. We should be aware that the various words used to describe those in public life who have gained notoriety, that is, those who are generally known and talked of, are not precise synonyms. There is a difference in meaning among the following: *well known*, *famous*, *celebrity*, and *star*. The difference may not be obvious if one consults a thesaurus or a dictionary; those words are normally used interchangeably in daily discourse. However, this book strives to present the concept of celebrity precisely so that it may be clearly understood. This means we must be careful in how we use words that are related but may not have exactly the same meaning. For example, Lai (2006) makes an interesting distinction between the terms *star* and *celebrity*. While acknowledging that scholars often disagree on the distinctions between the two, "in general, celebrity is used to refer to anyone who has achieved widespread renown, either by merit, accident, or notoriety. Star is more frequently used to refer to individuals who have become famous via their activities in the art and entertainment industries . . ." (p. 229). For example, the Dalai Lama is a Tibetan spiritual leader. He is committed to promoting compassion, forgiveness, tolerance, contentment, and self-discipline. He travels widely, receives awards for his work, appears frequently in the news, and even has his own Web site (www.dalailama.com). The Dalai Lama is, by our current definition, a celebrity, but he is not a star; in all likelihood, he would reject both the celebrity and star labels as being inappropriate for a spiritual leader. On the other hand, Kevin Bacon, who once claimed to have worked with everyone in Hollywood, is an accomplished actor. He is a celebrity, but because his activities occur in the entertainment industry, he is also a star. The Kevin Bacon Game, sometimes called the Six Degrees of Kevin Bacon, allows one to link Bacon to any other actor in fewer than six movies (http://oracleofbacon.org/). Additionally, Bacon has teamed with his brother Michael to form a band called The Bacon Brothers. This adds to Bacon's popularity and creates a sort of mystique around him.

Herwitz (2008) has a slightly different view of a star. He believes a star is a cultural icon, that is, a symbol of an idea or concept, or an individual idolized by some. To be a star, a synergy must exist between one's performance and one's personal life. Princess Diana is a good example. Before her untimely death in 1997, Diana was married to Prince Charles, the future king of England, and carried the title Princess of Wales. With her husband and sons, William and Harry, Her Royal Highness represented a fresh face and a welcome change from what many considered the stuffiness of royalty. Her personal life as wife and mother was supplemented by her work for many charitable causes. She was seen embracing an AIDS patient, talking with a leper, and cradling children whose limbs had been damaged by land mines (Leslie 2004). Her performance in these and other instances blended nicely with her personal life as a member of England's royal family. This synergy made her not only a celebrity, but also a star. Given the outpouring of grief at her death, it is safe to say that she was idolized by many the world over.

The Remarkable 21st Century

Because we are living in it, the 21st century may not seem all that amazing to us. We may be victims of the boiled frog phenomenon. You've probably heard the story before, but it bears repeating here because it is a likely explanation of why we are so blasé about living in contemporary culture. If you take a frog and place it in a pot of extremely hot water, the frog will try to jump out of the pot. But if you put that same frog in a pot of tepid water and gradually increase the heat, the frog will sit quietly in the pot, adjusting easily to the small increases in temperature until the water is warm enough to induce unconsciousness, allowing the frog to ultimately be boiled to death (Pollard 2004). It is unclear whether scientists have ever conducted this experiment; nevertheless, the story makes a valid point. Many people are relatively unaware of the true significance of the steady advance of cultural change. Sure, people recognize, even embrace, change. They know, for example, that the wireless cell phone is replacing the old home landline, that the microwave or convection oven is squeezing out the old electric range, that the computer has replaced the electric typewriter, and that the iPod has replaced the home phonograph. People relish these changes but lack a complete understanding of the way they fundamentally change our lives. Take the cell phone, for example. The cell phone is an excellent example of a technology illustrating the law of unintended consequences; it's not a real law, of course, but a principle that can be seen at work in contemporary culture. Briefly stated, the law of unintended consequences suggests the "actions of people always have effects that are unanticipated or unintended" (Norton n.d.). Who could have anticipated that cell phone use while driving would increase the likelihood that you'd have a traffic accident? One research study found that test subjects were "faster to brake and caused fewer crashes when they had a .08% blood-alcohol content than while sober and talking on a cell phone" (Cruz and Oloffson 2009, 46). Texting (sending text messages on a cell phone) is even worse. A study by the National Highway Traffic Safety Administration (NHTSA) "identified the cell phone as a serious safety hazard when used on the road." Several states and the District of Columbia have passed laws imposing a ban on texting while driving (Cruz and Oloffson 2009, 45). Surely no one intends to have a traffic accident while talking on a cell phone! Now that we know the dangers of cell phone use while driving, can we anticipate problems? Yes. Will we change our behavior? No! A headline in the July 30, 2009, edition of the *St. Petersburg Times* sums up the typical reaction to all those research studies: "Dangerous, yes, but who cares?" What does all this have to do with celebrity? Quite a bit, actually, as we shall soon see.

We have firmly established that media, and specifically media visibility, is a key component of celebrity. Without media, celebrities are not celebrities at all, but merely individuals who are successful, well known, or famous. As noted earlier, celebrity is fame modernized. In 21st-century America, modern means new media, a cadre of celebrities, and a host of celebrity pretenders. The development of new media has absolutely changed our definition of celebrity. Is it now possible for anyone, or everyone, to become a celebrity? Are we living proof that pop artist Andy Warhol was prophetic years ago when he said that one day everyone in the world will be famous for 15 minutes? We'll treat this issue in some depth in Chapter 2. However, at present, it is enough to say that as new media appear, our concept of celebrity changes. We, like the frog, may not be much aware that the changes around us—in our case, changes in media and our perception of celebrity—will have a major impact on our lives.

What is meant by the term new media? Well, computers and the Internet certainly qualify; they were around and in use at the end of the 20th century. Today, the computer is essentially an appliance, as necessary to a home as a television set, a washer/dryer, a coffee maker, or a toaster. But computers are constantly changing. Whether it's a desktop or a laptop, your computer may already be obsolete. Smaller, more efficient, and less-expensive machines appear on a regular basis. They have more memory, better software, quicker processors, and a host of other features. You can continue to use your present machine in the near term, but, before long, you'll want to "upgrade." Your friends, family, or business associates may have newer models, and you'll feel the pressure to join them in exploring all that is available online. What happens to your old machine? Recycle it if you can, but one computer technician, when asked what could be done with an old computer, remarked, "it makes a good doorstop."

What does a computer have to do with celebrity? A computer, connected to the Internet and accessing the World Wide Web, is the doorway to new media content. It is this content that will define celebrity in the 21st century. Electronic mail (e-mail) is routine these days. We get some important messages via this technology, but we also get spam and a variety of messages designed to steal our identities or personal information or implant a virus on our computer hard drives. We'll acknowledge e-mail's occasional usefulness, but dismiss it as having much influence on celebrity. Most of the action is on the larger, more complex World Wide Web. We'll discuss some of the problems and controversies relating to Web sites, online activities, and celebrities in Chapter 2. But now, let's take a broad, general look at the Web and identify some things with the potential to change not only the way people use and view media, but also the way we view celebrity.

The World Wide Web has enabled anyone with a computer to come forward as a potential celebrity. You can establish your own Web site. You can blog, that is, provide opinions, ideas, or information about your daily life in an online diary or journal. You can often comment on the blogs of other people. You can usually comment on news or human interest stories in the space provided at the end of an online article; these comments are collected by the Web site and are available to all readers. You can shoot your own video and upload it to YouTube where it can be seen by anyone accessing the site. You can join one of several social networks, such as MySpace or Facebook, or join the business and professional network LinkedIn. In short, there is almost an unlimited amount of content that gives you access to information about relatives, friends, neighbors, co-workers, politicians, newsmakers, lawbreakers, and yes, even celebrities. You can join this parade of personalities by getting involved in Web activities. You can increase your visibility in the world, or at least in the online world. You can present yourself as successful, rich, talented, and important, even if you are none of these. The truth is very slippery online.

Don't like to surf the Web? Would you prefer something a little more personal? The 21st century has it. It's a cell phone, and yes, we acknowledge what was said earlier about driving and cell phone use. But when you are not driving, the device can be used in a somewhat smaller context than the Internet and with much the same benefit—increasing your visibility. "Today's phones come equipped with many useful calling and multimedia features, including a media player, camera, Web browsing, child-location, and call-management services" (*Consumer Reports* 2009). One popular cell phone activity is twittering. Twitter is a "real-time short messaging service that works over multiple networks" (Twitter n.d.). A short message—no more than 140 characters—is called a "tweet." If you send tweets to others on the network, you are said to be a "tweeter "or to be "twittering." "Unlike most text messages, tweets are routed among networks of friends," or followers. Followers can be strangers "who choose to receive the tweets of people they find interesting" (Twitter 2009). So, Twitter is another media service that allows one to make oneself visible and important to others in any desired way. Some critics feel that most tweets are mundane and unimportant; an Ohio man expressed the opinion of many. He asked, "Do we really need to know that you just put your pants on, just brushed your teeth, just ordered a hamburger, just finished dinner, just walked out of the bathroom?" (Swartz 2009). Nevertheless, the service is extremely popular, particularly among politicians and celebrities. One study found that politicians spent most of their Twitter time promoting themselves (World in a Snap 2009). A Georgia man noted that Twitter is "a look-at-me-technology that seems to be more about vanity and competition than about information." If Twitter is about vanity and self-promotion, it is made to order for celebrities. Actor Ashton Kutcher has more than 3.2 million Twitter followers. Still, Twitter use by celebrities "has led many of their fans to the misguided impression that they're on a first-name basis" with the stars they follow (Swartz 2009, 3B). What we are seeing is that new media technology is making it relatively easy to become highly visible in the 21st century, even if you are not famous or well known, but particularly easy if you *are* famous or well known. It is possible that media visibility may soon become the only characteristic of a celebrity (see Chapter 2).

What about recorded music? Is it still important in the 21st-century celebrity world? It is. Although compact discs (CDs) are still popular, many people are turning to an iPod for music. "The iPod is a portable digital music and video player made by Apple . . . designed to work with the iTunes media library software, which lets users manage the music libraries on their computers and their iPods." A song can be downloaded to an iPod often for less than a dollar. As one Web site says, "the iPod is gaining in popularity and you do not want to be left out in the cold. Face it, even the youngest of children are (sic) learning how to work these new devices with ease" (iPod basics n.d.). The music of popular recording artists is now available at your fingertips. You may not be able to "see" your favorite stars, but you can hear them. Thus, the iPod provides a slightly different, but still effective, medium for celebrity visibility.

It would be a mistake to assume that celebrity in the 21st century is dependent only on electronic media, that is, television, computers, cell phones, iPods, and the Internet. A growing magazine industry has become an important part of the celebrity world. The editors of AllYouCanRead.com, a magazine and newspaper online database, developed a list of the top 10 celebrity magazines: *In Touch Weekly*, *InStyle*, *Interview*, *J-14* (the #1 teen celebrity magazine), *Life and Style Weekly*, *OK! Magazine*, *People*, *Tatler* (from Great Britain), *US Weekly*, and *Vanity Fair*. Appearing on a magazine cover is, of course, extremely important, but being featured inside the publication isn't bad either. The recession of 2008–2010 took a toll on celebrity magazine sales; nevertheless, overall circulation "held up well despite the [economic] downturn" (Perez-Pena 2009).

It is obvious that the expansion of media in the 21st century provided additional opportunities for celebrities to become more visible and for some private individuals to become somewhat visible in the new media world. We have the means today to present ourselves to the world in ways that everyday people in the ancient civilizations of Egypt, Greece, Rome, and the Middle Ages could not even imagine.

A Celebrity Taxonomy

A taxonomy is a classification system. Although typically used to categorize plants and animals, it is also useful in organizing people and ideas. Based on the review of history and the rise of media presented earlier in this chapter, we can place the well known and the famous into distinctive categories. For example, although there were few well-known people in Ancient Egypt, those who did get recognition and a small measure of fame were primarily political, military, or religious figures. The taxonomy expands during the Greek civilization where—in addition to the well known and famous in politics, government, and the military—other individuals made contributions to architecture, sculpture, literature, philosophy, and education. Taking into consideration all we know up to the present, we can assign the well known, the famous, and most celebrities to one of the following eight categories:

TABLE 1.1
Eight Categories of Celebrity

Category	Specific Examples
Politics, Government	rulers, military figures, politicians
The Arts	writers, artists, musicians
Science, Medicine	scientists, physicians
Entertainment	film and television stars, sports figures
Academic	philosophers, teachers, scholars
Business	entrepreneurs, captains of industry
Religion	popes, preachers, religious leaders
General Public	reality show participants, newsmakers

This taxonomy provides a basic framework on which we can build. We'll be able to better understand the taxonomy in the chapters ahead as we explore the changing nature of celebrity—what it is and what it means in the 21st century.

If you read the list carefully, you will notice there is one category about which we have said little in terms of members of the category being celebrities: the general public. Is it possible for members of the general public to become celebrities? Yes, it is possible, but certain conditions must apply. Let's take a detailed look at this category and see just why some members of the public might be considered celebrities, or at least well known or famous.

To be sure, most members of the general public are not well known or famous, and thus cannot be celebrities. They lead quiet lives. They go to work, pay their bills, watch television, send e-mail, and take a vacation occasionally; they may be married or single; they may or may not have children. They are known to their co-workers, neighbors, family, and friends. They may be known socially by others outside their immediate sphere of influence, particularly if they attend religious services, join an exercise club, have their letter to the editor published by the local newspaper, or are active in community or civic groups. They may be known by those upon whom they depend for service; their doctor, dentist, banker, or hair stylist may know them by name. In short, these members of the public are known within the framework of their lifestyles. They are known, but not well known enough to be considered famous.

Members of the General Public as Seekers of Fame

Some members of the public are not satisfied to be known simply in their own milieu, that is, their own surroundings. They'd like to be better known than that, to be more widely recognized. These individuals might actually achieve some small measure of fame if they use the tools given them by 21st-century media. They can shoot a home video and upload it to YouTube, establish a Web site, or start a blog. They can apply to appear on one of several television reality shows in the hope of being selected as a contestant. Appearing on television is considered by many the quickest way to become famous. Tens of thousands of people regularly apply to television's reality shows: *Survivor, American Idol, Big Brother, The Amazing Race, The Bachelor,* and *So You Think You Can Dance,* among others. The few selected to appear on these shows will have their 15 minutes of fame, but probably no more than that. Once they've completed their time on the shows, they'll be quickly forgotten. Who remembers the person who won the million dollars on the second season of *Survivor*? Which team won the million dollar prize on the first season of *The Amazing Race*? A few television junkies, that is, those who gather and retain television trivia, may be able to identify these individuals, but the rest of us cannot. Their fame was limited to their time on television, and because they are no longer on television, they are no longer famous. They were never famous or well known enough to be classified as celebrities.

There is, however, an exception to the fleeting nature of reality show fame: *American Idol*. Winners on this show have often been signed to recording contracts, and some still remain famous; Kelly Clarkson and Carrie Underwood are good examples. These women were just small-town singers from Texas and Oklahoma until their appearance on *Idol*. Their success on the show propelled them to fame. Even some of the losers have become successful. Jennifer Hudson won an Oscar for her role in *Dreamgirls*, and Kellie Pickler became a country music artist. We'll give *American Idol* its due in helping to create some famous, well-known individuals, but, for the most part, the fame associated with television's reality shows is short-lived.

Members of the Public as Famous Newsmakers

There is another, somewhat-more-common way for members of the general public to become famous: in the course of your normal life, do something extraordinarily unusual or extremely illegal. Either consciously or unconsciously, behave in such a way as to draw considerable media attention. The key phrases in this subcategory are "extraordinarily unusual" and "extremely illegal." Many people do unusual things or break a law or two. Someone might walk from one end of a state to another in an attempt to raise money for a charitable cause—praiseworthy, but not all that unusual. Another person might go big-game hunting in Africa—interesting, but not truly remarkable. Still another might get a speeding ticket or be arrested for burglary—troublesome, but not significant enough to draw any sort of sustained media attention.

There are individuals, however, who were thrust into the media spotlight and became famous because they did something that was beyond the usual, or beyond small violations of the law.

Nadya Suleman made headlines in January 2009 when she gave birth to history-making octuplets. That event itself was extraordinarily unusual, but it was made even more so by the news shortly thereafter that Suleman already had six children, all of them born through in vitro fertilization. "Many people across the country expressed outrage at Suleman and the fertility doctor who impregnated her, saying it was irresponsible for a single woman to bring 14 children in the world without the means to care for them" (Ferran 2009). This situation was tailor-made for the news media who are always eager to exploit the unusual for the ratings it might generate. True enough, dozens of requests and offers poured in. ABC's *Good Morning America* was one of the first to call, asking for an interview. Suleman, now known as "Octomom," was eager to capitalize on her sudden fame. She sought to trademark the term *Octomom*. She explored the possibility of having her own television show and considered developing a line of diapers, dresses, pants, and shirts with the Octomom label (Duke 2009). Thus, we can see it is not all that difficult for a member of the general public to become famous—just do something really, really unusual and get a lot of media attention for it.

In the second part of this sub-category we find individuals who have broken the law to such an extent that they, too, became famous in the news media spotlight. Such was the case with two high school seniors in Littleton, Colorado. On April 20, 1999, Eric Harris and Dylan Klebold took the first steps on the road to fame. They conducted an assault on Columbine High School during the middle of the school day, wanting to kill as many of their fellow students as possible. The attack was poorly planned and some of the bombs they planted failed to detonate; nevertheless, when the smoke cleared, 12 students, one teacher, and both boys were dead (Rosenberg n.d.). The media quickly swung into action, covering every aspect of the situation, and passing along some incorrect information in the process. The Trench Coat Mafia (TCM) was said to be behind the killings. Although the boys were wearing trench coats, they were not part of any group calling itself the TCM; in fact, the TCM was largely a myth. The news media clearly contributed to the confusion surrounding the situation; they failed to ask basic questions about the boys and the group they were presumed to be part of. Later, law enforcement officials were accused of making mistakes in the investigation of the slaughter and of covering up those mistakes

(Cullen 2009). The Columbine school shooting was a far more complicated series of events, both before and after the actual gunfire, than we can deal with here. Still, the tragic event illustrates how an extreme breaking of the law—in this case murder—can make those who commit the act famous. Harris and Klebold dominated news coverage of the event for many days; reporters flocked to Colorado to interview anyone who would talk to them. Harris and Klebold became household names. They were featured on the cover of the May 3, 1999, issue of *Time* magazine, together with photos of the 13 people they killed. Yes, they were famous. Sadly, that fame came at a high price: the death of 15 human beings. It is so often the case. Law breakers become famous if their deeds involve the loss of life, particularly the loss of many lives. Timothy McVeigh took 168 lives when he bombed the Murrah Federal Building in Oklahoma City in April 1995. There are other examples, of course, but the point is that one way to become famous is to do something extremely illegal and gain significant news media exposure as a result.

Were Eric Harris, Dylan Klebold, and Timothy McVeigh celebrities? If we apply our definition of celebrity, we can see they fail to meet at least two, perhaps three, important characteristics. Their actions did not connect subconsciously in the sense that they embodied the dreams and aspirations of the public. No mentally healthy person wishes for the death of others. It could also be argued that the attacks at Columbine High and in Oklahoma City were not so much accomplishments as actions. The word *accomplishment* carries—as we have applied it to celebrities—the implication of something worthwhile, something positive. Murder is neither of these. It is unknown whether Harris, Klebold, and McVeigh were seeking to become famous. All three were pursuing personal goals, however twisted. McVeigh apparently wanted to get away with it; it is not clear what Harris and Klebold thought about the outcome of their actions. Nevertheless, the three killers do qualify as celebrities on some of the other qualities.

The Octomom, on the other hand, initially missed on only two characteristics: embodying the dreams and desires of the public, and seeking ways to be seen and heard. However, once her story was out, she did indeed seek to capitalize on her notoriety. Thus, she qualifies on five of the six characteristics. This raises an interesting question. Must one meet all six requirements to be considered a celebrity? You'll find the answer to that question in Chapter 2.

References

Biagi, Shirley. 2005. *Media/Impact*. Seventh edition. Belmont, CA: Thomson Wadsworth.

Braudy, Leo. 1986. *The frenzy of renown*. New York: Oxford University Press.

Campbell, Richard, Christopher Martin, and Bettina Fabos. 2007. *Media and culture*. Fifth edition. Boston: Bedford/St. Martins.

Cashmore, Ellis. 2006. *Celebrity/Culture*. New York: Routledge.

Consumer Reports. "Cell phones and services." [Online information; retrieved 10/01/09.] http:www.consumerreports.org/cro/electronics-computers/phones-mobile-devices/cell-phones-service.html.

Corliss, Richard. 2009. "Legend." *Time*, June 29.

Cruz, Gilbert, and Kristi Oloffson. 2009. "Driving us to distraction." *Time*, August 24.

Cullen, Dave. 2009. *Columbine*. New York: Grand Central Publishing.

Czitrom, Daniel. 1982. *Media and the American mind*. Chapel Hill: University of North Carolina Press.

Duke, Alan. 2009. "Octomom seeks to trademark nickname for TV, diaper line." [Online article; retrieved 10/06/09.] http://cnn.com/2009/us/04/15/octuplet.mom/index.html.

Dyer, Richard. 1998. *Stars*. London: British Film Institute.

Eisenstein, Elizabeth. 2005. *The printing revolution in early modern Europe*. New York: Cambridge University Press.

Encyclopedia Britannica. http://britannica.com/EBchecked/topic/125572/collective-unconscious.

Fang, Irving. 2008. *Alphabet to Internet: Mediated communication in our lives*. St. Paul, MN: Rada Press.

Ferran, Lee. 2009. "Octomom: I screwed my life up." [Online article; retrieved 10/06/09.] http://abcnews.go.com/GMA/Story?id=7762688&page=1.

Flora, Carlin. 2004. "Seeing by starlight: Celebrity obsession." [Online article; retrieved 09/29/09.] http://www.psychologytoday.com/articles/200407/seeing-starlight-celebrity-obsession.

Fussel, Stephan. 2005. *Gutenberg and the impact of printing*. Translated by Douglas Martin. Burlington, VT: Ashgate.

Herwitz, David. 2008. *The star as icon*. New York: Columbia University Press.

"ipod basics for the beginner." n.d. [Online information; retrieved 10/02/09.] http://technology.solveyourproblem.com/ipod/ipod-basics-beginners.shtml.

Kleinschmidt, Harald. 2000. *Understanding the MiddleAges*. Woodbridge, Suffolk, England: Boydell Press.

Lai, Adrienne. 2006. "Glitter and grain." In *Framing celebrity*, eds. Su Holmes and Sean Redmond, 215–230. New York: Routledge.

Leslie, Larry Z. 2004. *Mass communication ethics: Decision making in post-modern culture*. Boston: Allyn & Bacon.

McCutcheon, Lynn, John Maltby, James Houran, and Diane Ashe. 2004. *Celebrity worshippers: Inside the minds of stargazers*. Baltimore: Publish America.

Menache, Sophia. 1990. *The vox dei*. New York: Oxford University Press.

Miller, James, and John Thompson. 2006. *Almanac of American history*. Washington, DC: National Geographic Society.

Munck, Thomas. 2000. *The enlightenment*. New York: Oxford University Press.

Norton, Rob. n.d. "Unintended consequences." [Online article; retrieved 09/30/09.] http://www.econlib.org/library/Enc/Unintended Consequences.html.

Perez-Pena, Richard. 2009. "Celebrity magazines post a downturn in sales." [Online article: retrieved 10/02/09.] http://www.nytimes.com/2009/02/10/business/media/10mag.html.

Pollard, David. 2004. "The boiling frog." [Online article; retrieved 09/30/09.] http://blogs.salon.com/0002007/2004/02/06.html.

Ponce de Leon, Charles. 2002. *Self-exposure: Human-interest journalism and the emergence of celebrity in America*. Chapel Hill: University of North Carolina Press.

Roberts, J. M. 1993. *A short history of the world*. New York: Oxford University Press.

Rodman, George. 2006. *Mass media in a changing world*. New York: McGraw Hill.

Rosenberg, Jennifer. n.d. "Columbine massacre." [Online article; retrieved 10/06/09.] http://history1900s.about.com/od/famouscrimescandals/a/columbine.htm.

Schickel, Richard. 1985. *Intimate strangers: The culture of celebrity*. Garden City, NY: Doubleday & Company.

Simpson, John, and Edmund Weiner. 1989. *The Oxford English dictionary*. Second edition. Volume II, V. Oxford: Clarendon Press.

Steele, Margaret. 2009. "The psychology of celebrity worship." [Online article; retrieved 09/29/09.] http://health.usnews.com/articles/health/healthday/2009/06/26-the-psychology-of-celebrity-worship.

Swartz, Jon. 2009. "Twitter haters see no point in tweeting." *USA Today*, August 25, 3B.

Thomas, Rosalind. 1992. *Literacy and orality in ancient Greece*. New York: Cambridge University Press.

Twitter. 2009. [Online information; retrieved 10/02/09.] http://topics.nytimes,com/top/news/business/companies/twitter/index.html.

Twitter. n.d. [Online information; retrieved 10/02/09.] http://twitter.com/about.

Woolf, Alex. 2008. *A short history of the world*. New York: Metro Books.

World in a Snap. 2009. "Pols can brag in 140 characters or less." *St. Petersburg Times*, September 19, 4A.

2

Problems, Controversies, and Solutions

This chapter explores several current issues involving celebrity and suggests how some of the more interesting, perhaps one could say the more troublesome, can be satisfactorily resolved. Where possible, both sides of an issue will be presented. In some cases a solution will be offered; in others, readers will be on their own to determine which arguments are most convincing.

Is Celebrity Finite?

Does celebrity have definite, recognizable boundaries or limits? In other words, can we determine when celebrity begins and when it ends? Chapter 1 presented six characteristics an individual should have to be considered a celebrity. One must lead a public life or work in the public sphere, accomplish something of importance and interest to the public, be well known or famous, seek celebrity by being seen and heard regularly, be highly visible in the media, and connect with the public by embodying its dreams and aspirations. If one accepts those characteristics, then celebrity begins when all six are met. Note that celebrity does not depend on age, gender, place of birth, talent, or skill, although these qualities may be more helpful to some people than to others. Celebrity depends on the *action* taken by individuals, that is, how they use their talent, skills, age, gender, and so forth. Notice some of the verbs in the list of characteristics: work, accomplish, seek, connect. These require considerable effort and energy. Having youth and talent will not get you very far unless you do something with that youth and talent. In today's popular terminology, you must be proactive. Passivity won't work to your advantage. If one accepts the six characteristics as determining celebrity, it becomes quickly obvious that not all those in public life are celebrities. It is possible to have some, even most, of the traits and still fall short of celebrity. One can be famous and well known, but not a celebrity. One can have significant work accomplishments and still not be a celebrity. In short, our requirement that an individual meet all six characteristics makes becoming a celebrity more involved that one might expect.

On the other hand, some people might feel that a list of qualities one must have to become a celebrity is too complicated, too analytical, too academic, too confusing. If you were such a person, you might pose some interesting questions. You might ask, "Why not simplify celebrity? In our technologically heavy society, doesn't it make sense to say that if one is highly visible in the media, that's enough to make that person a celebrity? Hasn't that person already met most of the other characteristics? Moreover, because contemporary society values everyone's opinion, if my opinion is that someone is a celebrity, it's a done deal! Why can't I say who is and who is not a celebrity in the same way I choose which songs to include on my iPod? It's all about individual choice today. Celebrity should not be any different. Why should other people make decisions about anything, including celebrity, I can make for myself?" This argument has considerable appeal. It is straightforward and doesn't demand the kind of time and effort applying a set of characteristics requires. The argument is supported, to some degree, by the technological determinism theory, developed by Marshall McLuhan, a Canadian professor of culture and technology. Although McLuhan died in 1980, his work remains a major influence in helping us understand popular media culture. McLuhan believed that media technology determines how people think, feel, and act. In other words, the messages we receive through media are so influential in our lives that we are no longer aware that our feelings, ideas, and opinions are being shaped by technology and the messages it carries. Thus, technology is the determining factor, that is, the unstoppable, unavoidable authority in establishing how we perceive the world. Not all scholars agree with McLuhan, but many do. In any case, McLuhan's theory offers some support to the notion that being highly visible in media is all that is necessary to make one a celebrity. In short, media exposure alone—because of technological determinism—is the definitive element in celebrity. This argument makes valid points about the power of the individual and the power of media. We are taught that our ideas, opinions, and choices do not hold absolute truth; others rightfully have different ideas and opinions and make different choices. Diversity is highly valued in contemporary multicultural society. Furthermore, we live in a media-rich culture of computers, smart phones, iPods; we blog, we tweet, and we upload to YouTube. New media, particularly, are quite powerful.

The conclusion to be drawn from these two arguments is, of course, a matter of individual choice. However, the stronger argument appears to be the one requiring celebrities to meet the six characteristics developed in Chapter 1. These qualities represent a set of standards, that is, a way of determining what a thing should be. If celebrities are role models or individuals the public holds in high esteem, they should meet some basic standards. Life is full of standards. There are standards for obtaining a driver's license, standards for earning a high school diploma or college degree, standards for entering adulthood, and standards for entering many professions. One cannot just arbitrarily do these sorts of things. There are criteria to be met. Even the media have standards: a television show that fails to attract a large number of viewers will not get high ratings and will likely be cancelled; an album recorded by a popular music group will not be designated "gold" or "platinum" if it fails to meet certain sales goals. In a world where standards are firm for many of the things with which we have contact, we cannot abandon celebrity to the whim of the individual. Furthermore, celebrity would be too easy to achieve if it depended solely on the opinion of an individual. Nothing worthwhile is easy. This brings to mind the 1992 movie *A League of Their Own*, a film about the first female professional baseball league in the 1940s. When a player complains about how hard it is to play, actor Tom Hanks, as team manager Jimmy Dugan, says, "It's supposed to be hard. If it wasn't hard, everyone could do it. The hard . . . is what makes it great." Meeting the six celebrity characteristics is hard; not everyone can do it. That's what makes celebrity special!

When does celebrity end? The quick answer is that it ends when an individual fails to meet the six celebrity characteristics. At first glance, one would be tempted to say that celebrity ends when an individual ceases to become highly visible in the media. That's true, but other factors may also be at work. Take Gary Coleman, star of the popular television sitcom *Diff'rent Strokes* in the late 1970s and early 1980s. Although Coleman died in late May 2010, his later life provides a good example of how celebrity can slip away. Coleman had financial problems for almost 20 years before he finally filed for bankruptcy in 1999. The few roles he got on television or in films were minor ones; for example, he played the pizza guy in the 2007 B-level film *A Christmas Too Many*. That was not enough for him to maintain celebrity status. Were it not for his apparent suicide attempt and a charge of assault on a fan, he would have been entirely out of public view. In any case, he no longer had accomplishments of interest and importance to the public. He did not embody the dreams and desires of those young people who were fans of his television show. In short, he failed to meet several celebrity characteristics and was therefore considered a former celebrity.

We mean no disrespect to Coleman. He has a lot of company in the former-celebrity category. Willie Aames, another popular sitcom star in the late 1970s and 1980s (*Eight is Enough*), has also fallen on hard times; he filed for bankruptcy in 2007. Richard Hatch, the winner on the first season of CBS's reality show *Survivor*, received a 51-month prison sentence for failing to pay taxes on his million dollar prize (Spears 2009). However, having money trouble is not the only way to lose celebrity status. In the 2007 Miss Teen USA pageant, South Carolina teen Caitlin Upton was an on-stage celebrity for perhaps an hour until she tried to answer a question about why a fifth of Americans are unable to locate the United States on a world map. In an answer peppered with *uhs* and *ums*, she said it was because "U.S. Americans don't have maps." She plowed on, referencing South Africa and "the Iraq." The video was uploaded to YouTube and received hundreds of thousands of hits, but her celebrity was not real. She had no accomplishments, was the object of nationwide ridicule, and certainly did not embody anyone's dreams and desires. Then there's the case of Olympic figure skater Tonya Harding. According to her Web site (www .tonyaharding.com), she is one of the most influential and controversial figures in sports history, second only to boxer Muhammad Ali. Most people would probably agree with the controversial part. She conspired with her ex-husband and two others to attack competitor Nancy Kerrigan at an Olympic practice session in 1994. Kerrigan was injured in the attack and did not place first in the

U.S. figure skating finals that year. Harding and her ex-husband also appear in a sex tape, presumably made on their wedding night. More recently, she turned to boxing and, according to her Web site, hopes to make enough money to retire and "live alone with her Persian cat." In the minds of the general public, she retired from celebrity long ago! Aames, Hatch, Upton, Harding, and a host of others, once celebrities, now fail to meet several of the required characteristics. They are former celebrities.

There are other ways, of course, that an individual's celebrity can come to an end. Although not common, a few individuals have chosen to leave the media spotlight and essentially abandon their celebrity. This was the case with Bobby Fischer. Fischer won the World Chess Championship in 1972 and then dropped from sight for almost 20 years. Fischer was quirky, cranky, and somewhat reclusive before the championship match, but the competition seemed to bring out his other negative qualities. He complained about first one thing, and then another, during the match. He returned to competition briefly in 1992 by playing a match in Yugoslavia, but disappeared again for several years before moving to Iceland where he died in 2008. Fischer was the first American to win the World Chess Championship and could have capitalized on his celebrity, but he chose not to.

Obviously, death can bring an end to celebrity, although a celebrity's reputation and work may live on. Take Michael Jackson, for example. Although the King of Pop died in June 2009, fans still buy his music, and his brothers and sisters make regular public appearances discussing Michael's life and the impact of his death. Four months after Jackson's death, his friend Kenny Ortega released a film comprised mainly of video clips from rehearsal sessions for Jackson's planned concert series. *This Is It* was well received by both critics and fans. *Forbes* magazine reported the Jackson estate earned $90 million in a recent year. The estates of other dead celebrities also managed to do well: Beatle John Lennon $15 million, Dr. Seuss (Theodor Geisel) $15 million, singer Elvis Presley $55 million, and fashion designer Yves Saint Laurent $350 million (www.forbes.com). In short, death may remove celebrities from the media spotlight, but their work and their earning power may live on.

Advancing age is also a factor in bringing celebrity to an end. Dozens of the famous and well known are over the age of 85 and, although still alive, have faded into the celebrity background.

For example, actresses Olivia de Havilland (*Gone with the Wind*) and Joan Fontaine (*Suspicion*) are in their nineties. So are actors Harry Morgan (*M*A*S*H*) and Frank Cady (*Green Acres*). These and other elderly celebrities are rarely seen. Their names are recognized only by people of a certain age; today's younger generation knows little or nothing about these senior celebrities.

To answer the question posed at the beginning of this section, yes, celebrity is finite. Celebrity has boundaries. Becoming a celebrity means meeting all six of our characteristics; the end of celebrity is less definite and includes factors, such as age, that are not part of the list of required celebrity qualities.

Celebrities Who Violate Social or Moral Norms

A norm is a principle of correct action held by members of a society that guides, controls, or regulates behavior. Here's a simple example. Time was, men stood aside respectfully and held doors open so women could pass through first. This practice was considered entirely appropriate; failure to follow this norm was the epitome of rudeness. A few old-timers still follow this practice today, but contemporary society is egalitarian; some women might feel they are being treated as the "weaker sex" if they are not allowed to open their own doors. Other women may simply not pay much attention to who goes through a door first. Nevertheless, norms still exist in contemporary society. What happens to a celebrity when the individual violates a social or moral norm?

Although there are violations of social and moral norms in all areas of life, most high-profile violations for celebrities seem to occur in politics and entertainment. Politicians are often not precise in their comments about pending legislation, government policies, the behavior of peers, or their own actions. This sometimes gets them into trouble because they violate a norm, that is, a standard of behavior expected of everyone. Take, for example, Rod Blagojevich who, in 2008, was the governor of Illinois. On the morning of December 9, he was arrested at his Chicago home and charged with "conspiring to commit mail and wire fraud and soliciting bribes" (Scherer 2008). Of particular interest to federal officials was his apparent attempt to "sell" an appointment to the U.S. Senate. Recorded conversations appeared to show that in order to be nominated for the vacant Senate seat, one had to contribute a large sum of money (reportedly $1.5 million) to the governor's campaign fund. You don't have to be a legal expert to see that this appears to be bribery, and bribery is not only illegal but also violates moral and social norms. We expect individuals to acquire jobs on merit; we expect those in public office to work for the common good, not their individual good. Our expectations are not always met, but they are worthy goals; we, as members of society, expect our leaders to behave properly. In this case, Blagojevich ignored a host of norms: legal, political, social, and moral. The Illinois legislature apparently agreed with this assessment and removed him from office early in 2009.

More often than not, politicians violate what might be termed "the marriage norm." Marriage norms require, among other things, that one "forsake all others" and be faithful to one's spouse. More than a few politicians have trouble with the "forsaking" business. South Carolina Governor Mark Sanford, Nevada Senator John Ensign, former presidential candidate John Edwards, and New York Governor Eliot Spitzer were discovered to have had sexual relationships with women to whom they were not married. All confessed to their wrongdoing and offered apologies. Only Spitzer resigned his position. It is safe to say that these men were diminished in the eyes of the public because they were unfaithful to their wives; adultery is still a serious violation of social norms in contemporary society. Whatever celebrity these men might have enjoyed as high-profile public office holders has slipped away.

Although the media pay close attention to the negative things politicians do, they give even greater attention to the misdeeds of entertainment celebrities. But unlike politicians, celebrities who violate social or moral norms do not necessarily lose or diminish their celebrity. The case of recording artists Chris Brown and Rihanna, R&B's most famous couple, is a good example. Grammy awards are given for outstanding achievement in the music industry. On Grammy day in 2009, Brown turned himself in to police and was booked on suspicion of making criminal threats. Further investigation revealed that his girlfriend Rihanna had bruises on her face as a result of an apparent early morning confrontation with Brown. One report said Rihanna had been hospitalized as a result of the attack. Neither performer appeared at the Grammy ceremony (Errico 2009). Several months later,

Brown reportedly asked his now ex-girlfriend to keep details of the attack private in her interview with ABC's Diane Sawyer. She didn't, admitting to Sawyer that Brown bit her, "put her in a head lock and punched her several times in the face" (Michaels 2009). Brown released a new CD late in 2009, and although a singing appearance on ABC's *Good Morning America* was cancelled, his in-depth interview with ABC's Robin Roberts for *20/20* was not. For her part, Rihanna also released an album in late 2009. Critics did not like it; one said it "sucked." Still, critics said they liked her personally, but disliked her musical performance on the new album. Clearly, it is not socially acceptable to attack one's girlfriend. Brown violated a social norm and appears to be less popular than before. Nevertheless, the careers of both singers seem to be moving forward, and the two recording artists' celebrity seems to be holding up. The question here is whether this violation of social norms *should have* led to diminished celebrity. On the one hand, one could argue that no one is perfect and that humans make mistakes, especially when strong emotions are involved. On the other, abuse of any sort violates contemporary social norms and should be punished. Professional football star Michael Vick went to prison for his role in promoting dog fights; our culture is not willing to ignore animal abuse. Are we willing to ignore the abuse of a girlfriend (or boyfriend)? What punishment, if any, should Brown be assessed as a result of his violation of a social norm? In theory, Brown deserves some punishment, but in practice, the general public is not inclined to deal harshly with celebrity misbehavior. Remember that celebrities embody the dreams and desires of many members of the public. We feel close to celebrities; many are role models. We resist making judgments that might destroy our relationship with them, however illusory.

Other entertainment celebrities have violated social or moral norms, yet they, too, seem to have survived with most of their celebrity status intact. Paris Hilton had the advantage of being born into a well-known family. The Hilton family is both rich and famous, best known for its worldwide chain of hotels. Paris considers herself a model, actress, singer, and fashion designer. She has her own line of fragrances. Others believe her to be a socialite, that is, an individual who is prominent due to social or financial status but who may have few real accomplishments. That assessment may be a bit harsh because Paris has some accomplishments. She appears regularly on television, both in the United States and elsewhere. She starred in her own television show, *The Simple Life*;

she appeared in several B-level films. Paris works hard and is willing to make personal appearances even in small venues. But Paris has a history of violating social and moral norms. In 2003, just before *The Simple Life* began its 56-episode run on television, a sex tape involving her and then-boyfriend Rick Salomon began circulating on the World Wide Web. Paris has some company on the sex tape list: Tommy Lee and Pamela Anderson's honeymoon sex tape (apparently stolen from their home), and Kim Kardashian's 2007 tape with then-boyfriend Ray J (before Kardashian became well known). Public display of sexual activities violates social and moral norms; everyone knows humans are sexual beings, but intimate behavior should be private.

Hilton violated another social and moral (and legal) norm by driving with a suspended license. She lost her license because of "alcohol-related reckless driving" after she was stopped for weaving down the street in her Mercedes. She was also sentenced to three years probation. Nevertheless, several months later she was stopped by police who discovered her license had been suspended. This landed her in jail. Originally sentenced to 45 days for driving with a suspended license, Paris served only four days and was released to home confinement with an ankle tracking device after "extensive consultations with medical personnel" (Nizza 2007). Reckless driving, driving while intoxicated, and driving with a suspended license violate social, moral, and legal norms. The public found these incidents somewhat entertaining but was disturbed that because she was a celebrity, Paris served less time in jail than she should have. Any member of the general public would almost certainly have had to serve more than four days. This raises the "double standard" issue. Should celebrities be held to the same standards as common folk? Paris doesn't think so. She told CNN's Larry King that she got a "raw deal." Many people would disagree; celebrities get lots of breaks when it comes to violations of the law or violations of social and moral norms. Most members of the public would not get similar breaks in similar situations. There is a simple answer to the double standard question: everyone should be treated equally when it comes to violations of the law; social and moral norms are not as firmly established as laws and thus violations should be subject to more flexible treatment. But the simple answer will not hold in today's complex culture. The double standard will continue primarily because, as everyone knows, the rich are different! So are celebrities!

Pop singer Amy Winehouse has been described as "troubled," "a train wreck," and "self-destructive." Winehouse has a history of bizarre behavior. At a jazz festival in the spring of 2009, she stopped singing in the middle of a song, "stared at the ground for 30 seconds and walked off stage—leaving her backup singers looking as confused as she does on a regular basis" (www.tmz .com/category/amy-winehouse). She sought and was awarded an injunction against the paparazzi; they must stay at least 100 meters away from her London apartment. She was acquitted of assault charges lodged against her by a fan who said Winehouse punched her in the face. Admitting to alcohol abuse, Winehouse took an eight-month vacation on a Caribbean island, stopped drinking, and emerged from the "rehab" experience looking refreshed. The celebrity gossip world promptly began buzzing about her apparent breast augmentation and her apparent new addiction— exercising. Determining the truth is hard here, obscured as it is by the hype and spin of her supporters and the delight some Web sites take in trashing her. Has Winehouse violated social or moral norms? Probably, but the public may have some sympathy for her; it is well known that alcohol abuse is a problem at every socioeconomic level of society. Your next-door neighbor or your cousin or your best friend could have a drinking problem. While no one likes to see another in a state of intoxication—or be on the receiving end of some drunken behavior—people tend not to condemn the person but to urge the individual to seek help. Is there a difference between the behaviors of Paris Hilton and Amy Winehouse? Yes, there is. Paris was essentially found to be driving under the influence (DUI) of alcohol, but is not known to be addicted to drink. Winehouse was addicted to it. Addiction is a serious problem worldwide. The public favors helping first, but stands ready to reassess its opinion if an individual either refuses help or returns to the addiction. Winehouse wasn't much of a celebrity to begin with, but her lifestyle has pushed her into the media spotlight in a way her singing career has not.

The list of entertainment celebrities who have violated social or moral norms is a long one. Not all of them can be profiled here, but a few more will serve to illustrate the point. Actress Lindsey Lohan was given an extra year of probation by a judge who discovered she had failed to attend alcohol education classes for her two DUI convictions. Lohan explained she was out of the country working; the judge ordered her to get court approval before leaving town or face time in jail (Gillin 2009). CBS's David

Letterman was the apparent victim of an extortion attempt, but cooperated with authorities in a sting that resulted in charges against Robert "Joe" Halderman, a veteran CBS news producer. In the course of the investigation, authorities found the extortion attempt was based on information the producer had about Letterman's sexual liaisons with some of the women who had worked for him on the *Late Show*. This news was, of course, not well received by Letterman's wife. Nevertheless, Letterman confessed on-air to the affairs and apologized for his behavior. Ratings for the *Late Show* improved for a week or so, but settled to their former levels when the story disappeared from newspapers and entertainment-news television programs. Neither Lohan nor Letterman appears to have diminished their celebrity status. We may be at the point in the culture where people just accept the fact that celebrities do these sorts of things and that celebrity social and moral norms are flexible. Often the best we can hope for is an apology and a return to normal life.

The case of professional golfer Tiger Woods raises another issue regarding celebrities who run afoul of social and moral norms. Can celebrities choose when to make information about their lives public and when to keep information private? In other words, should celebrities be permitted to control their celebrity status, that is, seek recognition and respect for their work in the public sphere, but withdraw from the celebrity spotlight when it is convenient for them? The concept of privacy is important to most Americans. To some extent, one's privacy is protected by law. But the law also makes a distinction between public and private figures. Private individuals, that is, those who do not lead public lives and "invite" public attention to themselves or their work, are entitled to a great deal of privacy. They have a right to be "let alone" and to be secure from outside interference in their work, homes, and possessions. Individuals in the public sphere are entitled to privacy but must understand that living a public life requires them to give up some of it. Celebrity depends to some degree on public opinion. A public hungry for information may go to unusual lengths to take a celebrity's picture, get an autograph, find out whom the celebrity is dating, learn what the celebrity likes to eat, and so forth. Because they lead public lives, celebrities must tolerate this "special" attention. Most ordinary citizens would call police if someone was lurking outside their home trying to snap a photo of them. Nevertheless, the degree of privacy to which one is entitled is an issue frequently argued in court. Let's take a closer look at privacy by examining the case involving Tiger Woods.

On the Friday after Thanksgiving 2009, at 2:30 in the morning, Tiger Woods had a single car accident in his suburban Orlando neighborhood. He struck a fire hydrant and then rammed a nearby tree. Woods suffered cuts and bruises but no permanent injury. Woods, exercising his right under Florida law, refused to speak with law enforcement about the accident. The questions came quickly. Did Tiger and his wife have an argument? Did he leave the house in anger? Exactly how did he manage to hit both a hydrant and a tree and do considerable damage to his vehicle? Where was he going at that time of night? Tiger was silent for more than 48 hours. On the following Sunday afternoon, he posted a statement on his Web site. "This situation is my fault, and it's obviously embarrassing to my family and me. I'm human, and I'm not perfect. I will certainly make sure this doesn't happen again," Woods wrote. This explanation satisfied almost no one. It failed to answer any of the questions the public and the media had posed. During the next couple of days, rumors about possible extra-marital affairs and domestic violence began to swirl. Woods described the rumors as "malicious" and reaffirmed his belief that the situation was a private matter and, furthermore, he intended to keep it that way.

This situation clearly illustrates a problem celebrities sometimes have. They may want to control or manage what the public knows about them. To some extent they can do this by being well behaved and having a good publicist, but their power is limited; celebrity, as we noted in Chapter 1, depends to a large extent on public opinion, often formed as a result of media coverage. Celebrities, as a rule, cannot control what media say about them or in what context media choose to feature them. Thus, celebrity control of a situation often ends when the television cameras roll. Nevertheless, Woods clearly violated a social norm: explaining the accident to law enforcement. Many people believe that if you have nothing to hide, why should you fear talking to police? Others might wonder whether a traffic citation would be issued if they talked. Is it best to talk or remain silent? In Woods's case, sportswriters were divided on the issue. One said the accident details were "none of our business." Another said the "none of our business" argument is the proper one and is justified under the circumstances (Farris 2009). But others said the matter is indeed the public's business: Woods has made millions being a public figure and cannot suddenly become a private figure when he has a traffic accident. Mike Paul, a public relations consultant, suggested Woods surrendered his privacy "when he turned pro in 1996 and signed his first Nike endorsement contract." "The good news is," Paul continued, "you're getting a lot of money. The bad news is: Privacy? Are you kidding me? It just went out the window" (Brady and DiMeglio 2009). Woods's Web site statement appeared on Sunday and the media and Internet buzz about Tiger continued on Monday and Tuesday. Woods remained silent . . . until Wednesday.

On Wednesday, *US Weekly*, a popular celebrity magazine, revealed that Woods would be featured in its December 14 issue. Woods appeared on the magazine cover along with the caption "Yes, He Cheated." The story inside the magazine contained new information, specific enough to further tarnish Woods's reputation. It should be noted here that until the time of the auto accident, Woods had a sterling reputation as a professional golfer, a husband and father, and a supporter of important charities. As the first sports billionaire, he was thought to be leading the perfect life: attractive wife, great kids, golf talent, and rich beyond anyone's wildest dreams. He was featured in many product commercials including Nike, Gatorade, and EA Sports. His failure to provide details about the accident would probably not have done much damage to his reputation; his celebrity would have remained intact. His violation of a social norm (refusing to talk to police) was a minor one and likely to be quickly forgiven (or forgotten) by the public. However, the information in the *US Weekly* story almost certainly damaged both his reputation and his celebrity status.

The magazine reported that Woods had an on-going relationship with Jaimee Grubbs, a woman he met at a Las Vegas nightclub in 2007. The story also included a word-by-word transcript of a voice mail message Woods apparently left on the woman's phone asking her to take her name off the phone because his wife went through his phone and might be calling her. The voice mail message itself was played by the broadcast media; the voice sounded like Woods's, but the Associated Press reported it could not confirm Woods was the caller. Another report said that there may have been as many as 300 text messages exchanged between Grubbs and Woods, although none of the texts was quoted. There were indications that Woods may have had relationships with other women, although the magazine's focus was on Grubbs. Almost immediately after the *US Weekly* story broke, Woods made a public apology and appealed again for privacy. Woods acknowledged that he had let his family down by committing "transgressions." "I have not been true to my values and the behavior my family deserves," he said. "I will strive to be a better person and the husband and father that my family deserves. For all of those who have supported me over the years, I offer my profound apology," he concluded.

Woods's statement had the effect of admitting the affair with Grubbs; it provided evidence that he violated a social and moral norm—being faithful to one's spouse. Although Woods received unqualified support from other sports figures, not everyone agreed that life would soon return to normal, he would continue to win golf tournaments, and his celebrity status would be as good as ever. The public expects an apology from those who have violated social and moral norms. Once an apology is given, reputations can be repaired. The same can be said of one's celebrity. An apology goes a long way in helping one maintain celebrity status. As a practical matter, however, neither one's reputation nor one's celebrity status can be totally restored. Woods's control of information about his life and activities slipped away quickly following the car accident. Just a few days later, he had little control over the information about him. Woods seemed to blame the media for this. *USA Today*'s Christine Brennan noted that his statement also contained an attack on the media "for having the audacity to invade his privacy, as if to say, 'How dare you do this to me'?" (Brennan 2009). While celebrities have a great deal of authority and prestige, those who gave them prestige and authority cannot be ignored. An aggressive media and public opinion are powerful forces. Even the world's greatest golfer cannot stand against them. If the media report your wins, they'll also report your sins. This is the nature of celebrity in the 21st century. In early December, Woods, essentially acknowledging multiple outside "relationships," announced he was taking an indefinite leave from professional golf in order to work on some issues with his family. Shortly thereafter, the sponsors for whom Woods does endorsements began to reassess their relationship with him. Several indicated they still supported him; several distanced themselves by shelving commercials featuring the golfer; a few severed their relationship with him, one noting that he was "no longer the right representative" of the company's values. Woods's troubles seemed to multiply with each passing day. Public opinion polls showed a significant decline in his popularity. Nevertheless, the Associated Press named him the 2009 Athlete of the Year; just a few days later he was named the PGA Tour Player of the Year. These awards were based on his year-long golfing performance. Thus, Woods is still a celebrity but, in the minds of many, not the celebrity he was when we all sat down to dinner on Thanksgiving Day 2009. Woods and his wife divorced in late August 2010.

We have seen that, overall, violating social and moral norms is frowned upon by the public, regardless of whether one is a politician, an entertainer, or active in some other profession. Celebrities can usually maintain their status by explaining what happened and apologizing for their inappropriate actions. Failing to make apologies and explanations can further damage a celebrity's reputation. The public is less forgiving, however, when celebrities violate a legal norm and are given special treatment because of their celebrity status. Nevertheless, celebrity rarely ends as a result of violating a social or moral norm.

Celebrity Endorsement

One of the most popular advertising techniques worldwide is to have a celebrity endorse a product. Celebrity endorsement is usually only a part, but an important part, of a larger product marketing campaign. In addition to being well known and famous, celebrities are attractive, likeable, and trustworthy—at least in the minds of the public to whom the advertising message is directed. The hope is that the celebrities' qualities will be "transferred" in some way to a product and stimulate sales (Erdogan 1999). Advertisers avoid celebrities, such as O. J. Simpson, who have negative reputations. However, very little research has been done on the issue of celebrity endorsement. Scholars have discovered only a few things of note. One important finding is that celebrity endorsement is culture specific, that is, celebrity endorsement is most effective in the celebrity's home country. For example, an American celebrity endorsing a product in an advertisement broadcast in Austria was less effective in fostering an intent to purchase than a non-celebrity native spokesperson, making the country of origin (COO) an important factor in endorsement decisions (Chao, Wuhrer, and Werani 2005). Other scholars see celebrity endorsers as "cultural products" of their respective countries that are particularly effective if their countries are political and financial powers (Chung 2003;

Choi, Lee, and Kim 2005). In a capitalistic society, it just makes sense to use celebrities to sell products or services. Capitalism has always made maximum use of the tools it has available to pursue profit. However, there are less-visible issues here that make celebrity endorsement problematic.

The most obvious question that arises from celebrity endorsement is this one: What expertise does the celebrity endorser have? Returning to Tiger Woods, for a moment, could it be said that when he endorses Gatorade, he is an expert and thus qualified to make the endorsement? The consumer presumes so, given the fact that Gatorade was originally developed for and is regularly consumed by all types of athletes. Actress Jennifer Love Hewitt has appeared on behalf of Hanes lingerie. The implication is she wears the undergarments she is endorsing. But what about celebrities endorsing products with which they have no apparent expertise? Chrysler removed ads featuring singer Celine Dion after she failed to increase sales of the Chrysler Pacifica. The connection between the celebrity and the automobile was not strong enough to motivate sales of the Pacifica, but may have increased interest in Dion's music. The singer may have been seen as having little or no expertise in automobiles. McCracken (1989) suggests that there are a variety of endorsement modes: explicit ("I endorse this product"), implicit ("I use this product"), imperative ("You should use this product"), and co-present (that is, merely appearing with the product). Ultimately, the mode of endorsement may not mean as much as the credibility of the endorser. A highly credible (and likeable) celebrity could probably endorse a product in any of the aforementioned modes with positive results. In any case, endorsement of a product the celebrity has no direct connection to may be troublesome in terms of generating product sales, but probably has little effect on the celebrity's status.

A related issue involves ethics. Is it ethical for celebrities to endorse products they do not use or have no expertise in? As a rule, ethical behavior is expected of individuals, groups, and corporations in all walks of life. As a practical matter, however, people are willing to stretch this ethical rule, or perhaps ignore it altogether, if it is convenient for them or makes their lives easier. In traffic, some motorists regularly run red lights; in parking lots, some drivers park in fire lanes; in department stores, some shoppers return an article of clothing they purchased the previous day and wore the previous night; in the job market, some workers inflate their resumes—listing jobs they have not had or degrees they have not earned. The actions of "some" often impact the lives of "others." Because most of contemporary society tends to see ethics as relative (flexible), those who see ethics as absolute (firm), are often considered out of step. After all, many argue, there is no clear right and wrong, no clear black and white; the world is gray. Relativists would say it is acceptable for celebrities to endorse products they do not use or have no connection to; absolutists would say the practice is not acceptable. The culture and the law have almost always given advertisers the freedom to advertise products in their most appealing light. For example, a fast-food hamburger advertisement on television might show the burger as a hot, juicy slab of beef, paired with a rich, red slice of tomato, and accompanied by a deep-green leaf of lettuce, all on a fresh bun. A consumer purchasing a hamburger would likely find it is not much like the one advertised: the beef is barely warm, the tomato barely ripe, the lettuce slightly brown at the edges, and the bun stale from sitting under the kitchen's heat lamp. Yet consumers buy these sorts of burgers by the millions daily. Consumers do not require their burgers to match the ideal one they saw on television. Thus, as a people, we accept puffery, that is, the exaggeration of a product's qualities or benefits, as a necessary part of advertising. This is welcome news to celebrities. They need not fear that the products they endorse will cast them in a negative light if those products do not perform as promised. It's ironic, in a way. A celebrity can endow a product with positive qualities, but a product's negative qualities will not adversely affect a celebrity's status. With all due respect to the ethical absolutists, the relativists win here. Celebrity endorsements do little harm and are ethically acceptable to most consumers.

Fictional and Cartoon Celebrities

Must a celebrity be a real person? Up to this point, we have assumed so. However, a closer look at popular culture reveals some celebrities are not real people. Take, for example, Homer Simpson, the bumbling father on the highly rated animated television sitcom *The Simpsons*. Homer is so well known that some of his favorite utterances have made their way into regular human conversation. "D'Oh" and "Mmm donuts" are two examples. At special events, an individual who wears a Homer Simpson costume is popular with the younger set. No one cares to know the name of the person wearing the costume; Homer is the celebrity. The same could be said of Marge, Maggie, Lisa, and Bart, the other Simpson family members. Most viewers of the program probably couldn't tell you whose voice is behind each of the characters. Homer Simpson is famous and well known, highly visible in the media, and seeks to maintain his status, but meets none of the other standards for being a celebrity.

Other fictional characters have captured the attention of the public, or at least the younger segment of the public. Like some other fictional film or television stars, SpongeBob SquarePants has his own line of merchandise, such as pillows, bed linens, clothing, and backpacks. Individuals dressed as SpongeBob are popular wherever they go. Even some parents have been known to watch the SpongeBob program with their children. Then there's *South Park*. Although not written for children, the program is highly popular among younger viewers; however, many of them may not understand the program as satire. Nevertheless, Stan, Cartman, Kyle, and Kenny, the *South Park* third graders, are celebrities. Kenny is particularly well known for dying in almost every episode, giving rise to the popular statement, "Oh my God, they killed Kenny!" SpongeBob and the South Park kids are recent additions to a tradition of fictional celebrities. Older adults will remember the Flintstones, Road Runner, Bugs Bunny, Elmer Fudd, Foghorn Leghorn, as well as Mickey Mouse and other early Disney characters. Should the celebrity label be applied to these and other cartoon characters? If the answer is yes, then a different list of celebrity characteristics must apply. As noted earlier, only three of our current celebrity characteristics fit fictional characters: being famous and well known, being highly visible in media, and seeking to maintain status. There seems to be no harm in this. Adults know the difference between a real and a fictional celebrity. Children may not know the difference, but it probably doesn't matter.

On the other hand, some people might say, "No, fictional characters should not be celebrities. Children need to be taught the difference between the real and the pretend world. Cartoons are a good place to start. Children should learn that cartoon characters can do things real people cannot, such as return from the dead for the next *South Park* episode or drink lots of beer as Homer Simpson does with no real consequences. Reality triumphs fiction. Therefore, celebrities must be real people." This argument makes a good point. Some children do mimic what they see on television and viewing cartoon or other fictional characters as celebrities can have tragic consequences. For example, a 12-year-old Maryland boy committed suicide and left a note for his parents, telling them to watch *South Park* to learn why he took his life. The note specifically mentioned Kenny, the character who is killed in most episodes (McManus 1998). Scholars are divided on the causal connection between media consumption and human behavior. Some say the connection is strong; others say media may only be one of a number of factors in an individual's decision to act in a certain way. However, most scholars agree that a child's view of the world can be properly adjusted if parents watch programs with the child, ask questions about the child's beliefs, and intervene when needed. Parental influence is becoming an increasingly important part of a child's experience with media. This is particularly true since there appears to be no shortage of real people playing fictional celebrities who can be seen by the young as role models: Spiderman, Harry Potter, the Incredible Hulk, the *X-Men*'s Wolverine, and Hanna Montana, among others.

Fictional and cartoon personalities are often a significant part of a youngster's life. Calling these characters celebrities appears to do little harm, particularly if parents monitor a child's media experiences. However, not every cartoon or fictional character can qualify as a celebrity. To be considered a celebrity, the character must possess three of our celebrity characteristics: be famous and well known, be highly visible in media, and seek to maintain status.

Source and Quality of Celebrity Information

The general public gets most of its information about celebrities from the media, relying on celebrity magazines, celebrity television programs, and the Internet for the latest "scoop" on what a favorite celebrity is doing. A celebrity may occasionally make the more formal "evening news," but, as a rule, celebrity media (magazines, television programs, and the Internet) are the source of most current celebrity information. An individual does not have to monitor all celebrity media, of course, to stay informed. Friends, family, and co-workers regularly pass on what they know or have heard about celebrities. It might be revealing to look at each celebrity medium with a view toward understanding what and how information is presented.

Celebrity Magazines

What follows are brief content descriptions of six of the most popular celebrity magazines (four weekly and two monthly) in December 2009. The information, photos, and other material in each magazine appear to be typical of the magazine's regular content.

The December 21, 2009, issue of *OK Weekly* featured Tiger Woods and one of his alleged girlfriends on the cover. Inside, a fashion layout was first, revealing the different tastes and styles of actresses Penelope Cruz, Kate Hudson, Kristen Bell, Nicole Kidman, Drew Barrymore, as well as singer Carrie Underwood and bad-girl Lindsey Lohan. A photo spread featured recent shots of Tom Cruise, Katie Holmes, and daughter Suri; Brad Pitt, Angelina Jolie, and son Maddox; Paris Hilton and her new boyfriend sledding in Canada; and several cast members of television's *Glee* enjoying a break from the show's shooting schedule. That was followed by photos of couples: Hillary Swank and her new boyfriend, George Clooney and his new girlfriend, Jack Black and his wife, and Britney Spears and her new boyfriend. Each of the photos had either a short caption of explanation or a slightly longer sidebar of information. This photo-and-caption technique is highly popular with celebrity magazines. It is quick and simple. A single celebrity photo takes up little space leaving room for other celebrity photos. The cover story about Tiger Woods was longer, of course, but there was no shortage of photos of Tiger, his wife and children, and his alleged mistresses. As one moved on, the number of photos and snippets of information multiplied. The magazine covered celebrity holiday preparations, celebrity rumors, celebrity travel, and celebrities "after hours." Featured celebrities included singer Susan Boyle, Chef Gordon Ramsay, singer Lady Gaga, actress and model Pamela Anderson, actress Julia Roberts, singer Taylor Swift, singer Madonna, actresses Brooke Shields, Rosie Perez, Jane Lynch, Jennifer Aniston, and Anne Hathaway, among many others.

In Touch Weekly's December 21, 2009, issue also featured Tiger Woods and one of his alleged girlfriends on the cover. A fashion layout was first inside, featuring many of the same celebrities and the same clothing featured in *OK Weekly*. Short features followed revealing actress-singer Miley Cyrus's new tattoo, the popularity of spiked clothes (singers Rihanna and Adam Lambert, actress Kristen Stewart), and the silly faces made by the young children of celebrities. Did *American Idol*'s Simon Cowell wax his chest hair and have Botox treatments? Perhaps, as a before-and-after photo comparison showed. A favorite section in many celebrity magazines might be called "out-and-about." Photos are presented showing celebrities engaged in simple, everyday activities—much like any member of the public. We see celebrities getting coffee, standing in line at a grocery or convenience store, shopping, or playing with their children. The photos are, of course, accompanied by brief captions. Apparently, singer LeAnn Rimes, actress Jennifer Lopez, singer Marc Antony, singer Gwen Stefani, and actresses Hayden Panettiere and Ellen Pompeo are just like us! They walk, they play with dogs, they buy bread, they push their children on playground swings. Actress Kristen Chenoweth is seen eating a pretzel; actor Jerry O'Connell is pictured leaving the post office with stamps and other mailing supplies in hand. Yes, indeed, just like us! Next, the Tiger Woods cover story is presented. It's longer and includes numerous photos of all those involved in the scandal. Additionally, some significant space is given to a story about Amanda Knox, the student in Italy who was convicted of murdering her roommate. Fashion layouts are next, featuring the Real Housewives of New Jersey. The cast of MTV's *Jersey Shore* gets some attention; upcoming movies are reviewed.

Tiger Woods did not appear on the cover of *Life and Style Weekly* for the week of December 21, 2009. What celebrity pushed Tiger off the cover? Actress Sandra Bullock. Her battle to help her husband (television personality Jesse James) gain custody of his son from a previous marriage was the magazine's featured story. First inside was a fashion layout featuring the 10 best dressed female celebrities of the week. Much like the ones in the two previous magazines described, the layout featured the usual suspects: actresses Penelope Cruz, Kate Hudson, and Drew Barrymore, among others. The reader is shown the best photos of the week: actress-singer Miley Cyrus, singer Carrie Underwood, actress Paris Hilton, the New Jersey Housewives, actress Halle Berry, Brad Pitt with Angelina Jolie, Tom Cruise and Katie Holmes, and Jennifer Lopez with Mark Antony. The reader discovers that Brad and Angelina have been a couple for five years. It's their anniversary. Will the relationship last? Has actor George Clooney finally met his match in model Elisabette Canalis? Next, information about the Tiger Woods situation is presented; the emphasis is on whether his marriage will survive his alleged infidelity. Elsewhere in the magazine, the reader will find bits of information and photos of MTV's *Jersey Shore* cast, go behind the scenes of the upcoming movie *Sex and the City 2*, ponder whether actress Cameron Diaz and singers Courtney Love and Madonna have had "cheek-plumping" surgery, as well as examine wedding dress fashions, jewelry, fragrances, footwear, hair styles, and makeup advertisements featuring celebrities as models.

People magazine (December 21, 2009) took a slightly different approach by featuring Elin Woods on the cover. Deep inside the magazine, the full Woods story was presented, but the emphasis appeared to be on what she would (or should) do as a result of her husband's apparent infidelity. But first inside the magazine were photos of celebrities out-and-about: actress Halle Berry and daughter, singer Gwen Stefani and son, actor Simon Baker and son, television's David Letterman and son, the Tom Cruise family, and Brad with Angelina. Fashion photos revealed the particular clothing styles of actresses Kate Hudson, Penelope Cruz, Nicole Kidman, Kate Beckinsale, and singers Carrie Underwood and Miley Cyrus. A section titled "Scoop" presented the latest information on actress Jennifer Aniston, singer Susan Boyle, actress Reese Witherspoon and actor Jake Gyllenhaal, singer Taylor Swift, and singer-actress Jessica Simpson. Celebrities were shown wearing spiked clothing. Movie reviews were presented for a half-dozen upcoming films. The year's best kid's television shows were listed as well as significant upcoming television programs. Alicia Key's music was discussed. On the more serious side, an in-depth article explored the effects of the recession on Wilmington, a small Ohio town. Chaz (formerly Chastity) Bono—daughter-now-son—of singers Sonny and Cher was profiled with emphasis on the impact of gender change. A Top Chef recipe was presented as were numerous advertisements for lingerie and jewelry with celebrities as models.

The following conclusions can be drawn from the examination of the four weekly celebrity magazines:

- They are more similar than different.
- They present hundreds of photos and bits of information.
- They limit longer features to current, "hot" celebrity personalities.
- They mostly feature entertainment celebrities.
- They are supportive, not critical, of celebrities.

Each of these statements requires explanation. First, the four weekly celebrity magazines are more similar than different. In all but one case, the ones examined had the Tiger Woods situation as the cover story; they all had introductory fashion layouts utilizing most of the same female celebrities; they all had what we are calling "out-and-about" photos showing celebrities in real life situations; most of the photos were exactly the same from magazine to magazine, but where there was a difference, the photos appeared to have been taken only seconds apart. With only a few exceptions, the same celebrities were featured in all four magazines. Only *People* magazine devoted space to a "common" topic: the recession in a small town.

The photos in each magazine number in the hundreds. To an infrequent or new reader, the photos and accompanying bits of information seem to be overwhelming. An experienced celebrity magazine reader will think nothing of it. Page after page contains photos, large and small, fitted as neatly together as a completed jigsaw puzzle. But the eye moves quickly, the information is absorbed, and the reader moves on. Furthermore, with the exception of the staged fashion layouts, the photos depict reality. In other words, they are true representations of what was actually happening at the time the photo was taken. Captions identify the celebrities and the event or location at which they were photographed.

Selecting a current or "hot" personality for the cover and for a detailed story is not only a good marketing ploy, but also an indication that the magazine is up to date on celebrity culture. Cover photos are eye-catching and usually accompanied by a few words indicating "the issue" to be discussed inside. There are cover similarities among the magazines, especially if a celebrity has been the subject of much public interest. But the stories inside are usually different in both tone and approach. A cover story may be accompanied by one or two shorter pieces, with photos, highlighting other celebrities who might be considered "runners-up" in a competition to appear on the magazine's cover.

We know there are celebrities in almost every profession. The taxonomy developed in Chapter 1 clearly indicates that. However, celebrity magazines routinely ignore celebrities in other professions and concentrate on only those in entertainment. A quick look back in this chapter will reveal the celebrities mentioned are actors, actresses, singers, models, or television stars. Finding information in the magazines about celebrities in politics, business, science, or one of the other categories is almost impossible. In other words, the magazines have a narrow celebrity focus. This is probably to their advantage; entertainment celebrities are more likely than celebrities in other fields to pique the interest of a typical reader. Still, shouldn't a celebrity magazine provide broader coverage? Admittedly, these magazines have a limited number of pages; they can't cover everything. Printing deadlines require articles and photos to be prepared well in advance of the publication date. Editors and publishers may ask themselves what they can include in a magazine that typically runs about 80 pages and must contain a significant number of advertisements. Who will generate the most interest, and the most sales? The answer, of course, is entertainment celebrities.

It is not at all surprising that celebrity magazines support, rather than criticize, the celebrities they feature. No one likes criticism, particularly if that criticism is directed at a favorite celebrity. Remember that a celebrity can embody the dreams and desires of many members of the general public. Criticizing a celebrity can be seen as criticizing the reader. That's not as farfetched as it might seem. Many people identify closely with celebrities. People buy their music, attend their concerts, watch their movies, and purchase products they have endorsed. These bonds are not easily broken. Celebrity is powerful in the 21st century. The magazines recognize this and rarely make a critical comment. If on occasion they do offer one, it is often mild and related to a social or moral norm. For example, *In Touch Weekly* ("Miley: 17 going on 37?") wondered whether actress-singer Miley Cyrus's tattoo was "age-appropriate." Perhaps the magazine did not realize that tattooed teens are not all that unusual today. Cyrus's ink was relatively benign: just breathe. However, the magazine also questioned her pole dancing at the Teen Choice Awards, her leather clothes, and her "itsy-bitsy" bikini. The mild criticism was offset to some degree by the almost full-length, half-page photo of Miley in that bikini. High school boys all over America would probably spend a little time looking at that photo. Okay, so she's growing up fast. Who doesn't these days?

Two other celebrity magazines were reviewed, *In Style* and *Vanity Fair*. Although these magazines are among the top-selling magazines in the country, they are issued monthly; this presents a number of challenges. Because of printing deadlines, they cannot cover what celebrities did or said last week or perhaps even last month. Also, when information about events or situations is presented, the accompanying photos reveal that the celebrities mentioned may not be celebrities at all. How many people would recognize Pepe Fanjul or Irina Lazareanu? Who are they? Few people know, but one magazine says they (and other unknowns) attended a dinner at the Monkey Bar, hosted by a New York fashion house. Many of the recognizable celebrities who appear on the pages of these magazines are typically used as models in advertising. A reader will occasionally get information on the comings-and-goings of well-known celebrities, but most are endorsing some product. For example, actress Zooey Deschanel appears in an ad for cotton fibers and actor Matthew McConaughey in an ad for a men's fragrance. A first-time reader of these magazines might be left with two impressions. First, the articles and information in the magazine are simply overwhelmed by advertisements. Second, the magazines seem to be written for the "in-crowd," wealthy, hip, connected individuals who live, work, and socialize in the New York metropolitan area. Only once in a while will one discover an article that might be interesting to Americans who live in what has been called "flyover country," that is, the middle part of the United States that East Coasters jet over on their way to Hollywood, America's other mecca, on the West Coast. In short, these magazines are slick, glamorous, wish books, filled with products and services typical Americans neither want nor can afford. The apparent emphasis on New York personalities makes the magazines seem snobbish. In any case, because they do not deal with current well-known celebrities in the same way the weeklies do, we will not consider them further.

So is there a problem with celebrity magazines? Some critics might say there is more than one problem with the magazines. First, the information they provide is sparse. It is true every photo has a caption, but the captions don't tell us much. Features do provide some in-depth information, but if one already knows about the individual or situation featured, these extended pieces add little new information and tend toward speculation. If we already know the facts from other sources, what's left to say? "Well, *if* such-and-such happens, then *maybe* this will happen." This is not good journalism. In fact, some critics would say, it isn't journalism at all. Journalists once prided themselves on writing fair, balanced, objective stories. Stories in celebrity magazines are not necessarily unfair, but they often lack balance and objectivity. Moreover, at its best, journalism provides important news and information we *need* to manage our lives, not trivial information we *want* about celebrities. However, what does one expect? You can buy a celebrity magazine for about $3. Information-wise, celebrity magazines are like cotton candy: tasty and fun, but not nutritious. Second, there is an obvious redundancy across all celebrity magazines in photos and information. In spite of the fact that some of the magazines have the word *style* in their name, the reality is that the magazines have no unique style. The same photos are used, the same information is conveyed in captions, the same advertisements appear, and the same individuals are often on the cover. The magazines look pretty much alike. Tear a page from one of the magazines and show it to a regular celebrity magazine reader; chances are the reader could not tell you from which magazine it was taken.

On the other hand, some people might feel critics of the magazines are unduly harsh. So what if the magazines are cotton candy? We need cotton candy. There's a time and place for it. It is not supposed to be a breakfast food. Similarly, celebrity magazines are not supposed to provide a reader with the latest world and national news. Get information on wars, the economy, and government from other sources. Celebrity magazines are light and frothy, just what some readers want and need to take their minds off their (or the world's) troubles. In short, celebrity magazines have a narrow, specific goal and they are strikingly good at achieving that goal. Additionally, there is nothing wrong with repetition of photos and information. Not everyone purchases all the magazines; a reader who purchases only one will not notice the repetition. Besides, people enjoy having a choice among similar products. That's why there is more than one type of bread on grocery store shelves.

Readers wanting a different type of celebrity information often turn to the supermarket tabloids. A tabloid is a small-format, newspaper-type publication featuring "screaming headlines . . . large photographs and stories about sex, violence, and celebrities" (Biagi 2005). For example, the cover of one *National Enquirer* issue showed several hip and leg photos of celebrities together with the headline "Stars with Cellulite!" The cover also promised that a story inside would reveal "Charlize Theron's Shocking Secret Life." *The National Examiner* and *The Globe* are two other well-known tabloids. There is some debate about whether these publications are newspapers or magazines. They use newsprint and look like a newspaper, but rarely follow standard journalistic rules of truth, balance, and objectivity. It seems more appropriate to call them entertainment magazines. These publications occasionally turn to the bizarre. For example, past headlines have revealed "Noah Had Dinosaurs on the Ark," "Bigfoot Kept Lumberjack as Love Slave," and "Man Sets Lard Eating Record." Supermarket tabloids are not serious sources of information, but they can be escapist fun. They are not important enough to contribute anything useful to our discussion of celebrity.

Celebrity magazine circulation declined during the recession of 2008–2010. Several magazines suffered from poor management practices. The conclusion some experts draw from these problems is that there are too many celebrity magazines and "consolidation is inevitable as advertising and circulation erodes" (Stableford 2009). Nevertheless, celebrity magazines in some form are here to stay. They are popular with readers and usually sell well, especially when placed near the checkout lanes of book and grocery stores. In a culture stressing the importance of diversity in all things, celebrity magazines, perhaps downsized, fewer in number, or offered in electronic form can take their rightful place among the other specialty magazines. Historically, many magazines with a modest target audience (sports, bridal, automotive, fashion, and cooking) have survived. Many general interest magazines (*Life, Saturday Evening Post*) have not.

Celebrity Television Programs

As it is used here, the phrase "celebrity television programs" refers not to shows *starring* celebrities, but to shows *about* celebrities. These half-hour programs can often be seen daily in what is called "prime time fringe," the time between the end of the evening news broadcasts and the beginning of network programming service. Local stations must fill this time each day with programs they have purchased through syndication. Some stations run off-network shows such as *Friends*, while others prefer first-run game shows, such as *Wheel of Fortune* or *Jeopardy*. Celebrity television programs are popular choices for prime time fringe. They are fresh and topical. Two mid-December broadcasts of four popular celebrity television shows (*Extra, Inside Edition, The Insider,* and *TMZ*) were examined to determine what and how information was presented as well as provide material for comparison with celebrity magazines.

Inside Edition is hosted by Deborah Norville, former host of NBC's *Today* show and a former television journalist. In a Tuesday episode, the Tiger Woods scandal was the hot topic; events related to his situation were summarized. A summary of the Golden Globe Award nominees was presented. A short feature followed on an Oklahoma woman who saw a burglar leaving her house with the family's Christmas presents and pursued him until he was captured by police. A second short feature speculated on the whereabouts of a Salt Lake City woman who mysteriously disappeared. Was her marriage on the rocks? Why did her husband go camping in bad weather and leave her home alone? The next program segment listed the year's top sex scandals. Celebrities on the list included television talk show host David Letterman, sports broadcaster Steve Phillips, South Carolina Governor Mark Sanford, and actor Josh Duhamel, among others. Actress Kate Hudson was shown working out at a New York gym, the video having been shot through a rain-speckled window. Film stars Sarah Jessica Parker and Hugh Grant were shown promoting their new movie. The show concluded with a short video clip of an octopus using two coconut shells as a house. Wednesday's episode began by rehashing Tiger Woods's troubles. A feature on ESPN sports reporter Erin Andrews followed. Andrews was secretly videotaped in the nude in her hotel room. She was seen leaving the courtroom after confronting Michael Barrett who pleaded guilty to the crime. Next, a short piece introduced the viewer to Tom Smallwood, a man who, after losing his job, pursued his dream of becoming a professional bowler. Numerous shorter items followed, all but two of them featured celebrities, including Kate Hudson (no longer with New York Yankee boyfriend Alex Rodriguez), singer Taylor Swift (soon to be on the cover of *People*), and the cast of MTV's *Jersey Shore* (wondering why a female cast member was punched in the face at a bar). One exception to this laundry list of celebrity activities involved a grandmother who was kidnapped, beaten, and kept in the trunk of an automobile for 26 hours but survived. She warned viewers to be wary of strangers knocking on their doors. The second exception, and perhaps the most unusual snippet of information in the show, revealed that a government employee had received an honor. The Federal Reserve's Ben Bernanke was reported to have been named *Time* magazine's Person of the Year. Government employees are usually not considered celebrities unless they are involved in some scandal that has significant consequences. No matter, the Bernanke item took fewer than 10 seconds of program time.

Film and television actor Mario Lopez hosts *Extra*. A Tuesday episode of this show began with questions about the Tiger Woods situation. Did he pay off one of his mistresses? Will there be a court battle with his wife over the children? The Golden Globe nominees were summarized and Sarah Jessica Parker and Hugh Grant were interviewed as they were out and about promoting their new movie. Viewers got a behind-the-scenes look at the popular television program *NCIS* and were then treated to photos of a fashion layout featuring singer and model Rihanna. Couples news was next. Kate Hudson and Alex Rodriguez may have split; the Reese Witherspoon-Jake Gyllenhaal romance may be over. Actor Mel Gibson, however, is apparently still with singer-girlfriend Oksana Grigorieva. They have a new baby girl. Wednesday's program began with another summary of the Tiger Woods scandal, but asked a new question: Did Woods have an affair with singer Jessica Simpson? Although the two posed for pictures at some event, that's apparently all it was—two celebrities meeting and agreeing to have their picture taken together. The movie *Nine* was reviewed. The Kate Hudson-Alex Rodriguez breakup was announced. Short pieces followed on David Letterman, comedian George Lopez, actress Helen Mirren, and the dancing kids in the television commercial for GAP clothing. Holiday makeup tips were given, followed by a promotional announcement for FOX's *So You Think You Can Dance*?

The Insider features Lara Spencer and her colleagues as co-hosts. Spencer has been host of several television programs. One of her co-hosts is Star Jones, a lawyer and former co-host of the popular daily morning talk show *The View*. Celebrity followers may know Spencer and Jones, but the other co-hosts (they often vary from time to time) are mostly young, attractive, unknowns. The program presents itself as a forum for arguments about celebrity news and frequently asks the question, "Which side are you on?" The Tuesday episode began by asking two guests (a comedian and a lawyer) to argue this question: If Tiger Woods is found to have taken performance-enhancing drugs, is he finished as a celebrity? The "argument" between the two guests consisted mostly of gossip and did little more than generate laughs and further speculation about Woods. The viewer was next informed that "a friend told us" Kate Hudson and Alex Rodriguez were finished as a couple. Famous New Jersey housewife Bethenny was seen posing for a picture in the nude in New York. The Golden Globe award nominees were announced, and Rihanna was shown in a fashion shoot for *GQ* magazine. The program listed its Top Newsmakers of 2009. The list included actress McKenzie Phillips (at #4) who wrote a book about her life and the sexual relationship she had with her father. The program scolded her for revealing such intimate facts and suggested that she included the incestuous relationship with her father simply to sell books. The top newsmaker in 2009, according to the program, was singer-dancer Michael Jackson. The program concludes each episode by naming the best and worst celebrities of the day. On Tuesday, singer Susan Boyle was the best; singer Courtney Love was the worst. Wednesday's show began with the news that Reese Witherspoon and Jake Gyllenhaal had split. Tiger Woods's problems followed. One item about Woods was delivered as if it were breaking news. "This just in" is a phrase used several times in the program to alert viewers that new information is to follow: Tiger Woods's jet plane flew across the country . . . but Tiger was not on board. With that trivial bit of information delivered, the program moved on to discuss why men "marry high, but cheat low." Kate Hudson and her co-stars next promoted their new movie. Actor Johnny Depp and actress Anne Hathaway were seen in a trailer from the movie *Alice in Wonderland*. The top celebrity babies were featured, and the gossip and innuendo about Tiger Woods and Jessica Simpson was presented. "I have a source who has a friend who told me . . ." Woods and Simpson exchanged text messages! The day's best celebrity was actress Emma Watson; the worst was country singer Toby Keith.

Harvey Levin's *TMZ* is, in many respects, unlike other celebrity television programs. First, there is no host, *per se*. Levin and his employees at TMZ.com gather around a couple of office cubicles and share information about celebrities. They are just "hangin' out" and swapping stories. The program often plays for laughs by using oversized graphics and distorted or high-pitched voices in pre-taped inserts. Sometimes the overall effect is to ridicule the subject—at others merely to parody what some celebrity has said or done. A Tuesday program in mid-December began with a photo showing singer Miley Cyrus apparently holding a cigarette. But, no, she wasn't smoking; the photo had been cropped. The original photo showed a woman standing next to Cyrus holding the cigarette. Short video clips followed. Singer Britney Spears was shown buying an orange drink at a convenience store; Elin Woods was seen taking her children out to lunch. A longer video piece featured young singer Justin Bieber performing at a

Los Angeles mall. The cast of MTV's *Jersey Shore* was interviewed with particular emphasis on the female cast member who was punched out in a bar. A favorite TMZ technique is the "ambush question." TMZ cameras are apparently almost everywhere celebrities are so it's relatively easy to catch a celebrity going from one place to another, walk along with the celebrity, and ask a question or two. Actor-director Ron Howard was caught in this fashion and asked whether he'd make a movie about the Tiger Woods situation. Howard was noncommittal. Asked what the movie's title might be, Howard responded, "Smooth Swing." A short video clip revealed that actress Renée Zellweger and actor Bradley Cooper were seen (from across the street) either arguing or house hunting—hard to tell. A Wednesday show revealed that Tiger Woods may have been spending time on his luxurious yacht. This gave rise to a musical parody sung to the tune of *Gilligan's Island*. Next, the ambush question technique was used on singer LeAnn Rimes and California first lady Maria Shriver. Singer Rod Stewart and his wife Penny were seen dancing and being pursued by a drunken fan. Young singer Jason Bieber was ambushed at the airport and asked if he was ready to date. The *Jersey Shore* cast made another appearance. A photo of Nicole Kidman was shown and comments made about her makeup—too much white. John Lithgow was ambushed on the street and asked about his role in the television show *Dexter*. Actor Tim Robbins was seen riding his bike. Robbins stopped to take a question about a possible movie. The program ended with a photo of a statue of Marilyn Monroe, made entirely of jelly beans. In each case, on both days, when a photo or video clip was shown, it was followed (or preceded) by light banter between Levin and one or more of his employees.

Celebrity television programs are often referred to as "news magazines." In a way, they are. They do provide news, but it's a specialized type of news. It's entertainment news, usually only about celebrities; it's not information members of the general public *must have* to manage their lives. There is repetition of information, some of it little more than gossip; much of it is simply trivial. The programs feature many of the same celebrities the print magazines do, but feature fewer celebrities in one show than their print cousins feature in one issue. However, the television programs move at a faster pace and, because they have shorter production deadlines, are consequently more current. Still, like their print counterparts, celebrity television programs provide little information, lack balance and objectivity, and—with the exception of

evening newscasts (ABC, CBS, NBC, PBS). Once cable television became popular, new sources of information became available, often linked to a traditional service. FOX is the exception here; the network provides some prime-time programming but no evening newscast. FOX does, however, have a popular cable service, FOX News. CNN (Cable News Network) is another exception. It is a stand-alone cable news service. For a time, these traditional news outlets seemed to meet the public's needs. However, the Internet and its related peripherals have changed the traditional media world, perhaps forever. It is widely known that newspapers are in financial trouble; most have reduced the size of their papers and/or laid off workers; some have gone out of business. Fewer subscribers want the print editions of a paper, preferring instead to go online and get their news from a newspaper's Web site or from an online news aggregator. Online news is mostly free; subscriptions to a print edition may cost as much as $200 or more per year. Additionally, the network evening newscasts have been losing viewers for several years. Cable news is still popular, perhaps because it is available 24 hours a day. Nevertheless, more and more people are turning away from traditional news sources in favor of news they can get online via a computer or cell phone. The most sophisticated cell phones can do many amazing things. Using a 3G network, phones can not only make calls, but also access the Internet, play music, serve as a GPS device, and do dozens of other things by simply touching the screen to load an app (application). Moreover, you can do this from almost anywhere you are; you do not need to be sitting in front of a television set to get the latest news and information.

Celebrity requires media exposure. A changing media environment can influence the frequency and quality of celebrity information the public receives. Traditionally, celebrity news has been only a small part of the information provided by print newspapers. The early newspapers, you may remember, provided bits of information about the well known and the famous. Sometimes the information was gossip; sometimes it was factual. But as newspapers developed, such news was relegated to inside pages, or perhaps a small weekend section. It rarely detracted from a newspaper's primary mission: delivering information the public needs to make decisions about their lives, the "yellow journalism" period (overly dramatic, highly sensational stories about crime, scandals, and celebrities in the late 1800s) being the exception. Some yellow journalism can be found today. Still, the decline of print journalism in the 21st century makes newspapers less important to celebrities than they were at one time.

News magazines, because they publish weekly, are also less important to celebrities. They cannot keep pace with celebrity television programs and can, at best, only summarize what we already know about celebrities from other sources. Moreover, their sometimes in-depth treatment of celebrity issues appears to be at odds with the reading preferences of many individuals. Few people want to take time to read four pages, but might read four paragraphs, or—more likely—four lines. If print is mostly irrelevant when it comes to celebrities, what about television? Network evening newscasts have little time for routine celebrity news, but may devote a minute or two to an individual or situation that has captured the public's interest. On the other hand, cable news outlets, because they operate 24 hours a day, have plenty of time to cover a wide range of celebrity issues. Most cable news services have a regular, short entertainment news segment each hour. The information provided is often fact-based but, at times, relies on rumor, gossip, and innuendo. Some viewers find this sort of information less compelling than celebrity information they find elsewhere. Thus, we can see that when they were the only media available, traditional news outlets were important sources of celebrity information. However, the media landscape has changed.

New Media Information Sources

The development and growth of the Internet and of electronic devices used to access it have given rise to new sources of celebrity information. Newspapers were somewhat reluctant, at first, to put their news online, but fell into line quickly when they discovered hundreds of millions of people were using the Internet for all sorts of things, including getting the latest news. Metropolitan newspapers such as the *New York Times* and the *Washington Post* established Web sites that carried many of the stories found in their print versions. Other papers, in markets large and small, followed. Most daily newspapers now have an associated Web site; some have a webmaster whose job it is to keep online information current. While some celebrity news finds its way onto these Web sites, the majority of material relates directly to news of local, national, or international interest.

The television and cable news services also have Web sites that publish information, typically stories, or versions of stories, news anchors and reporters have read on the air. The information on these Web sites is usually organized according to content. For example, a Web site might begin with the latest news—usually no more than three or four stories—at the top of the page. Introductory paragraphs are offered and links provided to the full stories. Further down the page, a reader will often find sections devoted to national, international, political, economic, sports, and entertainment news. It is in the entertainment section that one finds most celebrity information. Each section usually contains several headlines that readers can click on to get details. On a Monday in late December, a survey of five Web sites (msnbc. com, abcnews.com, cbsnews.com, cnn.com, and foxnews.com) revealed the following:

- All five Web sites had entertainment news sections
- Four Web sites provided information on the previous weekend's most successful movies
- Five Web sites covered the arrest of actor Charlie Sheen for domestic violence; they disagreed, however, as to whether Sheen and his wife were headed for counseling or divorce
- Two Web sites reported that Ivana Trump, former wife of billionaire Donald Trump, had been escorted from a plane by police; she apparently became angry and argumentative when she lashed out at young children who had been running and screaming in the aisles
- Three Web sites contained information on the year's celebrity deaths
- There were some interesting differences among the five Web sites.

None of the Web sites missed "breaking" celebrity news; the differences were mostly in the choice of subject. For example, cbsnews.com included a story titled "Love and Sex with Robots," asking the question, "Can robots be more than friends?" Over on abcnews.com, readers learned that actor Tim Robbins and actress Susan Sarandon had split; a story summarizing the lives of stars who died young was followed by another story asking whether pharmacy shopping, that is, the practice of getting prescription drugs from several different doctors, could have contributed to the stars' early deaths. A preview of upcoming NBC television shows had a prominent place on the msnbc.com site. Foxnews. com reported singer Mary J. Blige punched her husband at a bar they were in after she apparently caught him flirting with a waitress. Both Blige and her husband reportedly left the bar rapidly after the incident. Nicolas Cage's financial problems were the subject of a cnn.com story; Cage was being sued by a real estate company for $36.7 million.

So this is progress—news Web sites consider celebrity and entertainment news important enough to place it alongside news from politics, government, the economy, and world affairs. Some people might wonder why these Web sites take the trouble to include celebrity news. After all, there are many Web sites devoted entirely to celebrities (see Chapter 7). If one is hungry for celebrity news, those Web sites are chock-full of all sorts of information. Furthermore, celebrity information on news Web sites pales in comparison to what is available in celebrity magazines and on celebrity television shows. Old-timers might raise the issue of whether celebrity news belongs anywhere near the "real" news. We need information vital to the functioning of individuals in a democracy—that's news. Information that feeds our vicarious or leisure lives is not news—that's entertainment. Some see the line between news and entertainment as important as the line between truth and fiction. Sadly, those lines are increasingly blurred. Younger people, however, have a much broader view of news. To many of them, news is information of any sort. They'd argue that it's the information, not the categorization, that's important. This dichotomy of views is more than a mere academic argument. How we define news, what we want from news, and where we get our news will shape the media world as well as both our behavior and our knowledge in the years ahead. What role will celebrities play in the news? No one knows for sure, but chances are, celebrities will continue to be influential and people will want to know more about them as we move ahead in the 21st century.

Social Media and Celebrities

The term *social media* "describes the collaborative process that creates meaning and community online through the exchange of text, photos, or videos . . . [and] includes blogs, video-sharing sites, social networks, message boards, and social news sites" (Burns 2009, xii–xiii). The remarkable thing about social media is that "users" control content. Anyone can contribute anything to the Internet world through one or more of the social media outlets. This differs significantly from the world of newspapers, magazines, television shows, and news Web sites where content is closely controlled and where consumers have little input.

The development and use of social media has resulted in several issues of interest to our discussion of celebrity. First, social media, particularly blogs, and to some degree MySpace and Facebook, have enabled people to comment freely about celebrities and get feedback from readers. Until social media developed, media critics working for newspapers, magazines, and television or cable outlets were responsible for commenting on the lives and work of celebrities. Blogs are a forum for the exchange of ideas and information about many things, including celebrities. Today, anyone can comment on the latest celebrity movie, romance, or hairstyle; however, much of what one finds on blogs is opinion, and one must be careful not to interpret everything one reads as fact. Blogs may actually benefit celebrities, keeping their names and activities in focus and important to many readers. Although MySpace and Facebook are the two top social networking sites, there are others, including Bebo, Cyworld, Friendster, Twellow, Classmates.com, and Xanga. LinkedIn is predominantly a business networking site. MySpace and Facebook have the most members and are therefore important sources of information. Many celebrities, particularly those in entertainment, have a MySpace or Facebook page and some allow individuals to sign up as "friends," enabling them to follow celebrities more closely than might otherwise be possible. Admittedly, some of the information posted to these sites is trivial and mundane, but trivial and mundane information is often accepted as worth knowing in today's postmodern culture.

The apparent generational differences about social media have less to do with the concept than with the execution. In other words, communication among family, friends, and associates is important; using electronic technology and establishing systems to facilitate such communication is also to be valued. So, too, is the freedom to express one's ideas and opinions on any subject, including celebrities. However, these positives may be tempered by the poor quality of most social media communication. Clarity and correctness are often missing from material posted on social media sites. Many blogs, messages, and the like are full of grammatical errors. Call it old-fashioned if you will, but there is value in using language correctly. Any argument or opinion piece is less important to a reader if it is poorly organized, has misspellings, and lacks proper capitalization or punctuation. You don't have to be an English teacher to appreciate good writing; moreover, good writing goes a long way toward making an argument persuasive. Would you be convinced of an argument's validity if a blog about Britney Spears spelled her name Brittany Speers? Is Ms. Spears's celebrity status enhanced or diminished by the error, assuming a reader notices the error?

Another significant problem relates to threaded discussions on message boards, but is also in evidence elsewhere, particularly on news Web sites where reader comments about stories are encouraged and posted. In threaded discussions a user can post a comment and get responses to it from other users. A reader is able to see the original post and subsequent replies, and, if the reader so chooses, add to the discussion. There are two problems here. First, replies to the original post may, for a time, comment on the topic. However, before long, many users begin to write, not about the topic, but about another individual's comments. This seems acceptable up to a point, but wandering away from the topic often dilutes its significance. Try this: log on to a message board and look at the most recent comment in a threaded discussion of celebrities. Can you tell, from the most recent comment, what the original post said? You might say, yes, the original post was about celebrities. Well, that may be true, but what about celebrities exactly? Can you tell from the last post whether the original mentioned a specific celebrity, was pro-celebrity, anti-celebrity, or just raising an issue for comment? What key idea was expressed in the original post? Chances are the latest post will not tell you much about the original. Is this important? Yes, it is. In order to understand fully any idea, comment, or perspective, one must see it in context, that is, how it is connected or related to other ideas, comments, or perspectives. You could get the context by reading *all* the posts about celebrities, but sometimes there are hundreds, even thousands, of them. Who has the time to read them all? Well, some people apparently have a lot of time and spend hours posting comments here and there—first one place, then another. What quality of life is inherent in following celebrities by spending hours and hours staring at a computer screen or pounding on a keyboard?

The other problem with threaded discussions is misinformation. As we have seen, rumor and gossip about celebrities is everywhere. If a rumor gets a thorough workout in a threaded discussion on a message board, a news Web site, or elsewhere, it often takes on the cloak of truth. If everyone is talking about it, it must be true, right? Wrong. The volume of comments does not confer truth. Furthermore, as we have seen with exchanges of information on MySpace and Facebook, much of the information in threaded discussions borders on the trivial and mundane. It is difficult to see how trivial or misinformation serves celebrities unless one believes British writer Oscar Wilde was correct when he said, "the only thing worse than being talked about is not being talked about."

Overall, social media seem, at present, to play a moderate role in the lives of celebrities. There is much diversity of opinion among social media outlets and consensus is rare. Celebrities may not be well served by information about them on social sites, but they are not likely to be much hurt. Misinformation, particularly rumors and gossip, can be mitigated to some extent by traditional media's presentation of the facts. More and more people are turning away from traditional media, however, and this makes grasping the truth about any celebrity a slippery enterprise. One would do well not to consider social media as the only source of information. Nevertheless, given the power of the Internet and the increasing popularity of some Web sites, the day may come when social media are the only "news" media we have. On that day, in the absence of traditional media, if celebrities wish to maintain their status, they all may have to take more responsibility for connecting with the public by becoming regular bloggers, designing their own message boards, and initiating threaded discussions. This will mean closer public contact and spending more time online, something with which not all celebrities will be comfortable.

Misconceptions about Celebrity

There are several misconceptions about celebrity worth noting. First, simply calling oneself a celebrity does not make it so. In a recent cable television commercial, author and fitness expert Jennifer Nicole Lee, appearing on behalf of a brand of fitness machines, was identified as a "Fitness and Exercise Celebrity." In the fitness world, she is probably well known. Her Web site (jennifernicolelee.com) indicates she "has become an icon for women and fellow moms across the world with her amazing 70-pound plus weight loss success story." Furthermore, she has shared her weight loss story with Oprah Winfrey, *Inside Edition*, and *The Early Show* on CBS. Promoting a healthy lifestyle is praiseworthy, but with all due respect to Ms. Lee, she is, at best, a limited celebrity, known primarily in the fitness and exercise world. True celebrities are more widely known than Ms. Lee. Suppose one were to obtain photographs of Ms. Lee and a widely known celebrity such as Paris Hilton, Angelina Jolie, or even ABC News's Barbara Walters or CBS News's Katie Couric. Show the photos to 100 people on the street (or to 20 friends) and see how many recognize Lee. It's not scientific research, but it would likely reveal that more people know Hilton, Jolie, Walters, or Couric than know Lee. This simply means that Lee's celebrity is limited. She barely meets our list of celebrity characteristics, and only if we broadly expand some criteria to include her accomplishments. There are many individuals who qualify as limited celebrities: reality show contestants who did not win, most cable television news anchors, winners of a state or national lottery, and so forth. Of course, we cannot prevent individuals from calling themselves celebrities, but we should be aware that language is important. Celebrity is a powerful phenomenon in the 21st century. We should be careful on whom we confer celebrity status.

Second, and related to the one just discussed, is the misconception that any member of the general public becomes a celebrity by doing one thing and having that one thing viewed or acknowledged by a large number of people. Take, for example, the videos uploaded to YouTube and available for viewing worldwide. Many videos are funny, entertaining, or unusual. However, even if a video has been viewed by 17 million people in 20 countries (Burns 2009), that doesn't mean the video producer is a celebrity. Many videos are poorly photographed, lack proper audio, or treat trivial subjects. Some viewers may watch a video several times, but rarely pay attention to or remember who produced the material. Realistically, uploading a video to YouTube is not a real accomplishment. Anyone can do it. Those who put their work on YouTube do not live and work in the public sphere, have no real accomplishments worthy of continued attention, are not well known or famous, and do not embody the dreams and desires of the public. Clearly, they meet none of the characteristics required of celebrities.

Here's another misconception: celebrities are superior to the rest of us. It's a fact that many of them are talented, rich, have luxurious homes, and live exciting lives. Their lifestyles are different from, and in some ways more comfortable than, the lifestyles of the rest of us. Still, they are just people; they have many of the same flaws and problems you, your neighbors, your co-workers, your boss, or your friends have. During the first decade of the 21st century, more than a few celebrities were arrested on charges ranging from driving under the influence, drug possession, reckless driving, and assault to child molestation and gun possession. The list of celebrity names connected to these charges reads like a *Who's Who* in the celebrity world: Robert Downey Jr., Nick Nolte, Wynonna Judd, Michael Jackson, Macaulay Culkin, Mel Gibson, Paris Hilton, Nicole Richie, Kiefer Sutherland, Lindsay Lohan, Heather Locklear, O. J. Simpson, Andy Dick, Lil Wayne, and Phil Spector, among others (Gillin 2010). Celebrities are just as likely to break the law or engage in unethical behavior as any group of people anywhere in the world. In short, they are like the rest of us, except when they're not.

Are we being too harsh and judgmental? Perhaps. Accepting the diversity in our culture and the vagaries of life makes us a richer, more complex society, a society where we enjoy life, feel comfortable about ourselves and others, and have much freedom of movement and expression. Maybe we'd be better off to just "chill" (to use an old term) and let things be, particularly when it comes to celebrities. On the other hand, celebrities play an important part in the lives of many people. Some serve as role models, others as leaders. We spend money to see, hear, or be near them. If celebrities are important to the culture, shouldn't they at least meet a minimum set of standards that qualifies them to exercise such influence? Many things in our society are based on merit. You can't justifiably put an MA after your name unless you have *earned* a master's degree, or justifiably call yourself "General" unless you have served in the military and earned the rank. Of course, people assign themselves unearned or undeserved titles all the time, but that does not make it right. In short, if one is going to be considered a celebrity, shouldn't the individual have earned that status? Celebrity status can be earned by meeting all six of our celebrity characteristics.

We are thus presented with a difficult choice in the 21st century. Should we accept the most inclusive view of celebrity by agreeing that anyone can be one, small accomplishments matter, inappropriate behavior should be ignored, and lists of characteristics are unimportant, or should we differentiate among those who wish to be celebrities by establishing standards, holding them accountable for their behavior, critically evaluating their accomplishments, and separating the little known from the widely known? Tough question. Some people will prefer the first choice; this book, of course, prefers the second.

Summary and Conclusion

There are, of course, other celebrity issues and problems. As the 21st century progresses, new concerns will almost certainly arise. This chapter has, however, covered some important and controversial ones. It has shown there is a beginning and an end to celebrity: celebrity begins by meeting the six celebrity characteristics developed in Chapter 1; its end depends on different factors, including age and/or lack of media attention. We noted celebrities, like many of the rest of us, often violate social or moral norms and, if they publically apologize, lose little of their celebrity status. Celebrities who violate legal norms and get special treatment may face diminished celebrity status. In general, celebrities who endorse products do not suffer if the products endorsed do not perform as promised; moreover, celebrities may, but are not required to, have expertise with the products endorsed.

Fictional and cartoon celebrities are important to children, but do not damage their perception of the real world if parents or other adults interact with them, stressing the difference between the cartoon and the real world. Celebrity magazines are popular and very much alike, supporting, rather than criticizing, celebrities, but may face consolidation due to declining revenues. Celebrity television shows are similar in many ways to celebrity magazines, but are often more up-to-date. Celebrity information provided by both magazines and television is often trivial and little more than rumor or gossip. Celebrities depend on media exposure, and with the decline of interest in traditional media, now find that new media are important, that is, being seen and heard by individuals using the Internet and social media Web sites. Finally, several misconceptions about celebrity revealed a divergence of opinion about whether celebrities are special and whether celebrity should be earned, inclusive, or restrictive.

References

Biagi, Shirley. 2005. *Media/Impact*. Seventh edition. Belmont, CA: Thomson Wadsworth.

Brady, Erick, and Steve DiMeglio. 2009. "How much privacy do public figures deserve?" *USA Today*, December 3, A1.

Brennan, Christine. 2009. "Tiger's sorry statement illuminating." *USA Today*, December 3, 3C.

Burns, Kelli S. 2009. *Celeb 2.0*. Santa Barbara, CA: ABC-CLIO.

Chao, Paul, Gerhard Wuhrer, and Thomas Werani. 2005. "Celebrity and foreign brand name as moderators of country-of-origin effects." *International Journal of Marketing* 24(2).

Choi, Sejung Marina, Wei-Na Lee, and Hee-Jung Kim. 2005. "Lessons from the rich and famous: A cross-cultural comparison of celebrity endorsement in advertising." *Journal of Advertising* 34(2), 85–98.

Chung, Heejoon. 2003. "Sport star vs. rock star in globalizing popular culture." *International Review for the Sociology of Sport* 38(1), 99–108.

Erdogan, Zafer B. 1999. "Celebrity endorsement: A literature review." *Journal of Marketing Management* 15(4), 291–314.

Errico, Marcus. 2009. "Chris Brown arrested after alleged Rihanna assault." [Online article; retrieved 12/01/09.] http://www.eonline.com/uberblog/b99069_police_looking_chris_brown_after.html.

Farris, Gene. 2009. "Juicy details, on a want-to-know basis." *USA Today*, November 30, 3C.

Gillin, Joshua. 2009. "Lilo gets more probation." *St. Petersburg Times*, October 17, 2B.

Gillin, Joshua. 2010. "Celebrity slammer." *St. Petersburg Times*, January 1, 2B.

McCracken, Grant. 1989. "Who is the celebrity endorser? Cultural foundations of the endorsement process." *Journal of Consumer Research* 16(3), 310–321.

McManus, Mike. 1999. "Puzzled about teen violence? Have you seen 'South Park'?" *Tampa Tribune*, May 31, C6.

Michaels, Sean. 2009. "Chris Brown: Rihanna assault should remain private." [Online article; retrieved 12/01/09.] http://www.guardian.co.uk/music/20089/nov/09/chris-brown-rihanna-assault.

Nizza, Mike. 2007. "Paris Hilton leaves prison for house arrest." [Online article; retrieved 11/30/09.] http://thelede.blogs.nytimes.com/2007/paris-hilton-is-reportedly-freed.

Scherer, Michael. 2008. "Governor gone wild: The Blagojevich scandal." [Online article; retrieved 12/01/09.] http://www.time.com/time/nation/article 0,8599,1865781,00.html.

Spears, Steve. 2009. "Top 5: What's super hot . . . for the moment." *St. Petersburg Times*, November 2, 2B.

Stableford, Dylan. 2009. "DeSilva + Phillips report: Turnaround 'slow, painful, and partial at best.'" [Online article; retrieved 01/04/10.] http://www.foliomag.com/node/34098.

3

Worldwide Perspective

Many of us would be interested to know what the future holds, that is, what lies ahead in our lives. Will we be successful, healthy, happy? It is not possible, of course, to predict the future when it comes to human beings. There are simply too many variables in life to make any sort of accurate prediction. Some people get enjoyment out of dreaming what they might do and be if they won, say, their state's lottery. But we don't really expect it to happen. Often the best we can do is make choices intelligently and with an eye on the possible consequences. It often comes as a surprise, therefore, when someone predicts something and that something comes true.

You met Canadian media theorist Marshall McLuhan in Chapter 2. Much of what McLuhan predicted in the 1960s about media and popular culture has, in fact, become reality. He made many of his predictions when television was in its infancy and 20 years before the development of the personal computer (Kappelman 2001). Of most interest in this chapter on celebrity from a worldwide perspective is McLuhan's notion of the world as a *global village*. The term is a metaphor suggesting that new technologies have the ability to electronically link the world (Zechowski n.d.). In other words, electronic technology, primarily the media, function as an electronic nervous system enabling people to experience—in real time—events from other parts of the world. As a result, "information about people of different cultures, in different countries thousands of miles away, becomes as meaningful to media consumers as things happening in their own neighborhoods" (Rodman 2006, 452). Because we live in a global village, celebrities today are no longer bound by the borders of their home countries. In Chapter 1, we noted that the early civilizations may have had famous or well-known individuals, but they were not widely known beyond their own spheres of influence because there was no way to communicate information across long distances. Did the ancient Chinese culture know about the famous playwrights of ancient Greece? Probably not. Would Chinese citizens today know about a devastating earthquake in Greece that destroyed part of an ancient Greek theater? Yes, they would if they were in contact with the rest of the world through today's complex electronic media and chose to access that information. People from many parts of the world have laptops, cell phones, and the like that connect them to the Internet, which has essentially become the world's electronic nervous system.

Your parents or grandparents probably enjoyed chatting with their neighbors over the backyard fence. Today, if you are in France, you can chat with friends in Australia just as easily. If you are in Japan, you can communicate with acquaintances in California. Obviously, the global village provides us the opportunity to communicate over long distances by simply striking a few keys, touching a screen, or activating a voice-recognition system. There are limits to what we can do, however. Not all countries in the world are economically and politically stable enough to participate fully in today's electronic community. There are many places on earth, most of them in third-world countries, where the tools of technology are simply not available. Nevertheless, communication today is easier than it has ever been and distance is usually not a problem. This benefits us as individuals because we can pass along personal information, but it also benefits celebrities in that they can become better known worldwide as information about them and their accomplishments is readily available through a variety of electronic devices. It is doubtful McLuhan thought much about the impact of the global village on celebrities, but the impact has been substantial.

Entertainment Celebrities

Entertainment is a worldwide phenomenon. Whether it's a simple tribal dance in some less-developed part of the world or a rock-music concert in Europe, people enjoy being entertained. Film and television stars, major sports figures, and recording artists move easily from one part of the world to another. It is usually not important from what country these celebrities come; the importance lies in the fact that they provide entertainment, a pleasurable diversion from the often mundane routine of life. Movie viewers, for example, may not know or care that the main characters in a film are from countries other than their own. Just because someone in a film speaks with a British accent does not mean the individual is a native of Great Britain. Accents can be learned or mimicked; after all, that's part of what acting is all about. The National Basketball Association (NBA), America's professional basketball league, has a number of players from countries other than America. No one seems to care about where these sports figures are from; they do care about how many points these players score in a game. To further illustrate the point, let's look at some specific examples. Tennis celebrity Maria Sharapova is from Russia but plays in tournaments and makes public appearances in many other parts of the world. British soccer star David Beckham and his wife Victoria, a former member of the music group Spice Girls, are a celebrity couple whose fame extends beyond the playing field or the recording studio. Actress Salma Hayek was born in Mexico; actresses Nicole Kidman and Naomi Watts are from Australia; supermodel Gisele Bundchen is a native of Brazil; rock star Bono is from Ireland. These and other entertainment celebrities are widely known and much esteemed anywhere in the world they choose to go. The global village thus provides the famous and well known in the entertainment industry the opportunity to become celebrities not only in their native countries, but also in many other countries around the world.

Celebrities and Politics

Appearing on the world's stage as they do, many celebrities cannot resist the impulse to comment on or participate in the world of politics. American celebrities are particularly noted for their political activism. They have a wide range of interests and opinions and are not shy about communicating them when an opportunity presents itself. Many members of the general public, however, are not all that pleased about celebrities' political activism. Many people wonder why celebrities think they are qualified to tell us how to vote. Time after time, public opinion polls have shown that a majority of people feel celebrities should stay out of politics. Ironically, one actor summed up the feeling of more than a few members of the public when he said, "Hollywood activists should keep their mouths shut."

Celebrity activity in politics is not limited to America, of course. "Recently, there has been notable involvement of Latino celebrities within politics" (Velasquez 2008). This may be the result of the rise of a number of specific issues, like immigration, of interest to the Latino community. For example, comedian George Lopez and television actor Adam Rodriguez came out in support of Senator Barack Obama when he was running for president; actors Lorenzo Lamas and Eduardo Verastegui supported Senator John McCain. Television actress Eva Longoria Parker is also active in support of Latino causes. When asked about it, she said she just wanted to make people aware of the importance of registering to vote and helping others register to vote. Parker also said she feels "empowered" by participating in the political arena and that it is her "responsibility to do so" (Velasquez 2008).

Talking about politics is one thing, but running for political office is quite another. Several American celebrities have run for office, and a few have been successful. The most notable examples include actor Ronald Reagan who became president, actor Jesse Ventura who served as governor of Minnesota, and actor Arnold Schwarzenegger who was elected governor of California. Other famous or well-known Americans have been elected to Congress. Finnish distance runner Lasse Viren won gold medals at the Olympic games in 1972 and 1976. He set an Olympic record in the 5,000 meter race in 1972, giving Finland its first gold medal in 36 years. Yet his 1976 win was controversial. He won the 10,000 meters, but took off his shoes and held them over his head during a victory lap. He was accused by the International Olympic Committee of advertising a product; the logo on the shoes could be clearly seen as he held them high. Viren denied the charge, saying he had a blister. He was also involved in blood boosting, a practice that involves freezing blood and then returning it to the body later to improve the blood's oxygen content. Though controversial, the practice was not illegal at the time (Viren n.d.). Viren was, nevertheless, highly popular in Finland and was elected to the Finnish Parliament where he served from 1999 to 2007.

Moores (1991) suggests that one reason celebrities find running for public office so attractive is that political candidates often use many of the same public relations and promotional campaigns that celebrities do in order to project an image; many feel, therefore, that making the transition from celebrity to elected official will not require a complete change of identity. Celebrities in some countries, however, have not had much success in running for office. For example, in 1981 Coluche, a popular French comedian who died in 1986, ran for the French presidency. Public opinion polls gave him 16 percent of the vote even though he proposed no social or political policies upon which a voting decision could be made (Moores 1991). Apparently, his support was based solely on his celebrity status as a comedian.

Not all celebrities are interested in running for public office, but many of them do promote their pet projects. Sometimes it seems as though "celebrities today are obsessed with trying to move the global agenda" (Drezner 2007). They raise money for a variety of humanitarian causes such as hunger and stem cell research. "Celebrity activism is nothing new. In 1971, Beatles star George Harrison performed a concert for Bangladesh to raise money for starving refugees" and later persuaded Bob Dylan, Ringo Starr, and others to join him in a concert to raise money for the United Nations Children's Fund. In the eight-year period from 1973 to 1981, Harrison raised about half a million dollars a year to fight hunger. U2 singer Bono created an organization to fight poverty and toured Africa in "an effort to encourage debt relief for poor countries" (West 2007). Although Bono's debt-relief campaign was considered successful, "his (Product) Red campaign, which aimed to generate money for the U.N. Global Fund to Fight AIDS, Tuberculosis, and Malaria" was a disappointment. There are obviously limits on what a celebrity can do. "Promoting a policy agenda is one thing; implementing it is another thing entirely. A celebrity who harps on a cause risks generating fatigue with the general public" (Drezner 2007).

As we noted in Chapter 1, celebrities depend on media exposure to assist them, not only in becoming celebrities, but also in remaining celebrities. The media appear all too willing to provide the needed assistance. Drezner (2007) suggests that "the power of soft news has given stars new leverage." Today, it seems that much of the news we see is about what we *want to know* rather than what we *need to know*. Cable television, talk shows on radio and television, Internet blogs, YouTube, and a host of other media outlets appear to have blurred the line between news and entertainment. We apparently know less about important political and social issues than we do about the lives of celebrities. A Nielsen poll in Australia, for example, found that "fewer people—across age groups—could correctly answer political questions than popular culture questions about actors, models, and sporting figures" (Sheridan 2009). None of the respondents to the survey could name the leader of Australia's NSW National Party; only 25 percent could identify the country's health minister. However, 60 percent could name two songs by Lady Gaga, 85 percent knew that a comic actor had lost lots of weight, and every respondent knew that two popular Australian radio disc jockeys had been recently suspended. One psychologist noted that many people shy away from discussing current political and social issues because they fear exposing their ignorance; they'd rather stick to safe, popular topics such as the dramatic weight loss of a television personality (Sheridan 2009).

Limits on Worldwide Celebrity

We noted earlier in this chapter that because the world is a global village and because we have the means to communicate over long distances, celebrities are no longer bound by the borders of their home countries. This is true, but only to the extent that well-known or famous people have spent a significant amount of time on the world stage and drawn a correspondingly significant amount of attention and exposure from the media. For example, one could easily argue that Katarina Witt, an Olympic gold medal–winning figure skater, and Boris Becker, a world-class tennis professional, are worldwide celebrities in addition to being celebrities in their native Germany. Professional tennis matches and the Olympic Games get a tremendous amount of media coverage. But are Oliver Kohn and Franz Beckenbauer also worldwide celebrities? Both are German football stars, but because German football does not get much media attention worldwide, these two men are not widely known in the global village. This phenomenon is in evidence elsewhere. In Spain, Rafael Nadal Parera is a famous tennis player, and Fernando Diaz is a well-known Formula One driver. The former is a worldwide celebrity; the latter is little known outside his home country. The amount of worldwide media coverage given to individuals has a direct impact on the degree to which they will (or will not) become worldwide celebrities. Here's another example. Stefka Kostadinova holds the world's record in women's high jumping, but would not draw a crowd if she came to New York City; her accomplishment is praiseworthy and she is undoubtedly famous in her home country of Bulgaria, but she is not a "media star" and thus not a worldwide celebrity. Our examples here are from sports, but the principle holds true for other occupations. Did you know that Bulgaria's Veselin Topakov is a chess grandmaster and a former FIDE world champion? Thus, there is a clear distinction between individuals who are worldwide celebrities and those who are merely famous or well known within their home countries.

It should be noted that what might be called the "stay-at-home-celebrity" phenomenon is often a choice celebrities make. Some prefer to live in their home countries, content to get considerable recognition there among their fellow countrymen with perhaps only an occasional, brief moment in the world spotlight. Others seek wider fame by relocating to another country, typically the United States. The United States is considered the leader in the production of media product, that is, movies, television programs, videos, books, magazines, and the like. This is not to say that other countries do not have media product or that their products are less important, but the sheer volume of media output in America makes relocating here a key factor in a celebrity's pursuit of worldwide fame. Take, for example, the case of Renny Harlin. Born in Finland, Harlin relocated to America and became a well-known Hollywood director, producer, actor, writer, and cinematographer. He directed several popular movies, including *Die Hard 2* (with actor Bruce Willis), *A Nightmare on Elm Street 4: The Dream Master*, and *Exorcist: The Beginning*. In all, he has more than three dozen films as well as many short video clips and production pieces. He moved to celebrity status when he married American actress Geena Davis in 1993; they divorced in 1998. Although Harlin made some films in his native Finland, he is best known for his work in the United States.

There are, of course, other examples. Australian actor Heath Ledger moved to America after a rather mediocre career in Australian film and television. His performance was not particularly noteworthy in the American film *10 Things I Hate About You*, but he did much better in *The Patriot* (with actor Mel Gibson). Some critics say his best performance was in *Brokeback Mountain*, a movie about two cowboys who fall in love in the American West. Ledger died in New York in January 2008 from an overdose of prescription drugs; he was posthumously awarded an Oscar for Best Supporting Actor in his final film role: the Joker in *The Dark Knight*.

A Look at the Worldwide Celebrity Taxonomy

You may recall the celebrity taxonomy described in Chapter 1, showing eight celebrity categories: politics and government, entertainment, the arts, science and medicine, business, academia, religion, and the general public. Thus far in this chapter, our discussion has centered primarily on celebrities in the entertainment field; however, there are worldwide celebrities in the other categories. Before looking at those, we should recall the definition of celebrity developed in Chapter 1. A celebrity leads a public life or works in the public sphere, has accomplishments of interest and importance to the general public, is considered well known or famous, seeks to maintain status as a famous or well-known person, is highly visible in or on media, and connects with the public by embodying their dreams and desires. Some of the individuals discussed in the sections that follow meet all six celebrity characteristics; others meet only the first four. You'll see some individuals fall short of worldwide celebrity because they are not highly visible in the media or because they do not connect with the public's dreams and desires. Furthermore, we are setting aside the "general public" category because the individuals in that category are mostly of local—or at best regional—interest. For example, backpack serial killer Ivan Milat is famous in his home country of Australia, where he is said to have killed more than 20 women. Milat is not, however, known outside Australia and, furthermore, his actions do not reflect the public's dreams and desires. We don't add much to our discussion of worldwide celebrity by tracking down individuals who are mostly of local interest.

There is another issue we need to consider, too, as we move forward through the taxonomy. According to Brown and Fraser (2008), researchers have "provided only a limited understanding of the central place of the celebrity in society and the appeal of celebrities across cultural, political, social, and economic boundaries" (47). Therefore, our look at the taxonomy of worldwide celebrities cannot be solely based on anything we absolutely know to be true; our understanding of celebrity is grounded mostly in what we can observe and infer from the information we do have.

Politics and Government

Although we have thus far resisted the temptation to say that well-known individuals in politics and government are celebrities, we must acknowledge that some of them are, in fact, famous enough to be worldwide celebrities. South Africa's Nelson Mandela is a good example. "Mandela is one of the world's most revered statesmen . . . [he] led the struggle to replace the apartheid regime of South Africa with a multi-racial democracy" (BBC News 2008). He campaigned against segregation and discrimination early in his career and was charged with treason by the government. Convicted and given a life sentence in 1964, he was freed from prison in 1990. Mandela won the Nobel Peace Prize in 1993 and was elected his country's first black president one year later. Although he retired from public life in 2004, he continues to be active in the Mandela Foundation, a charity he founded. He formed a group known as The Elders, leading world figures who are willing to offer their time and expertise in solving some of the world's toughest problems (BBC News 2008). There can be little doubt Mandela's life and accomplishments have earned him a place as one of the few in politics and government who can be considered celebrities.

It almost goes without saying that Queen Elizabeth of England and her relatives are celebrities. The English have a genuine fondness for their royalty. Crowds gather, in England and in other countries, when any member of the royal family, particularly the Queen or Prince Charles, the heir to the throne, appears in public. William and Harry, Charles's sons, are favorites among young people. You may recall the worldwide outpouring of grief at the death of Princess Diana, Charles's former wife. Is the royal family's celebrity status based more on tradition than on accomplishment? Perhaps it is, but most members of the Queen's family are involved in civic and charitable causes worldwide.

Others in this category, however, owe their rise as celebrities to activities that have little to do with their accomplishments as politicians or heads of state. Nicolas Sarkozy is president of France. Elected in 2007, he worked diligently to promote social and political reform at home while enhancing the image of France abroad. But it is his "private life that has enthralled the media." Shortly after his election to the presidency, Sarkozy divorced Cecilia Ciganer-Albeniz, a former model and public relations executive. Four months later, he married model-turned-singer Carla Bruni.

"The publicity surrounding the romance between Sarkozy, 54, and Bruni, 41, was a departure from the French tradition of keeping presidential private lives private." In terms of his work as president, he earned the nickname "hyper-president" because he was a workaholic, willing to tackle racism, the economy, illegal immigration, and a host of other problems. However, his taste for Rolex watches and luxury yachts earned him a less impressive nickname, "the bling-bling president" (BBC News 2009a). Thus, his work as president has made him famous in France, but the media's attention to his personal life has made him a celebrity, both in France and in other parts of the world.

Controversial and flamboyant are words often used to describe Silvio Berlusconi, Italy's prime minister. In his seventies, Berlusconi is among Italy's richest men, worth more than $6 million, according to *Forbes* business magazine. His wealth comes from a business empire that includes media, advertising, insurance, food, and construction. Many Italians are unclear about his accomplishments as prime minister. Berlusconi has been accused of embezzlement, tax fraud, and bribery; in some cases he was acquitted; in others he was convicted but the convictions were overturned on appeal. He admits to having had cosmetic surgery, but denies allegations that he paid prostitutes for sex. Whatever positive accomplishments he might have as prime minister seem to have been largely ignored by the Italian media who would rather concentrate on his private and business lives. Some complain that "an Italian voter cannot escape blanket coverage favorable" to him. That is no surprise. Berlusconi's investment company controls three of Italy's biggest private television stations, and his political appointees control three public stations. His opponents are troubled by his control of the media, noting that comedians who made fun of him when he was last prime minister "never appeared on TV again" (BBC News 2009b). Berlusconi is famous in Italy, known worldwide, and gets significant media attention. He is clearly a celebrity.

There are other politicians and government leaders who are well known, perhaps famous worldwide, but they have not risen to celebrity status in the United States. Tony Blair, former prime minister of Great Britain, and Gordon Brown, who succeeded Blair, are familiar to many in Europe and North America. Great Britain has ties to the European continent, of course, and has almost always supported the United States in whatever foreign policy initiatives the American government promotes. However, because Americans and Europeans have their own politicians and government officials, it is unlikely that many citizens would call either Blair or Brown a celebrity. The same applies to German Chancellor Angela Merkel. She is the first woman to serve as Germany's head of government and has good working relationships with other European government officials, particularly on economic issues. However, she is still a relative newcomer to politics and has not risen to celebrity status. Notice that, in contrast to Sarkozy and Berlusconi, neither Blair, nor Brown, nor Merkel has a controversial private life. Must one have a splashy private life to become a celebrity? It would seem so. If you are a politician or government official, the nature of your work requires you to live something of a public life, that is, you'll attend meetings, hold news conferences, run for election (or reelection), and otherwise spend a considerable amount of time in front of media cameras. But conversations about monetary policy, government white papers, and the like are of so little interest to most people that these media appearances register not as individuals whose lifestyles we'd like to have, but as individuals doing their jobs. This alone cannot make them celebrities.

A few politicians and government officials are often in conflict with American foreign policy, are viewed with suspicion, and are not celebrities in the United States, although they may be well known and considered celebrities elsewhere. Chief among these is Mahmoud Ahmadinejad, the president of Iran. Readers who are acquainted with America's involvement in the wars in Iraq and Afghanistan will recognize the Iranian president as a problem for American foreign policy in the Middle East. Although he does not have tremendous support in Iran, Ahmadinejad was reelected in 2009 in what some say was a fraudulent election. Nevertheless, he remains popular in his own country and among Muslims throughout the world.

Cuba lies about 90 miles off the coast of Florida. One might think Cuba and the United States would be long-time friends, but the two countries have had a strained relationship for years, dating back to the 1960s and the administration of President John F. Kennedy. Cuban leader Fidel Castro is well known in the Western Hemisphere and may be considered a celebrity in some parts of South and Central America. Under his leadership, Cuba embraced communism, depended on the old Soviet Union—an American enemy in those days—for aid, and frequently stirred up trouble in the Caribbean. In declining health, Castro turned over the government to his brother Raul in 2006. Fidel's years as Cuba's head of state get mixed reviews. He did make some improvements in health care and education, but "the Cuban people still face food shortages, economic hardship, and little personal freedom" (A&E Television Networks 2006). Nevertheless, Fidel remains a popular celebrity in his country. Many smaller countries in the world appreciate the fact that he governed his own way and did not take direction from the more-powerful United States. Still, Castro is disliked by many Cuban Americans, particularly those living in Florida who think his repressive regime has harmed (and is still harming) their relatives and friends in Cuba. Under Raul, Cuba is attempting to moderate relations with the United States and there is optimism some of the problems between the two countries can be solved. However, unlike his brother, Raul is not a celebrity.

Venezuelan president Hugo Chavez is currently out of favor in the United States. Few Americans would call him a celebrity. He has both supporters and critics in his home country. His supporters see him as "a populist and a champion of the poor, while his critics call him anti-business and neo-fascist." Nevertheless, Chavez was reelected president in 2006 by a fairly wide margin (Pearson Education 2007). Even his critics would probably acknowledge that he has celebrity status in Venezuela. His relationship with America is quite another thing. He was a regular critic of President George W. Bush, accusing Bush of plotting to assassinate him. He "made suggestive comments about Secretary of State Condoleezza Rice, visited Fidel Castro in Cuba, bashed the United States on the al-Jazeera television network, and traveled to Libya to receive an award from Moammar Gaddafi." He also threatened to cut off Venezuelan oil shipments to the United States as a way to fight American power (Sullivan 2005). Chavez has been equally controversial in his comments about President Barack Obama. He called Obama an "ignoramus" for saying that Venezuela's socialist government exports terrorism and obstructs progress in Latin America (Daniel 2009). Although his verbal attacks on the United States have not endeared him to Americans, his willingness to insult America's politicians and government officials has made him popular in countries where anti-American feeling runs high. To many citizens of those countries, Chavez is a celebrity.

No discussion of worldwide politicians and government officials would be complete without including Russia's Vladimir Putin. Putin became Russia's president in 1999 and immediately set about restoring Russia's place as an influential world power.

He was reelected to a second term in 2004. Although the United States and Russia (the old Soviet Union) have had significant differences on most issues down through the years, the rise of Mikhail Gorbachev and then Boris Yeltsin to the Russian presidency brought a new era of cooperation between the two countries. However, relations cooled a bit when Putin became president. Because of term limits, Putin could not run for president again in 2008, but he ensured the election of his protégé Dmitry Medvedev and essentially appointed himself prime minister, thus maintaining control of the Russian government. The Russian system of government and even the lives of Russian citizens are something of a mystery to most Americans. Like many other countries, Russia has significant problems: high unemployment, food shortages, harsh winters, and an ever-watchful government. The Russian people have adjusted to these problems, but are not particularly happy about them. Yet it doesn't pay to criticize the government, the president, or the prime minister too much. Tales of the Russian secret police are still circulated. Thus, many Russians tolerate Putin and his ilk but do not consider them celebrities. Nevertheless, Putin is known worldwide not only as a firm and decisive leader but also as an adventurer who has tranquilized tigers and demonstrated the art of judo on DVDs. He is a celebrity in many parts of the world.

To be sure, there are other politicians and government leaders who are visible on the world's stage: North Korea's president Kim Jong Il, Afghanistan's president Hamid Karzai, Canadian prime minister Stephen Harper, Mexican president Felipe Calderon, and Chinese premier Wen Jiabao. For the most part, these men are well known, both inside and outside their countries, as many heads of state are. However, they have not risen to worldwide celebrity status.

Media Influence and Political Celebrity

Communication scholars regularly study the impact of all sorts of media messages on human behavior. It is a generally accepted notion that media influence is a fact of life. Consumers purchase many of the products and services they see advertised, youngsters often mimic actions they have seen or repeat speech they have heard on television, candidates for public office solicit the editorial endorsement of newspapers, and so on. McCombs and Shaw (1972) believe that although the media may not tell us *what to think*, they are quite successful at telling us *what to think about*. However, some scholars believe media messages are more powerful than we realize. There is widespread agreement, however, that causal relationships (A causes B) are difficult to prove; correlation (A bears some relationship to B) is sometimes the best we can do. Can a medium, say a magazine, make someone an international celebrity? If high media visibility is one of the requirements for becoming a celebrity, wouldn't it follow that significant exposure by a magazine would meet that requirement? And what is meant by "significant exposure?" Would appearing on the magazine's cover be significant? Would it be even more meaningful if the cover caption included the words, "She's a global celebrity?" What if the "she" referred to is U.S. Secretary of State Hillary Clinton?

The cover story in the November 16, 2009, issue of *Time* magazine is about Clinton and her service as secretary of state. Written by Joe Klein, "Hillary's Moment" examines the successes and disappointments of Clinton's first nine months on the job. Klein writes that Clinton "is the star of the Obama Cabinet and an international celebrity" and "the second most popular American in the world" (25–26). Klein acknowledges that Clinton "has no history as a global strategist" but is "an international celebrity with a much higher profile than any of her recent predecessors" (27). Some readers, maybe even many of them, will accept Klein's assessment of Clinton as a celebrity. But a closer look will reveal some problems with that assessment. First, Klein does not tell us what an international celebrity is, but he does tell us Clinton is one. Can we accept his word for it, or should he explain how she fits his (or any) definition of international celebrity? Clinton is the star of the Obama cabinet, he says. This claim may come as a surprise to some other cabinet members who may consider themselves the stars. Klein admits Clinton is not a global strategist but has a higher profile than other secretaries of state. Moreover, she is the second most popular American in the world, a claim Klein makes without any supporting data. On what did he base that claim? An international poll, perhaps? If so, where are the numbers showing the degree of her popularity? More likely, some world leaders know her best as the wife of former president Bill Clinton, but few would know of her accomplishments as the junior senator from New York. Therefore, based on Klein's article, we are led to think that an international celebrity is a political star with little or no worldwide foreign policy experience who maintains a high profile and is the second most popular person in the world from her country.

We have no particular quarrel with Secretary of State Hillary Clinton. We do have a problem with Klein's casual use of the phrase "international celebrity." As the preceding chapters in this book have shown, defining celebrity is not easy. Many variables are involved and these variables differ from culture to culture, country to country. Simply saying someone is a celebrity doesn't make it true. Additionally, Klein is a long-time political strategist, novelist, and journalist with ties to the Clinton family. The article does a disservice not only to our understanding of celebrity, but also to objective journalism. So, is Clinton an international celebrity? Yes, but not for the reasons Klein mentions. Clinton qualifies by meeting all six of our celebrity characteristics. The lesson here is that high media visibility comes with a caveat: examine media exposure critically and assess its reliability as an indicator of celebrity.

The Arts

Although the individuals in this category are all performers of sorts, that is, writers, artists, sculptors, and musicians, most of them lack the worldwide recognition that politicians and governmental leaders get. At best, those in this category who are extremely well known qualify as second-level celebrities. What is a second-level celebrity? The term is not meant to minimize either talent or contribution to cultural life. Used here, it denotes individuals who are celebrities in their own countries, but only well known in some parts (not all) of the world. George Hobeika is a good example. Hobeika is a famous fashion designer and is highly respected in his home country of Lebanon and in other areas of the Middle East. He is largely unknown to individuals who are not connected to the fashion industry. He is famous in Paris for his *haute couture*, or trend-setting fashions. It is unlikely, however, that his fame extends much beyond the fashion industry. Would his name be among those mentioned if a dozen Canadians (or Japanese or Austrians) were asked to name five fashion celebrities? Almost certainly not. Fashion is often unique to a country or a region (denim jeans being a notable exception). Chinese fashion is obviously different from African fashion, which differs from Brazilian fashion, and so on. There is no shame in being a second-level celebrity. Even if you are a stay-at-home celebrity, it means you've made enough of a mark in the world to be well known or famous among a select group of people elsewhere.

It might be useful to identify some individuals in the arts who are well known enough to be considered second-level celebrities. Googoosh (real name Faegheh Atashin) is a famous Persian and Iranian singer and actress. Georg Baselitz is a well-known German painter and sculptor. Fred Williams is an Australian painter and printmaker. Peter Abrahams is an award-winning South African novelist. So is Nigerian Chinua Achebe whose novel *Things Fall Apart* is required reading in many schools. Before her death in 2010, Dame Joan Sutherland was an Australian soprano famous in the opera world. Manuel de Elias was a well-known Mexican composer and conductor. Marwa Rakha is a famous writer, poet, and marketing personality from Egypt. Damien Hirst is a British artist. A few individuals in the arts category may be slightly better known that those mentioned herein: feminist writer Germaine Greer, art critic Robert Hughes, and award-winning authors Peter Carey and David Malouf, all from Australia. However, these names may be more recognizable to Americans than to some people in other parts of the world. Hughes, for example, was an art critic and writer for *Time* magazine; Greer's writing and lectures have attracted large audiences, particularly in the United States (African Writers Index 2000, Fanoos Encyclopedia n.d., Linkism n.d., White Hat 2009).

So what's missing? Why aren't these individuals first-level celebrities? The answer, of course, is that while these individuals are doing important work, they lack significant, continuing media exposure. Media in this case means primarily television. Perhaps this is a Catch-22 situation: they are not on television because people do not know much about them, and people do not know much about them because they are not on television. Thus, we echo previous statements in this book by noting that celebrity depends on high media visibility. The degree to which these individuals may or may not embody the public's dreams and desires is unknown.

Science and Medicine

It has become obvious that not all categories in our taxonomy contain worldwide celebrities. Although many people in the world consider science important, few have a complete understanding of it, and still fewer think much about scientists as celebrities. There are famous people in science, of course, but, with a couple of exceptions, their fame does not extend much beyond the boundaries of the profession. The same is true of physicians and others in the field of medicine. But let's look at scientists first, specifically those who are exceptions to the rule of limited fame.

Stephen Hawking is a British theoretical physicist. His 1988 book *A Brief History of Time: From the Big Bang to Black Holes* is a long-time best seller. He has written other things, of course, and has appeared in movies and on television, but it is his scientific work that has prompted some to call him a genius. His accomplishments are even more remarkable given the fact that he has amyotrophic lateral sclerosis (ALS), sometimes called Lou Gehrig's disease. He is wheelchair-bound and speaks through a computerized voice synthesizer (WGBH 1998). If there is any scientist who can be considered a worldwide celebrity, it is Stephen Hawking.

On February 28, 1953, two scientists in Cambridge, England announced that they "had found the secret of life." Indeed, they had. James Watson and Francis Crick had figured out the structure of deoxyribonucleic acid (DNA) and thus the key to life's hereditary information. *Time* magazine listed Watson and Crick as two of the 100 Most Important People of the [20th] century. There can be little doubt that both Watson and Crick, who died in 2004, are worldwide celebrities (*Time* n.d.).

For every Hawking, Watson, and Crick who become famous and get increased media exposure, there are dozens of scientists who work diligently without media attention. In paleontology, Dong Zhiming is known for leading numerous expeditions in his home country of China and for discovering a large number of dinosaurs. Argentina's Jose F. Bonaparte is said to be the most prolific paleontologist in South America, a claim based on the large number of dinosaurs he discovered and named. Rinchen Barshold's important fossil discoveries made him the most famous paleontologist in Mongolia. Before her death in 2008, Joan Wiffen of New Zealand was a respected self-taught fossil hunter (About. com n.d.) These scientists are well known, even famous, within the field of paleontology, but are essentially unknown outside the scientific community. They receive little media attention and are not celebrities.

Other scientists find themselves in a similar situation: famous within the scientific community, and, lacking media exposure, relatively unknown elsewhere. French developmental biologist Nicole Le Douarin and French geneticist Axel Kahn have significant accomplishments: the former for her work on animal nervous and immune systems, the latter an award winner for his work in genetics. Yet they are unknown to the world at large. Ireland's

Jocelyn Bell Burnell discovered (and continues to study) pulsars—rapidly rotating neutron stars. The general public, a key factor in someone becoming a celebrity, knows nothing about Burnell and even less about neutron stars. Australian Peter Doherty won a Nobel Prize for his work in immunology, and fellow Australian Tim Flannery is recognized as a groundbreaking environmentalist. But we don't know much about them (Reville 2000, White Hat 2009). Let's be clear. We are not minimizing the important work these scientists are doing. We are saying that the nature of their work makes them well known or famous among their fellow scientists, but their fame does not extend much beyond that. They lack high media visibility; they are not celebrities.

From time to time a relatively unknown scientist may temporarily garner headlines, usually for an important scientific discovery or accomplishment. On rare occasions, a scientist is exposed for wrongdoing. Such was the case with South Korean scientist Hwang Woo-suk who was found guilty in 2009 of "embezzling from his stem cell research fund and illegally buying human embryos." Hwang became a national hero in South Korea after he claimed to be the first to successfully clone human cells, but he partially fabricated his research results. He was given a suspended sentence of two years. Hwang apologized for his misdeeds, but that failed to stop Seoul National University from firing him from his professorship (Park 2009). This is, of course, not the sort of fame a scientist wants. His life as a celebrity in South Korea is over.

Let's turn our attention now to the field of medicine. The relationship between patients and their physicians has always been a private one. Individuals who have certain illnesses or diseases are often uncomfortable discussing those problems with friends or acquaintances, but are quite willing to discuss them with their doctors. They know their doctors will respect their privacy and offer medical advice on how to deal with health issues. It is extremely rare for a doctor or some other medical service provider to become a celebrity based on treatment of patients alone. A doctor may become well known in a community or a region if satisfied patients recommend the physician to others. This sort of word-of-mouth advertising is often effective in building a doctor's reputation for quality patient care.

For physicians or other individuals in the medical field to become celebrities, they must contribute to medical science in ways other than direct patient care. This usually means conducting research, inventing a surgical device, developing a treatment, discovering a disease, or in some other way contributing to the betterment of all patients with whom physicians might have contact. A few physicians achieved worldwide celebrity based on their work. South Africa's Christiaan Barnard performed the first heart transplant; America's Jonas Salk developed a polio vaccine. Like both Barnard and Salk, many important contributors to medical science have passed on, but their work is still in evidence. This is particularly true if a disease carries their name: Alzheimer's disease is named after Alois Alzheimer, Parkinson's disease is named for James Parkinson, Down syndrome after John Langdon Down, and so on. But for the most part, those who have made major contributions to medical science are unknown to the general public. For example, we all know that active people reduce their risk of heart disease and live longer, but how many of us know that the studies resulting in that principle were conducted by Ralph Paffenberger? Do we know that Trinidad's Lall Sawh is a surgeon and urologist who is well known in the Caribbean for his expertise in kidney transplantation?

Are there other ways for physicians to become well known, perhaps even celebrities? Yes, and it usually involves moving outside typical medical practice. Jack Kevorkian, known as "Doctor Death," is a well-known advocate of a patient's right to die and was convicted of assisting in the suicide of many terminal patients. He served a prison term but was released in 2007 due to ill health. Robin Cook is the author of bestselling medical novels. Deepak Chopra is an Indian American writer of motivational and health books. Other physicians have served in government, composed music, and become comedians or actors or athletes. Of course, almost none of these individuals is well known.

It is safe to conclude, therefore, that those in science and medicine have, at best, limited worldwide celebrity. They are well known, even famous, within their own specific occupational communities. Although their contributions may speak to the public's dreams and desires for a quality life, they remain mostly unknown to the general public. The primary reasons for their lack of worldwide visibility are the complex nature of their work and the lack of high media visibility.

Academia

It is fair to say that most people believe education is important. Countries all over the world invest millions of dollars annually in educating both the young and the old. Parents monitor the academic performance of their children, encouraging them to do well, and, perhaps, even helping them with homework. Getting a secondary school education is a must in most cultures, and a college degree is a goal worthy of much individual sacrifice. Although education is held in fairly high esteem worldwide, those who provide the instruction that comprises a large part of that education are not. Commonly referred to as *the academy* or *academia*, teachers, administrators, and other school officials—in elementary, secondary, and higher education—are under constant scrutiny and criticism. Truth be told, the academic world "is marked by venality, pretension, irresponsibility, and risible claims" (Fish 2009). Guess who wrote the quoted part of the last sentence? If you said "an academic," you are correct. Let's put that quote in more familiar words. The academic world is open to corruption, filled with overly ambitious workers (many of whom are untrustworthy), and makes laughable claims about the significance of its work. Although the previous sentence is not a precise paraphrase of the quotation in question, it captures its spirit. The academy is an insular world: narrow, limited, and self-absorbed. While not everyone feels that way about academia, many people do, and they are not shy about speaking up. There is a general notion that academics have cushy jobs, earn large salaries, work in "ivory towers" and are thus out of touch with reality, argue over meaningless theories, and, worst of all, have tenure that gives them lifetime job security. As a result of this widespread opinion of those in the academy, there are no worldwide academic celebrities. Like the physicians described previously, public school teachers and university professors may be well known, but their fame does not extend beyond the academy.

Rodden (1998) appears to disagree with that assessment, noting that "celebrity is a new and important phenomenon in the academy: significant changes have indeed occurred in the academy since the 1960s" (171). Rodden's view is more than a decade old; nevertheless, his notion that universities operate more as businesses than as "pastoral or utopian retreats" has merit; so does his observation that the absent-minded professor has been replaced by the career-minded professional. Still, regardless of the changes in the academy over the last dozen years or so, the celebrity scholars he identifies are almost all from American universities, thereby reinforcing our notion that their fame does not extend into the world much beyond the academy. Even if we accept the idea that there are academic celebrities, an idea we strongly dispute, it is not the same sort of celebrity garnered by those in, say, entertainment. Academic celebrities enjoy privacy, do not have to dodge the paparazzi, and need not worry about having their latest exploits exposed on a syndicated television "entertainment-news" program. Neither will they grace the cover of a pop-culture, celebrity magazine. It would be unfair, however, to say that academics never make the news. One did in the summer of 2009. African American scholar Henry Louis Gates Jr., a professor at Harvard, was arrested at his home by police investigating a possible break-in. Gates charged police with racial profiling; they charged him with disorderly conduct. An investigation revealed that it was all just a misunderstanding, and apologies were offered all around. The incident was a nightly feature on American newscasts for several days, but was not of much concern to people elsewhere in the world.

It might be useful to identify a few of the academy's high-profile scholars. Australia's Peter Singer, a professor of bioethics at Princeton University, is known for favoring the rationing of health care; Harold Bloom, a faculty member at Yale University, has made contributions to literary criticism; Princeton's Cornel West has been a champion of racial justice; Richard Dawkins, retired from the University of Oxford in England, is a writer well known for books critical of organized religion; David Lodge, retired from England's University of Birmingham, writes novels about academic life. Frenchmen Michel Foucault, Jean Baudrillard, and Jacques Derrida, all postmodernists, were popular in the academy beyond their home country, but all three are dead. Universities, however, are willing to accept outsiders, that is, those who are not trained academics, if they contribute significantly to the school's reputation. For example, former Mexican president Ernesto Zedillo directs a research center at Yale University. Jose Maria Aznar, former prime minister of Spain, is a distinguished scholar at Georgetown University. Salman Rushdie, a native of India who is known for his novels and essays, is on the faculty of Emory University.

The conclusion to be drawn about academic celebrities is rather obvious. Some scholars are well known, even famous, in the academy for their work. Only a few of them are known in countries other than their own. A college student in Hong Kong might be assigned one of Professor Bloom's books on William Shakespeare, but that does not make the gifted professor a celebrity. It simply makes him required reading. Academics are mostly unknown to the world at large; they lack high media visibility. It is fair to say that not many members of the public dream about becoming a teacher, professor, or philosopher. Therefore, there are no world-wide academic celebrities.

Business

One of the surest ways to become famous in the business world is to make lots of money. At the very least, you'd be identified as a billionaire in *Forbes* magazine and held in awe by most of the people in your home country; you would probably be a celebrity there. Americans will recognize the names of successful celebrity businessmen and women who have made important contributions to life and commerce in the United States and in the world: Warren Buffett, Bill Gates, Steve Jobs, Ralph Lauren, T. Boone Pickens, Martha Stewart, Steve Wynn, and Donald Trump.

There are, of course, others in the business world who have been just as successful as the Americans, but maybe not quite as well known. Richard Branson is a famous British entrepreneur and founder of the Virgin brand of products and services, among which are Virgin Records and Virgin Atlantic airlines. Branson owns a private island in the British Virgin Islands and has attracted considerable media attention for his publicity stunts. Giorgio Armani is a famous Italian businessman and fashion designer. Clothing designed by Armani is much in demand and being able to afford it signals one's good taste and high economic status. Both Branson and Armani are well known outside their own countries, but would not be considered celebrities in some others, particularly third-world countries where poor economic conditions make the services and products offered by the two men irrelevant.

A host of other successful businessmen are not as familiar to Americans, but there is little doubt they have celebrity status, not only in the business world, but also in their home geographic regions. Sergey Brin is a Russian Internet entrepreneur and computer scientist known for co-founding the Google search engine. Fellow Russian Roman Abramovich made his fortune in oil and is owner of the English football team Chelsea. Saudi Arabian real estate and stock mogul Alwaleed Bin Talal is a member of the Saudi Royal Family. Amancio Ortega of Spain is said to be that country's richest man, having made his fortune in fashion. China's Li Ka Shing, a billionaire businessman and philanthropist, is the richest man in East Asia. Mexico's communications and investment king Carlos Slim Helu is a billionaire. So is Sweden's Ingvar Kamprad, founder of the IKEA furniture brand. Taiwan's Jerry Yang is co-founder of Yahoo!

Billionaires are obviously famous among their fellow businessmen and well known enough to be considered celebrities in some parts of the world, particularly because many members of the general public dream of being rich and powerful. Money often attracts media attention. There appears to be a correlation between the amount of money you have and the degree to which you are a celebrity. This is bad news for your hometown realtor who struggles daily to sell houses, and is important to you if you are in the market for a new home, but is unlikely to achieve the recognition that Japan's Akira Mori, a billionaire real estate and hotel tycoon, has achieved. In short, money changes everything!

Religion

Can religious leaders be celebrities? Does the secular idea of celebrity conflict with the mission of spreading God's word and encouraging believers to lead more spiritual lives? Before answering these questions, we should remember that religion is a sensitive topic worldwide. Not everyone believes in God or a supreme being. Nevertheless, there may be as many as 10,000 different religions worldwide. Wars have been fought because of religious differences. These days, when someone brings up religion at a social or political gathering, tempers usually flare. There is often tacit agreement among friends or co-workers never to discuss religion at a party, at work, or during lunch. One's belief system is considered highly personal and few people want to argue the particular aspects of their religion with someone who holds different beliefs, particularly if the individual is disinclined to change, but quite willing to engage in a lengthy argument. Still, religion and celebrity may not be incompatible.

The degree to which religious leaders may become celebrities depends to a large extent on the general public. For present purposes, we can place members of the public in one of four categories: the believers, the atheists, the agnostics, and the uninformed. This typology is important because individuals in each category have a different view of religious leaders and that view will determine whether a religious leader can be deemed a celebrity. Because atheists do not believe in a supreme being, they are unlikely to care much about anything relating to religion. Believers, on the other hand, care a great deal about religion and hold many religious leaders in high esteem. Agnostics believe that the existence of a deity is unknown and, moreover, unknowable. Thus, they have no opinion about religious matters. The uninformed, as the name implies, simply lack information about religion and cannot, therefore, have a valid opinion about any religious leader or issue. We can collapse the atheists, the agnostics, and the uninformed into a single category: the indifferent. In other words, religion does not matter one way or the other to this group. They'll be of no help in determining whether a religious leader is a celebrity.

Time now to answer the two questions posed at the beginning of this section. Can religious leaders be celebrities? Yes, they can, but mostly among the believers. Does the idea of celebrity conflict with the mission of religion? No, not if celebrity assists in bringing a spiritual message to the world. There are probably only three worldwide religious celebrities: Pope Benedict XVI, the Dalai Lama, and Billy Graham. There are other religious leaders who are well known and famous to a lesser degree, but among believers, only three fit all six celebrity characteristics. Bear in mind that this overall assessment is based on the opinions of a section of the general public: the believers. Still, each of the three has captured the interest and attention of many other people worldwide. They work in the public sphere, have accomplishments of importance, are well known or famous, seek celebrity as a means to spreading the gospel, are highly visible in the media, and embody the dreams and desires of believers.

The Dalai Lama was briefly mentioned in Chapter 1. The Tibetan spiritual leader travels widely, appears regularly at conferences and religious gatherings worldwide, works for political change in his country, is frequently in the news, and has received awards for his work promoting a more spiritual life. Although he might be a little uncomfortable with being called a celebrity, he would likely acknowledge that being one enables him to bring his message of compassion, tolerance, self-discipline, and forgiveness to the attention of more people than might otherwise be possible.

As the head of the Roman Catholic Church, Pope Benedict XVI is a celebrity, not only to the hundreds of millions of Catholics in the world, but also to many Protestants. Many tourists visiting Rome make their way to the Vatican, hoping to catch a glimpse of the pope. He conducts public worship services regularly, travels the world with his spiritual message, and is a media favorite. The pope's role in world affairs may have been enhanced by the ministry of Benedict's predecessor, John Paul II, a man with an engaging personality who was much admired the world over. Benedict is a little less effusive than John Paul was, but still a major influence in religious matters (Mansfield 2005).

American evangelist Billy Graham is a celebrity, chiefly because his ministry conducted more than 376 crusades worldwide between 1947 and 1996. Graham preached to millions during that time. He is the author of two dozen books and has advised and counseled many American presidents (Graham 1997). Graham is often mentioned as the best-known spiritual leader in America, although he retired a number of years ago.

There are, of course, other well-known religious leaders whose work is recognized in countries other than their own, but who lack the high media visibility of the three leaders mentioned here. Desmond Tutu, the retired South African Archbishop of Cape Town, has a long, distinguished history of religious accomplishments. Teacher, priest, bishop, and then archbishop, Tutu dedicated his life to ending apartheid; moreover, he worked on behalf "of all the poor and oppressed wherever they might be" (Gish 2004, xii). A man with a sparkling wit and outgoing personality, he was awarded the Nobel Peace Prize in 1984. Even in retirement, he continues to work for freedom and justice for all.

Rowan Williams was officially confirmed as the 104th Archbishop of Canterbury in London in December 2002. As head of the Church of England, he has spoken out on both religious and political issues. Politically, he opposed the wars in Iraq and Afghanistan; socially, he is "opposed to abortion and believes consumerism exploits, corrupts, and causes a premature sexualisation of children" (BBC 2002).

As noted earlier, religion is a sensitive and controversial subject. Nevertheless, not all religious leaders are widely respected. Take, for example, televangelist and faith healer Benny Hinn. Considered a prophet by some, Hinn travels worldwide preaching to thousands who attend his crusades hoping to be healed. However, several investigations revealed that not even one healing has been objectively proved. "Instead, people apparently *feel* 'healed,' therefore they *are* 'healed' (emphasis added)." The media have examined his ministry and concluded that he is manipulating the faithful for his personal financial gain. His lifestyle is lavish ($1,000 a night presidential hotel suites; a house with seven bedrooms and eight baths; several BMWs). Still, his followers don't seem to mind that he spends a lot of money. One of the faithful noted, "It takes money to be on TV and to do crusades. Why is everyone hung up on money? The streets of heaven are paved with gold" (Ross 2002).

Summary

Electronic technology—particularly computers, the Internet, and cell phones—has made the world a global village. We have almost instantaneous access to information about other people and events worldwide. The famous and well known are no longer bound by the borders of their home countries; some have become worldwide celebrities. Some individuals in the entertainment field have become famous worldwide for promoting charitable projects. A few entertainers have run for public office; others have relocated to the United States in order to improve their visibility. Some in the entertainment field are content to be celebrities in their home countries only. In the area of politics and government, there are celebrities, but many of these are heads of state or other important governmental officials whose work automatically puts them at the center of attention. In addition, a few have interesting lifestyles, one of the factors influencing celebrity. The media provide those in entertainment, government, and politics with plenty of exposure and celebrity status is often the result.

Individuals in the arts, science and medicine, and education all share a common status: limited celebrity in their own areas of work. If you are an artist, a scientist, a physician, or a professor, you may be well known, even a celebrity, within your own field. It is extremely difficult to become known worldwide unless you receive a considerable amount of media attention for some major invention or accomplishment. Most individuals in these categories receive little media attention and are thus typically not celebrities.

In business and religion, however, things are a bit different. There are worldwide celebrities in these fields. Business is an important enterprise worldwide. As a result, those who have become successful business persons (especially those who make a great deal of money), are celebrities and more than a few are known beyond the business world. Religious leaders are, of course, well known or famous among their faithful believers, but only three currently have worldwide celebrity standing. The media give both business and religion considerable exposure.

Worldwide celebrities must work in the public sphere, have accomplishments of importance and interest, be well known or famous, seek celebrity status, be highly visible in the media, and embody the dreams and desires of the public. Many individuals meet some of these requirements; a smaller number meet them all. If one were to select the requirement that most distinguishes a celebrity from an almost-celebrity it would be this one: significant media exposure.

References

A&E Television Networks. 2006. "Fidel Castro." [Online information; retrieved 10/31/09.] http://www.biography.com/hispanic-heritage/fidel-castro.jsp.

About.com. n.d. "Famous paleontologists, dinosaur scientists, and fossil hunters." [Online information; retrieved 10/25/09.] http://dinosaurs.about.com/od/famouspaleontologists.

"African writers index." 2000. [Online information; retrieved 10/25/09.] http://www.geocities.com/africanwriters/AuthorsA.html?200925.

BBC. 2002. "Dr. Rowan Williams." [Online article; retrieved 11/11/09.] http://www.bbc.co.uk/religions/Christianity/people/rowanwilliams_l.shtml.

BBC News. 2008. "Mandelas's life and times." [Online information; retrieved 10/31/09.] http://news.bbc.co.uk/2/hi/africa/1454208.stm?ad=1.

BBC News. 2009a. "Profile: Nicholas Sarkozy." [Online information; retrieved 10/31/09.] http://news.bbc.co.uk/2/hi/europe/3673102.stm?ad=1.

BBC News. 2009b. "Profile: Silvio Berlusconi." [Online information; retrieved 10/31/09.] http://news.bbc.co.uk/2/hi/europe/3034600.stm?ad=1.

Brown, William J., and Benson P. Fraser. 2008. "Global identification with celebrity heroes." In *Heroes in a global world*, eds. Susan J. Drucker and Gary Gumpert. Cresskill, NJ: Hampton Press, 45–65.

Daniel, Frank Jack. 2009. "Venezuela's Chavez calls Obama 'ignoramus'." [Online article; retrieved 10/31/09.] http://www.reuters.com/article/topNews/idUSTRE52L19G20090322?sp=true.

Drezner, Daniel W. 2007. "Should celebrities set the global agenda?" *Los Angeles Times*, December 30.

Fanoos Encyclopedia. n.d. "Middle East celebrity." [Online information; retrieved 10/25/09.] http://www.fanoos.com/encyclopedia/middleeastcelebrity.

Fish, Stanley. 2009. "Academics under siege." [Online article; retrieved 11/04/09.] http://fish.blogs.nytimes.com/2009/10/19/academics-under-siege.

Gish, Steven D. 2004. *Desmond Tutu: A biography*. Westport, CT: Greenwood Press.

Graham, Billy. 1997. *Just as I am*. San Francisco: Harper/Zondervan.

Kappelman, Todd. 2001. "Marshall McLuhan: The medium is the message." [Online article; retrieved 10/18/09.] http://www.leaderu.com/orgs/probe/docs/Mcluhan.html.

Klein, Joe. 2009. "Hillary's moment." *Time*, November 18, 24–33.

Linkism. n.d. "Contemporary art." [Online information; retrieved 10/25/09.] http://www.linkism.com/visual_artists/famous-artists/contemporary/index/htm.

Mansfield, Stephen. 2005. *Pope Benedict XVI: His life and mission*. New York: Jeremy P. Tarcher/Penguin.

McCombs, Maxwell E., and Donald L. Shaw. 1972. "The agenda-setting function of the mass media." *Public Opinion Quarterly*, 36, 176–187.

Moores, Pamela M. 1991. "Celebrities in politics: Simone Signoret and Yves Montand." In *Political culture in France and Germany*, ed. John Gaffney and Eva Kolinsky. New York: Routledge.

Park, Ju-Min. 2009. "Disgraced cloning scientists Hwang Woo-suk guilty of embezzlement." [Online article; retrieved 11/01/09.] http://www.latimes.com/news/nationworld/la-fg-clone27-2009oct.

Pearson Education. 2007. "Hugo Chavez." [Online article; retrieved 10/31/09.] http://www.infoplease.com/biography/var/hugochavez.html.

Reville, William. 2000. "Ireland's scientific heritage." *The Irish Times*, December 14.

Rodden, John. 1998. "The scholar gypsies: Academic celebrity in America." [Online article; retrieved 11/03/09.] http://www.mmisi.org/ma/40_02/rodden.pdf.

Rodman, George. 2006. *Mass media in a changing world*. New York: McGraw Hill.

Ross, Rick. 2002. "Benny Hinn is raking it in." [Online article; retrieved 11/11/09.] http://www.cultnews.com/archives/000189.html.

Sheridan, Jennifer. 2009. "Celebrities, yes, but politics? Don't ask." [Online article; retrieved 10/22/09.] http://www.smh.com.au/national/celebrities-yes-but-politics-dont-ask-200090919-fw4d.html.

Sullivan, Kevin. 2005. "Chavez casts himself as the anti-Bush." [Online article; retrieved 10/31/09.] http://www.washingtonpost.com/ac2/wp-dyn/A35193-2005MAR14.

Time. n.d. "The Time 100." [Online information; retrieved 11/03/09.] http://www.time.com/time/time100/scientist/profile/watsoncrick.html.

Velasquez, Bertha. 2008. "Celebrities and their politics." [Online article; retrieved 10/22/09.] http://www.lavozcolorado.com/news.php?nid=2944&page0.

Viren, Lasse. n.d. [Online information; retrieved 10/22/09]. http://222.britannica.com/EBchecked/topic/629818/Lasse-Viren and http://www.spiritus-temporis.com/lasse-viren.

West, Darrell M. 2007. "Celebrity, politics, political celebrities." [Online article; retrieved 10/22/09.] http://www.britannica.com/blogs/2007/08/celebrity-politics-political-celebrities.

WGBH. 1998. "Stephen Hawking." [Online information; retrieved 11/13/09.] http://www.pbs.org/wgbh/aso/databank/entries/bphawk.html.

White Hat. 2009. "The white hat guide to 200 significant Australians." [Online information; retrieved 10/25/09.] http://www.whitehat.com.au/australia/people/People200.asp.

Zechowski, Sharon, n.d. "McLuhan, Marshall." [Online information; retrieved 10/18/09.] http://www.museum.tv/archives/etv/M/htm/mcluhanmars.

4

Chronology

Historical records do not tell us when the term *celebrity* was first used. We see the word and its cognates— *celebration, celebrated, famous,* and *well known*— in English literature as early as the 16th century. It may have been used in oral communication earlier than that. Determining a precise date for the widespread use of the term is not possible. If we accept Schickel's (1985) notion that prior to the beginning of the 20th century there was no such thing as celebrity, then fixing a precise date for the beginning of celebrity is easy; it's 1900. In a way, Schickel has a point. Celebrity depends on media exposure and media did not become highly developed until the 20th century. However, given the fact that some form of media has been around since the early civilizations, we prefer Ponce de Leon's (2002) idea that celebrity is fame modernized. Thus, any chronology of events relating to celebrity—such as the one this chapter provides—must take into account the historical, political, cultural, and social conditions resulting in improved communication and in the modernization of life in each historical period. You will, therefore, find information in the chronology detailing a variety of events for a given time period with particular emphasis, of course, on media.

Readers today are not particularly inclined to remember historical dates and events much beyond the birthdays and anniversaries of relatives and friends. Many adults remember being required to memorize dates, names, and other facts for exams they took as youngsters in school. Most of them hated memorizing names and dates. It was frustrating and seemed to make little sense. The younger generation is growing up with a similar distaste for knowing dates and events. Want to know when and where World War II started? No problem, just look it up on the Internet. Today, electronic technology puts us in touch with all sorts of information, most of it at our fingertips and available quickly. We have access to a great deal of information, but much of it is disorganized and offered with little or no context. Internet search engines fail to present information in any logical fashion. A single piece of online information rarely answers all one's questions. Moreover, it is not often placed in context with other, similar pieces of information. It is very much like dumping 1,000 jigsaw puzzle pieces on a table, picking up one or two, and trying to determine what picture is on the puzzle. In order to understand completely any person, event, situation, or phenomenon, we need context, that is, a framework allowing us to see our subject of interest and its relationship with interrelated subjects and conditions.

Celebrity is not a difficult concept to grasp, but our understanding of it can be enhanced by seeing the framework in which it developed. It did not spring full blown into the 21st century. Its development depended on many things, some directly and others indirectly important to its growth. This chapter provides a chronology of events, particularly the development of communication and media. Because celebrity is fame modernized, one must see it in its proper context. Media exposure is critical to modern-day celebrity.

BCE (Before the Common Era, dates approximate)

3500   *Date of earliest known writings in Mesopotamia.* A complex set of symbols, sometimes called pictograms, is developed. Messages are inscribed on clay tablets. Communication is primitive; almost no one is widely known.

2600   *Egyptian scribes use hieroglyphics.* Priests use these picture words and inscribe them on the walls of Egyptian tombs and on pottery. They also use a cursive form of hieroglyphics involving pictograms and consonants. However, most Egyptians cannot read and thus pay little attention to the writing. Some Egyptian rulers are known by the general public but are not considered famous.

2200 *Papyrus becomes popular.* The papyrus reed is plentiful on the banks of the Nile. Workers split the reeds into thin strips, place them close together in cross-rows, pound them into smooth sheets, and dry them in the sun. Scribes write on these sheets, using ink made from berries or soot. Daily life is difficult. People have little time to think about affairs other than their own. There are no celebrities and few well-known individuals.

800 *Greeks improve the Phoenician alphabet, adding vowels.* As literacy improves, the Greeks use papyrus, together with a simplified alphabet designed to better represent speech, and contribute to art and literature. The library at Alexandria has about 700,000 papyrus scrolls. The Greeks enjoy attending plays and political gatherings and understand the importance of oral communication. Influential writers, politicians, and military figures are well known among members of the general public.

200 *Romans use parchment and vellum.* Made from treated animal skins, these writing surfaces are popular among Roman writers. Many Roman citizens cannot read and thus hear official news and proclamations read aloud to them in public places. Romans share information with others, including travelers from other parts of the world. Major political and military figures are well known, some of them famous for their accomplishments.

CE (Common Era, most dates approximate)

105 *Chinese invent paper.* Ts'ai Lun, a government employee, mixes tree bark, hemp, and rags to make a smooth writing surface. It is cheaper to make than papyrus or parchment but is not as durable. Nevertheless, paper is not widely used in Western culture until the 13th century.

400 *Literacy advances.* Rome has more than 20 libraries containing about 20,000 scrolls each. Private schools are available for those who can afford them. Travel is easier and information sharing is common. The number of well-known writers, politicians, and others in public life increases. Some information is available on what is happening elsewhere in the world.

600   *Manuscript culture develops.* The number of books (papyrus scrolls) increases and literacy continues to improve. The Middle Ages era begins. Monks and other religious scribes produce illuminated manuscripts containing colorful designs on each page. Religion continues to be a dominant influence in the lives of many. The world expands beyond the Roman Empire. There is much political and social activity in Europe. Important contributions are made to art, music, and literature. It is easier for members of the public to become acquainted with important, influential individuals. Many people are considered to be famous or well known.

1453   *Printing press invented.* Using an old wine press, Johannes Gutenberg develops the printing press during the Renaissance era. Movable metal type, together with paper that has made its way west from China, allows Gutenberg to mass produce printed material. Although many Europeans cannot read, the printing press makes Europe a more literate society. The Bible is printed in several languages. Works of literature and philosophy are widely available. The word *famous* is used occasionally in literature. The general public, having seen, heard, or read about them, consider many of those in public life well known or famous. Oral communication is still a primary means of information exchange.

1632   *London coffeehouses become communication centers.* The importance of oral communication is evident as citizens gather to share information and ideas. In addition to art and literature, coffee drinkers talk about science and philosophy. The terms *celebration* and *celebrity* appear in some works of literature. In America, the New England colonies struggle to establish life in the new world. The first American newspaper is published in 1690. Several colonists are well known; only a few are famous.

1750   *The Enlightenment is in full bloom.* The world is expanding and the human spirit is awake! Writers, philosophers, musicians, artists, religious leaders, and politicians from many countries contribute to both their individual cultures and to worldwide culture. This rich intellectual and social environment makes it easier for individuals to become well known or famous.

A few are on the verge of celebrity. In the colonies, the Revolutionary Era is poised to begin. The Revolutionary War makes many colonists well known, particularly those in government and the military. Benjamin Franklin, Thomas Jefferson, and George Washington, along with others, become famous for their roles in establishing the United States as a nation.

1850   *Magazines and newspapers prosper in America.* After a modest start at the beginning of the 19th century, print media become influential. *The Saturday Evening Post* is a popular magazine and has nationwide distribution. Engravings and other illustrations are added to magazines. Newspaper circulation increases. Early experiments begin in what will become the radio and music industries. The public is aware of significant news events. Individuals in government appear to be well known, but a growing literary culture earns recognition; the works of Nathaniel Hawthorne, Edgar Allan Poe, Ralph Waldo Emerson, and Henry David Thoreau are widely read.

1861–1865   *War years.* The Civil War enables many in government and the military to become well known. Some military leaders are famous for their tactics or performance on the battlefield. Generals William T. Sherman, Robert E. Lee, and Ulysses S. Grant are widely recognized for their roles in the war. Writers and artists are also at work during these years, but the country's attention is focused on the war.

1900   *Media continue to grow.* By the time the 20th century begins, media seem to be everywhere in life. Newspapers suffer a bit from the effects of yellow journalism—a period of wild, sensational stories, perhaps a forerunner of some of today's celebrity publications. Paperback books are widely available. Many homes have phonographs. City dwellers see films in Nickelodeons. The public becomes more knowledgeable about important individuals in politics and entertainment. The Industrial Revolution brings the leaders of business and industry to the public's attention. John D. Rockefeller and J. P. Morgan become well known for their work in the oil and steel industries.

Alexander Graham Bell invents the telephone and Henry Ford establishes assembly line production of automobiles. The Wright Brothers test the first airplane. Because media are fairly robust and report every new development in the country, Rockefeller, Ford, and the others are celebrities.

1920   *More media.* With World War I over, Americans hope for a period of normalcy. Book clubs begin. *Ladies Home Journal, Time, Life,* and *Reader's Digest* are popular magazines. Radio is a full-time mass medium. The first experimental television signal is transmitted. Movies now have a sound track. For some individuals in public life or in the news, the growth of media during these years signals an upcoming transition; more well-known or famous individuals will soon become celebrities.

1930   *More celebrities.* Celebrity expands beyond government, business, and literature to include individuals in other areas of life. Baseball's Babe Ruth establishes the single-season home run record; Ty Cobb and Rogers Hornsby establish baseball records of their own. Major sports figures are well known and famous enough to be celebrities. Even those on the wrong side of the law become celebrities; Al Capone, a Chicago gang leader and racketeer, gains celebrity status. John Dillinger and Bonnie and Clyde are also celebrities.

1950   *Media become more organized and influential.* At mid-century, media have an important place in American life. The airwaves buzz with radio and television signals. The public knows about domestic and foreign political affairs, listens to music on vinyl discs, reads books, attends movies in theaters, reads magazines and newspapers, and—if they can afford a set—watches television. Color television is just a few years away. Well-known and famous individuals are celebrities because they benefit from regular media exposure. Celebrities can be found in politics, government, business, industry, sports, and entertainment.

1960   *The number of celebrities increases as media use increases.* Media are powerful forces in American life. Thousands of books are published annually. Newspapers benefit from wide circulation and report interesting, important world and national events. Radio's popularity increases with the coming of the Top 40 format and FM. Popular music is available on vinyl discs or on cassette tapes. Cable television systems eliminate the need for an outside antenna. Some television signals are relayed by satellite. Research begins for the Internet. The public becomes well acquainted with radio, television, and movie personalities as well as politicians and others in public life by reading about them in newspapers or magazines, hearing them on radio, or seeing them on television or in films. Individuals who seek and receive regular media exposure for their accomplishments are celebrities.

1970   *Print media begin to lose audience; celebrity depends to a large degree on exposure in electronic media.* Newspapers are steady, but general interest magazines (*Life, Look*) decline and eventually disappear. However, magazines designed to reach a "niche" audience, that is, an audience with special interest in a specific subject, remain successful. *People* magazine begins publication. With no commercial messages, National Public Radio (NPR) brings news and special features to its radio audience. Situation comedies are popular on television. Electronic mail (e-mail) and the microprocessor develop, adding important components to a young Internet. Many individuals in public life are celebrities. It is, in fact, rather easy to be a celebrity. One simply works in the public sphere, has a significant accomplishment or two, captures the imagination of the public, and appears regularly somewhere in the media (usually on radio or television, or in the movies).

1980   *New developments.* The *Columbus Dispatch* becomes the first online newspaper. Traditional print information sources seem less important to the public than the new electronic media. VHS videocassettes mark a major transformation in movies and video. Video cassette recorders (VCRs) are available for home use.

Cable television is increasingly popular. Fiber optic cable improves transmission of information on the Internet. These technological advances increase the public's ability to access information and entertainment in their homes. Most media personalities are celebrities; many high-profile individuals from business and government are also celebrities.

1990   *More progress.* The typical American home has five radio sets and access to more than 30 cable television channels. Television hits include *Seinfeld* and *Law and Order*. Talk radio becomes the most popular radio format. *Entertainment Weekly* magazine begins publication. *Dances with Wolves, Pretty Woman,* and *GoodFellas* draw well in theaters. Photoshop becomes available for computers, enabling users to manipulate images. Celebrity grows; hundreds of personalities from entertainment and politics, as well as a smattering from other fields, are held in high esteem by Americans.

1995   *A rich media environment enhances celebrity status.* Although traditional print newspapers begin to falter, other media capture the attention of Americans. Multiplex theaters provide several different movies in one location. Web browsers make it easy to navigate the Internet. Amazon.com begins online shopping. Television service is available by direct broadcast satellite (DBS). Jerry Springer, Jenny Jones, and Maury Povich host tabloid television talk shows. CNN becomes the most popular cable television news channel, largely due to its coverage of the Gulf War in 1991. *Comedy Central, SciFi Channel, Cartoon Network,* and *Court TV* are added to cable television systems. More than 65 million personal computers are in use, about 2 million of them connected to the Internet. The World Wide Web is available for general use. Compact disc music sales increase; cassette music tapes decline. More than 150 newspapers offer news content online. *Schindler's List, Sleepless in Seattle, Forrest Gump, The Lion King, Braveheart,* and *Pulp Fiction* entertain moviegoers. Television hits include *NYPD Blue, X-Files, Friends,* and *ER*. The video game industry earns about $3 billion. Although no one is counting, there may be a thousand celebrities.

In the minds of many members of the public, individuals become celebrities by appearing in one movie, or having one hit record, or starring in one television show. It doesn't take a record of accomplishments; just one will do.

2000   *Internet use increases; celebrity becomes commonplace.* At the beginning of the 21st century, the shift from traditional to new media is well underway. Some newspapers have closed; others publish only online editions. Network evening newscasts begin to lose audience. One-third of Americans use the Internet regularly. America Online (AOL) reports 15 million subscribers. Internet users can access more than 800 million Web sites. Some analog formats are replaced by digital. Digital video discs (DVDs) enable Americans to view movies at home on DVD players that offer better picture and sound quality than movies on VHS cassette tapes. MP3 players are popular with music lovers. The video game industry continues to grow in popularity and in revenue. Many Americans have cell phones. Lance Armstrong wins his second Tour de France race. Vladimir Putin is elected president of Russia. Author J. K. Rowling releases her fourth Harry Potter book. Winners of FOX's *Who Wants to Marry a Millionaire*—Darva Conger and Rick Rockwell—fail as a married couple. Rapper Eminem is arrested twice on weapons charges but has the #1 album on music charts. Because the public has access to so much media content, the celebrity label is quickly applied to most individuals who appear in movies, on television, in the news, or on the Internet.

2001   *Media cover the terrorist attacks; celebrity exposure increases.* George W. Bush is sworn in as the 43rd president. Oklahoma City bomber Timothy McVeigh is executed. Slugger Barry Bonds becomes the single-season home run champion with 73 homers. Sean Combs, also known as Puff Daddy, is acquitted of weapons and bribery charges and changes his name to P. Diddy. Hollywood stars Tom Cruise and Nicole Kidman file for divorce. Venus Williams wins the women's Wimbledon tennis championship.

Traditional media regain some ground in the fall of 2001 as Americans (and the world) turn to television for news and video of the terrorist attacks of 9/11. Newspapers, television networks, and cable systems are popular information sources about the terrorist attacks. The Internet, too, serves as a source of information, but is more instrumental in establishing memorial services and soliciting memorial funds for those killed in the attacks. Osama bin Laden is identified as the primary force behind the terrorist attacks and becomes famous in some parts of the world. The terrorist attacks have three effects on celebrity. First, they make some individuals heroes, particularly police, firemen, and other personnel involved in rescue efforts at New York's World Trade Center. Some rescue personnel lose their lives; others survive. A few become well known. Second, the terrorists who planned and carried out the attacks become well known in America and famous in some other parts of the world. Third, many celebrities (George Clooney, Jack Nicholson, and Bruce Springsteen, among others) appear on television commenting on the attacks or appealing for donations to help survivors or cleanup efforts.

2002   *Significant developments.* World Wide Web users create online journals, or Weblogs, and are called bloggers. E-mail is an increasingly popular form of communication. Satellite radio offers two services, Sirius and XM. *American Idol* begins its run on FOX. Movie industry revenue tops $33 billion worldwide; computer users can download movies and save them to DVD. File sharing is popular among computer users. Serena Williams defeats her sister Venus in the women's Wimbledon tennis final. The movie *Spider-Man* earns more than $400 million. Hollywood movie stars Denzel Washington and Halle Berry win Oscars. Celebrity is widespread among individuals in many fields.

2003   *Personal, electronic communication increases.* More than 150 million people worldwide use cell phones; some phones have Internet capability. The Internet is important in political campaign fund-raising. iTunes offers songs for 99 cents each, which can be downloaded to iPods. DVD movie sales outstrip box office sales.

More newspapers offer content online. The United States launches an attack on Iraq, citing that nation's weapons of mass destruction as a threat to world security. The Space Shuttle *Columbia* explodes, killing all seven aboard. Actor Arnold Schwarzenegger is elected governor of California. Singer Norah Jones wins five Grammy awards. *American Idol*, in its second season, increases in popularity.

2004   *More growth.* Most American homes have a color television. Three-fourths of Americans use the Internet. Online advertising rakes in $21 billion. Cell phones number 1.5 billion worldwide. iTunes sells its 200 millionth song. MySpace becomes an Internet social networking site. Mark Zuckerberg launches "thefacebook." Massachusetts Senator John Kerry wins 9 of 10 spring primaries to become the Democratic nominee for president, but loses in the fall to Republican George W. Bush. Business-woman and television host Martha Stewart is sentenced to five months in prison after being found guilty of charges related to illegal stock market activities. Singers Janet Jackson and Justin Timberlake experience a "wardrobe malfunction" during their halftime performance at Super Bowl XXXVIII when Timberlake rips the bodice of Jackson's dress, revealing her right breast; the Federal Communications Commission (FCC) fines Super Bowl broadcaster CBS half a million dollars for the incident. Filmmaker Michael Moore releases *Fahrenheit 9/11*, a film sharply critical of President George W. Bush and the Iraq war. Mel Gibson's film *The Passion of the Christ* stirs up religious controversy. Celebrities seem to be everywhere.

2005   *A troubled year.* Hurricanes Katrina and Rita strike America's Gulf Coast, destroying property and leaving many homeless and without help. A 7.6 earthquake in Pakistan's Kashmir region leaves more than 4 million people homeless. Pope John Paul II dies and is replaced by Pope Benedict XVI. The number of U.S. soldiers killed in the Iraq war reaches 2,000. CBS's Dan Rather steps down as evening news anchor after airing an erroneous story about President George W. Bush.

Peter Jennings, ABC's evening news anchor, dies. Actor Brad Pitt recovers quickly after his divorce from Jennifer Aniston by hooking up with Angelina Jolie, his co-star in the movie *Mr. and Mrs. Smith*. Actor Tom Cruise and actress Katie Holmes become engaged. ABC's *Lost*, *Desperate Housewives*, and *Grey's Anatomy* are popular television shows; performers on those shows become instant celebrities. *People*, the leading celebrity magazine, has a total paid circulation of more than 3.7 million.

2006   *Big numbers.* Millions of bloggers post information and opinion online for millions of readers. YouTube has more than 100 million videos, with tens of thousands added daily. Popular television programs are available on the Web. Facebook expands its membership to include anyone 13 years of age or older. Jack Dorsey creates Twitter, a free microblogging and social information service. Celebrity Web sites, like TMZ.com, are popular. CBS's Katie Couric becomes the first female evening news anchor. Bill Gates steps down as day-to-day manager of Microsoft. *Babel* and *Dreamgirls* are identified as two of the top films of 2006 by the American Film Institute. Saddam Hussein, former Iraqi dictator, is convicted of crimes against humanity and hanged in Baghdad. *Time* magazine lists actor George Clooney, actress Meryl Streep, television personalities Ellen DeGeneres and Rachael Ray, and comedian Stephen Colbert among the 100 people who are shaping our world. Some members of the public apply the celebrity label to anyone who posts a video on YouTube, but entertainment personalities are still the culture's primary celebrities.

2007   *Staying the course.* The War in Iraq continues. Gordon Brown replaces Tony Blair as British prime minister. Democrat Nancy Pelosi is elected the first woman Speaker of the House. *The Departed* wins the Academy Award for best picture. The Dixie Chicks win three Grammys: record, album, and song of the year. *People* magazine continues to be the top-selling celebrity magazine, but loses almost 200,000 in paid circulation. FOX's *American Idol* continues its run as the top television program, followed by ABC's *Dancing with the Stars*.

The popularity of these two television shows leads many of the participants to claim their 15 minutes of fame. Bloggers consider themselves famous for their work on the Internet. Facebook users consider themselves famous if they have lots of "friends." For many, "well known" means being acknowledged for an accomplishment, however small. The terms *well known, famous,* and *celebrity* appear to have the same meaning.

2008   *New developments.* The Taliban reemerge in Afghanistan. China hosts the Summer Olympics. Bank failures, subprime mortgages, and stock market declines contribute to a global financial crisis. Four important celebrities die: actors Heath Ledger and Paul Newman, comedian George Carlin, and NBC's Tim Russert. Britney Spears undergoes a psychiatric evaluation early in the year, but rebounds with a new album in the fall. *People* magazine continues to be the top-selling celebrity magazine. *US Weekly, Entertainment Weekly, and In Style* trail *People* by about one million in circulation each. *American Idol* dominates television ratings. Singer Taylor Swift tops the charts in America with more than 4 million albums sold. *The Dark Knight* and *Slumdog Millionaire* are the year's top movies. Senator Barack Obama, an Illinois Democrat, is elected president.

2009   *Oversaturation.* Too much media and too many celebrities characterize this year. Media dominate the lives of many Americans. Eighty-five percent of the public uses cell phones; more than 100 million Web logs are in cyberspace. Texting and twittering are daily, routine activities. Facebook is an obsession for the more than 300 million users worldwide. Google introduces Chrome, a faster Web browser. Use of digital cameras is widespread (no more film!). Although network television viewing declines, cable channel viewing increases with popular shows on Bravo, the Food Network, USA, AMC, HBO, and Showtime. News channels CNN, FOX, and MSNBC gain viewers. Digital Video Recorders (DVRs) allow users to record their favorite shows for later playback. Many television programs are available online. Most movie-rental outlets experience a decrease in rentals, leading some to close. Film lovers rent their favorite movie by mail or from a vending machine at local stores.

The ubiquity of media enables almost any member of the public to become a celebrity. Some individuals have noteworthy accomplishments; others have questionable ones. Chesley "Sully" Sullenberger, a 57-year-old U.S. Airways pilot, makes a successful emergency landing in the Hudson River and is hailed as a hero. Oprah Winfrey announces that the 2010 season will be the last for her syndicated television talk show. Susan Boyle's singing performance on the television show "Britain's Got Talent" lifts her to the top spot in YouTube video viewings and ultimately results in a best-selling album. Six-year-old Falcon Heene is a pawn in a balloon hoax designed to earn his parents a television reality show. It doesn't. Former Republican vice-presidential candidate Sarah Palin resigns as governor of Alaska, writes a book, and undertakes a speaking tour. Tareq and Michaele Salahi, a socialite couple from Virginia, breach White House security and attend a state dinner uninvited. Comedian David Letterman admits past affairs and is the victim of an extortion plot. Comedian Jay Leno is ousted from NBC's *The Tonight Show* in favor of Conan O'Brien; Leno is given a 10 p.m. prime-time weekday slot on the network. Singer Michael Jackson dies. Tiger Woods has multiple affairs, a traffic accident, and suspends his golfing career for a time. South Carolina Governor Mark Sanford admits an extramarital affair. South Carolina Representative Joe Wilson interrupts President Barack Obama's State of the Union speech by shouting, "You lie!" Clearly, there are more celebrity goings-on than the typical American can readily follow.

2010   *A busy, uncertain, troubling year.* Apple introduces the iPad, a multipurpose electronic device. A group of individuals unhappy with Washington politics formally organizes as the Tea Party and holds its first convention. Professional golfer Tiger Woods confesses to past sexual indiscretions and enters therapy. *The Hurt Locker* wins the Academy Award as best picture, edging out the popular *Avatar*. Earthquakes cause major devastation in Haiti and Chile.

Internet-search-engine-giant Google quarrels with China over government restrictions on Google access. Golfer Tiger Woods emerges from therapy and holds a small press conference but refuses to answer questions about some aspects of his behavior. Woods returns to the professional golf tour by entering the Masters in April, but he doesn't play well. The Democrat-controlled Congress passes major health care reform over the objections of Republicans. Actress Sandra Bullock, winner of this year's Academy Award as Best Actress for her role in *The Blind Side*, encounters domestic trouble when her husband, actor and motor-cyclist Jesse James, is discovered to have had several affairs, primarily with tattooed women, during his marriage to Bullock. Russia and the United States reach an agreement to reduce the number of nuclear missiles. Although its ratings slip a bit during the winter, *American Idol* continues to be the most-watched television program. However, most of the celebrity buzz is about *Dancing with the Stars*. Former Republican vice-presidential candidate Sarah Palin becomes a commentator on FOX News. The U.S. census is conducted with regular media announcements encouraging citizens to return the census questionnaire. War in the Middle East continues but the emphasis shifts from Iraq to Afghanistan. A volcano erupts in Iceland, spewing a debris cloud into the atmosphere where winds move the cloud eastward resulting in major flight cancellations, the loss of millions of dollars by the airlines, and major inconvenience for passengers affected by the cancelled flights. An oil rig explodes and sinks in the Gulf of Mexico off the coast of Louisiana leaking millions of gallons of oil into the water, endangering wildlife, commercial fishing, and tourism all along the Gulf Coast. Early attempts to stop the leak are unsuccessful. A terrorist bomb in an SUV in New York's Times Square fails to detonate and the perpetrator is caught trying to leave the country on a commercial airline. The stock market's Dow Jones average plunges almost 1,000 points in the spring on news that Greece may default on its debt obligations, although some observers blame a transaction typographical error for the drop.

The market slowly recovers only to fall again in early summer due to problematic world economic conditions. Gordon Brown resigns as Britain's prime minister and is replaced by David Cameron. Arizona passes an illegal immigration law; special interest groups protest, but polls show majority public support for the law. Heavy rains flood most of the Nashville, Tennessee, area, including the site of the Grand Ole Opry; country music celebrities help with the cleanup. Facebook, accused of selling users' personal information to advertising and marketing firms, struggles to revise its privacy policy. Golfer Tiger Woods and his wife Elin divorce; some sources say Elin may have gotten as much as $100 million as part of the settlement.

References

Campbell, Richard, Christopher Martin, and Bettina Fabos. 2007. *Media and culture*. Fifth edition. Boston: Bedford/St. Martins.

Fang, Irving. 2008. *Alphabet to Internet: Mediated communication in our lives*. St. Paul, MN: Rada Press.

Miller, James, and John Thompson. 2006. *Almanac of American history*. Washington, DC: National Geographic Society.

Ponce de Leon, Charles. 2002. *Self-exposure: Human-interest journalism and the emergency of celebrity in America*. Chapel Hill: University of North Carolina Press.

Schickel, Richard. 1985. *Intimate strangers: The culture of celebrity*. Garden City, NY: Doubleday and Company.

www.cbsnews.com/stories/2009.

www.infoplease.com/year.

5

Biographical Sketches

This chapter presents brief biographical profiles of 30 celebrities. These particular celebrities were selected for several reasons. They are all famous, well-known individuals with significant accomplishments. They are visible in or on media. They seek publicity opportunities for themselves or their work. Each connects in some way with the public, either as an individual whose lifestyle is admired or as an individual who embodies the public's dreams and desires. In other words, the 30 precisely fit the definition of celebrity developed and presented in Chapter 1. And, because this book is primarily about celebrity in the 21st century, celebrities who are dead or who are no longer in the pop culture spotlight for one reason or another are not included. However, you will notice some older celebrities in the group. Their work began in the 20th century and has continued well into in the 21st century. The expectation is they have more to contribute as the 21st century progresses. Additionally, this chapter does not include celebrities whose lives or activities were discussed at length in earlier chapters.

Glenn Beck (1964–)

Glenn Beck, a radio-television political talk show host and author, was born in Mt. Vernon, Washington, on February 10, 1964. His teen years were troubled. Glenn lost his mother when he was 13; she drowned in a bay near Tacoma. Shortly after his mother's death, one of his brothers-in-law committed suicide and another had a fatal heart attack. However, that same year, Glenn won a local radio contest and was allowed to work for an hour at a local radio station as a disc jockey. He graduated from high school in Bellingham, Washington, and set out to establish a career in radio, working at stations in both small and large markets. Glenn was well known in the radio industry, but not yet a celebrity. By age 30, he tired of radio and turned to alcohol and drugs for solace. He and his wife divorced after four years of marriage and two daughters—one of whom had cerebral palsy. Still battling substance abuse, Glenn decided to enroll at Yale University as a theology major; he lasted one semester. He began to turn his life around with the help of friends and Alcoholics Anonymous. Returning to radio, his "Glenn Beck Program" was soon heard on more than 40 stations. He went from a local radio personality to a national radio celebrity very quickly. Television followed soon after. His daily show on the FOX News cable channel is one of the network's most popular. Like some other political talk show hosts, Glenn is outspoken, conservative, and often inflammatory. Because of his widespread support among political conservatives, he is a media celebrity of considerable influence.

Beyoncé (1981–)

An American singer and actress, Beyoncé Giselle Knowles was born September 4, 1981, in Houston, Texas. As a preteen, she began singing with the popular R&B group Destiny's Child. Early on, their music was a rich mix of gospel, rhythm and blues, and hip-hop, but they settled mainly on R&B in 1995. Her father Mathew served as the group's manager. The group soon became well known, appearing on television's *Star Search*, but the singers had not yet become individual stars. The group's first two albums were overwhelming successes, both at home and abroad; concerts sold out. Internal conflicts in 2000 led to the group's breaking up; in 2004 Beyoncé won five Grammy Awards for her single "Dangerously in Love," firmly establishing her as a music industry celebrity. She also had an interest in acting, appearing in an MTV production before landing roles in the James Bond parody *Goldmember* (2002), *The Fighting Temptations* (2004), and *The Pink Panther* (2006). Her celebrity was enhanced in 2006 when she appeared in *Dreamgirls*, a film nominated for a Golden Globe award; her song "Listen" was nominated for an Academy Award. Beyoncé married hip-hop personality Jay-Z in

2008, making them one of the music industry's most powerful celebrity couples.

Kobe Bryant (1978–)

Kobe Bean Bryant is a professional basketball player for the Los Angeles Lakers. Born August 23, 1978, in Philadelphia, Pennsylvania, Kobe immediately became part of a sports family: his father, Joe, had played in the National Basketball Association (NBA), and his two older sisters were athletic. By age three, he was already playing basketball. After living and playing basketball for a while in Italy, Kobe returned to Philadelphia where he became a high school basketball star, winning several awards. He decided to turn professional right out of high school. This was unusual; most NBA players are drafted after their college careers. Nevertheless, he was drafted by Charlotte and traded to Los Angeles. In 1998, he was selected for the NBA All-Star team, the youngest all-star (at 19) in NBA history. Kobe helped the Lakers win three consecutive NBA championships and signed endorsement contracts with Adidas, Sprite, and other sponsors. At the pinnacle of his celebrity in 2003, he was charged with one count of sexual assault on a 19-year-old female hotel worker in Colorado. Kobe admitted to adultery, but denied the rape charge. The case was dismissed in 2004, but a civil lawsuit against him by the apparent victim was settled out of court. Understandably, the episode eroded his celebrity status and resulted in a couple of forgettable seasons on the basketball court. Still, he returned to form and helped his team to the NBA finals in 2008 and 2009. Kobe continues to be an influential celebrity in the sports world.

George Clooney (1961–)

George Timothy Clooney, born May 6, 1961, in Lexington, Kentucky, is an actor, director, producer, and social activist. Although he was not aware of it at the time of his birth, some members of his family were celebrities. Perhaps he was destined to become a celebrity himself. Nick, his father, was a celebrated television news anchor—first in Lexington, then in Columbus and Cincinnati, Ohio. Rosemary Clooney, his aunt, had been a popular singer in the 1940s and 1950s. For a time, Rosemary was married to José

Ferrer, a well-known actor. However, as a youngster, George was interested in sports. He played basketball and baseball during his school years and tried out for the Cincinnati Reds but did not make the team. As a student at Northern Kentucky University, George was known more for partying than studying; he quit before the end of his freshman year and moved to Los Angeles to pursue an acting career. Although he came from a family of celebrities, George was not an immediate success in Hollywood. He failed to get an acting job for two years, so he took construction jobs to pay for acting classes. He soon appeared in a few commercials and some minor television sitcoms. His big break came when he was cast as a doctor on *ER*, an NBC television drama where he quickly became one of the show's most popular characters. Although he had parts in several B-level movies during his *ER* stint, his success in films began in 1996 when he starred with Michelle Pfeiffer in *One Fine Day*. He played Batman in the 1997 film *Batman and Robin*. His popularity increased as a result of roles in *Ocean's Eleven* (2001) and *Michael Clayton* (2007). Total celebrity finally arrived for George in 2009 when he starred in *Up in the Air* and was nominated for an Academy Award as Best Actor. The film itself was nominated for Best Picture. George once described himself as "an actor, businessman, and a bit of a hothead."

Tom Cruise (1962–)

Thomas Cruise Mapother IV was born in Syracuse, New York, on July 3, 1962. Today he is a celebrated actor, but acting was of little interest to him growing up. His family moved often and he suffered from dyslexia. As a result, he did poorly in school, but tried to compensate by becoming active in sports, particularly wrestling. As a 14-year-old seminary student, Tom was deeply religious and felt destined to become a priest. However, he began thinking about an acting career, and—at age 18—dropped out of school and headed for New York. Within a few years, Tom was starring in some popular films, including *Top Gun* (1986), *The Color of Money* (1986), and *Born on the Fourth of July* (1989), and playing alongside some well-established film celebrities, including Dustin Hoffman and Paul Newman. Tom joined the upper-rank of celebrity with *A Few Good Men* (1992, with Jack Nicholson and Demi Moore), and *Jerry Maguire* (with Cuba Gooding Jr. in 1996). Since then, Tom has had one hit movie after another. However, as is so often the case, a celebrity's personal life becomes the center of public attention. Tom began dating actress Katie Holmes in 2005; the couple—dubbed "TomKat" by the pop culture media—had a daughter in April 2006 and married in November 2006 (his third, her first). Tom was widely ridiculed for his behavior on *The Oprah Winfrey Show*. He hopped up and down on the couch, proclaiming his love for Holmes. Critics have also quibbled about his height (5' 7") and his devout following of Scientology. Nevertheless, Tom remains a box office favorite and an influential celebrity in the movie industry.

Ellen DeGeneres (1958–)

Ellen Lee DeGeneres, a television talk show host and author, was born January 26, 1958, in Metairie, Louisiana, a suburb of New Orleans. Growing up she dreamed of becoming a veterinarian, but, feeling she was not "book smart" enough for that career, enrolled after high school at the University of New Orleans as a communications major. She dropped out after one semester and worked as a waitress, vacuum cleaner salesperson, house painter, and legal secretary before turning to stand-up comedy. She appeared on *The Tonight Show with Johnny Carson* in 1986. The appearance on the Carson show gave her immediate recognition and a limited sort of celebrity. Although her early work as a supporting actress in television sitcoms did little to enhance her celebrity, her own sitcom *Ellen* (1994) became a hit. The show was cancelled after the 1997 season because of poor ratings; nevertheless, Ellen made television history that year by revealing (on air) that she was a lesbian. Now she was really a celebrity; some critics wondered whether her show had been cancelled because of poor ratings, because sponsors withdrew from the program, or because of her sexual orientation. She returned to stand-up comedy for a while before attempting another show in 2001, *The Ellen Show*, but it, too, suffered from poor ratings and was cancelled. Never one to give up, Ellen returned to television in 2003 with a daytime television talk show. It was both a critical and commercial success, winning 15 Emmy awards in its first three seasons, including the award for Outstanding Talk Show host. She continued to ride the celebrity wave as host of the Grammy Awards show, Emmy Awards show, and the Academy Awards show. In 2008, Ellen married actress Portia de Rossi. In early 2010, she joined Simon Cowell and others on the *American Idol* judges' panel but left the show after one season.

Tony Dungy (1955–)

Anthony Kevin Dungy was born October 6, 1955, and grew up in Jackson, Michigan. The former professional football coach was a natural athlete as a youngster and often played with older children, relishing the challenge of competing with those older and stronger. He played football, basketball, and baseball in high school, leading his teams to eight championships. Tony's coaches were impressed by his leadership, preparation, intelligence, and natural ability. He played football at the University of Minnesota and was twice named the Golden Gophers' Most Valuable Player. Although he had impressive statistics as a college quarterback, he was not drafted by a National Football League (NFL) team. Nevertheless, he signed as a free agent with the Pittsburgh Steelers. He was subsequently traded to San Francisco, and then to the New York Giants who cut him prior to the 1980 season. Tony retired as a player but did not leave the game. He turned to coaching and held a variety of defensive coaching positions with the Steelers, Chiefs, and Vikings. At one time, he was the youngest and only African American defensive coordinator in the NFL. Although Tony was well known in NFL circles, he did not come to the attention of the sports public until 1996, when he became head coach of the Tampa Bay Buccaneers, where he established a strong defense and improved the team's offensive effort. Fired in 2001, Tony soon became head coach of the Indianapolis Colts. Under his leadership, the Colts won the 2007 Super Bowl. Tony became the first African American head coach to win a Super Bowl. At the height of his celebrity, he retired from coaching after the 2008 season. Tony has always been active in civic and religious activities, including the Fellowship of Christian Athletes and Big Brothers/ Big Sisters. A former player, when asked about Tony, said, "He's a man of integrity, he has a great deal of character. He has that aura. You want to do your best because of the type of guy he is."

Bill Gates (1955–)

Businessman, entrepreneur, and software developer William H. Gates III was born October 28, 1955 in Seattle, Washington. He enjoyed a normal childhood, active in sports and Cub Scouts. His family thought he might follow in his father's footsteps and become an attorney. However, by the seventh grade, Bill had developed an interest in computer science at Seattle's private Lakeside School. He met Paul Allen at Lakeside and the two became fast friends. At age 15, Bill and Paul (who was two years older) developed a traffic-monitoring computer program and earned $20,000 for their work. After graduating from Lakeside, he enrolled at Harvard University, still interested in a law career, but spent more time in the computer lab than in class. He dropped out of Harvard in 1975 and began a career in software design with his friend Paul, forming a company called Micro-Soft; the hyphen was soon dropped and the company became Microsoft. The two friends wrote programs for the early Commodore and Apple computers, but took a large step forward in 1980 with the Microsoft Disk Operating system (MS-DOS) for IBM. Between 1978 and 1981, Microsoft experienced unprecedented growth: the staff increased from 25 to more than 120 and revenue increased from $4 million to $16 million. Although Bill was certainly well known—and probably a celebrity—in the computer world, he was relatively unknown to the general public, which knew little about computers. However, the rest—as they say—is history! Computers eventually worked their way into the personal and work lives of everyday citizens and Bill's aggressive and sometimes ruthless approach to business made him the wealthiest man in America. He married Melinda French in 1994 and the couple established the Bill and Melinda Gates Foundation, focusing on improving the health care and education of children around the world. The foundation has donated billions of dollars to worthy causes. He stepped down as the day-to-day manager of Microsoft in 2000, but remains the company's chairman and chief software architect. With a unique combination of business and philanthropic success, Bill is a worldwide celebrity.

Al Gore (1948–)

Former U.S. Vice President Albert Arnold Gore Jr. was born March 31, 1948, in Washington, D.C. He presently serves as chairman of Current TV, a cable television news network. Al was born into a family already on its way to political celebrity. His father was in the U.S. House of Representatives and then was elected to the Senate in 1953. Although the family home was in Carthage, Tennessee, young Al spent the school year in the nation's capital, returning home in the summer. Al attended Harvard, graduating with a degree in government. He roomed with future actor Tommy Lee Jones. He enlisted in the army and served five months in Vietnam, returning home to Tennessee to work as a reporter for the *Tennessean* and to enroll in Vanderbilt University's law school. However, he quit law school to run for the U.S. House from Tennessee. Elected four times, he followed his father's path and ran for the Senate, where he remained until he was selected by Bill Clinton as the Democratic vice-presidential candidate in 1992. After serving two terms as vice president, Al won the Democratic nomination in 2000, but lost a close election to Republican George W. Bush. Serving as vice president and then running for president automatically made Al a political celebrity. However, his work since leaving politics propelled him to greater celebrity heights. His long-term interest in environmental issues motivated him to write a book on the subject and to make an Oscar-winning documentary film titled *An Inconvenient Truth*. In 2007, Al won a Nobel Prize for his work on global warming. He continues to speak and write on the dangers posed by climate change and is considered the nation's most important environmental celebrity.

Scarlett Johansson (1984–)

Scarlett Johansson was born November 22, 1984, in New York City to parents of Polish and Danish descent. The actress is the grandchild of Ejner Johansson, a well-known Danish screenwriter and filmmaker and was thus surrounded by creative people early in life. As early as age three she expressed an interest in becoming an actress. Scarlett's stage debut came at age eight when she starred with Ethan Hawke in an off-Broadway play. Her first film was Rob Reiner's *North* (1994). She had supporting parts in other films with movie celebrities Sean Connery, Sarah Jessica Parker, and Ben Stiller. She costarred with Robert Redford in *The Horse Whisperer* (1998) and was nominated for an award as most promising actress by the Chicago Film Critics Association. Scarlett was well on her way to becoming an accomplished actress. After graduating from the Professional Children's School in New York City, she applied to New York University's Tisch School of the Arts, but decided to focus on her acting career when she was not accepted. Although her appearance with Redford gained her some attention, her role with Bill Murray in *Lost in Translation*

(2003) established her as an important actress and set her on the celebrity path. Scarlett has worked steadily since age 12. When asked about her career, she said, "I have a hard time taking time off . . . There are so many great actors who are unemployed and seeing them makes you wonder why everything's happening for you . . . I'm just lucky."

Angelina Jolie (1975–)

Angelina Jolie Voight, actress and social activist, was born June 4, 1975, in Los Angeles, California, to parents who were already celebrities at the time of her birth. Her father is Academy Award–winning actor Jon Voight; her mother is French actress Marcheline Bertrand. Thus, growing up, she was no stranger to the celebrity spotlight. By age 11, Angelina was studying acting at the famous Lee Strasberg Theatre Institute. She studied film for a time at New York University, and at age 16, began a career in modeling. Of Czech, French-Canadian, Iroquois, and English ancestry, her exotic good looks made her particularly attractive to filmmakers. She appeared in several movies in the late 1990s, but was more famous for her off-screen relationships. She married and divorced actor Jonny Lee Miller and then actor Billy Bob Thornton. Her film celebrity caught up with her personal-celebrity in 2001 when she starred in *Lara Croft: Tomb Raider*. That movie was followed a few years later by *Mr. and Mrs. Smith* (2005) where she costarred with actor Brad Pitt, whom she married in 2008. The couple has three adopted and three biological children. Very much the social activist, Angelina has capitalized on her celebrity in drawing attention to the plight of the world's refugees. She was made a Goodwill Ambassador for the UN Refugee Agency in 2001 and was praised for her work on behalf of Cambodian refugees. In 2005, she received the Global Humanitarian Action Award from the United Nations for her work on behalf of refugee rights. She is a frequent subject in tabloid newspapers, which regularly speculate on when the Jolie-Pitt marriage will end.

Michael Jordan (1963–)

Michael Jeffrey Jordan, a businessman, actor, and former professional basketball player, was born in Brooklyn, New York, on

February 17, 1963, but grew up in Wilmington, North Carolina. As a youngster, he was interested in sports, primarily baseball. However, influenced by his older brother, he turned to basketball. He did not make his high school team as a sophomore, but eventually made the team and was named to the McDonald's All-Star Team as a senior. Accepting a basketball scholarship to the University of North Carolina, he helped his team win the 1982 NCAA Championship. Michael was the third overall pick by the Chicago Bulls in the 1984 National Basketball Association (NBA) draft. By the late 1980s, he had developed into a superstar and enjoyed the celebrity that came not only from his agility and leadership on the court, but also from several endorsement deals, particularly Nike. After the death of his father in 1993, he retired from professional basketball to pursue a baseball career. His performance in the minor leagues was less than spectacular; he returned to professional basketball in 1995, but retired again in 1999 as one of the greatest ever to play the game. His celebrity status was further enhanced in 2009 when he was inducted into the Naismith Memorial Basketball Hall of Fame. Although retired, Michael is still very much a celebrity. Recently, he has appeared with actor Charlie Sheen in television commercials for Hanes underwear.

Jennifer Lopez (1970–)

Born July 24, 1970, in the Bronx, New York, Jennifer Lynn Lopez is a singer, actress, and model. By age five, she was enrolled in singing and dancing classes. In high school, she played softball and tennis, and was interested in gymnastics. After graduating, she worked in a law office for a while and continued with dancing lessons. Her first break came in 1990, when she earned a dancing spot on the television sitcom *In Living Color*. After several small acting jobs, she jumped to the big screen with her first major film role alongside Wesley Snipes and Woody Harrelson in *Money Train* (1995). Two years later, she became a full-fledged film celebrity, playing the title role in *Selena*, a biographical film about Tejano pop singer Selena Perez who was killed by a crazed fan. While she enjoyed her movie work and had a couple of hit records, Jennifer was a dancer at heart. She was nominated for Best Dance Performance for "Waiting for Tonight," her second hit single; however, actress-singer Cher won the award. Nevertheless, Jennifer had established herself as a multi-talented celebrity. Appearing with

George Clooney in *Out of Sight* (1998), she became the highest paid Latina actress in history. At the height of her celebrity, she and then-boyfriend Sean "Puffy" Combs were involved in a 1999 shooting incident outside a New York City nightclub. Three people were injured; Combs was charged with gun possession and bribery but was later acquitted of all charges. Jennifer ended their relationship two months later. Other personal relationships kept her in the celebrity spotlight; she was linked romantically with dancer Cris Judd and actor Ben Affleck. She married singer Marc Anthony in 2004.

Stephenie Meyer (1973–)

Stephenie Meyer, a novelist, was born Stephenie Morgan on December 24, 1973, in Hartford, Connecticut. Her family moved to Phoenix when she was four. She graduated from high school in Scottsdale, Arizona, was awarded a National Merit Scholarship, and used it to finance her education at Brigham Young University, where she majored in English. She married "Pancho" Meyer in 1994; she had known him since she was four years old, primarily through church activities. She became a stay-at-home mother, taking care of her young sons. She had little thought of becoming a celebrity of any sort. However, that changed on June 2, 2003. Stephenie awoke that morning clearly remembering a rather remarkable dream. The dream nagged at her throughout the day until she finally sat down at her computer and began to sketch out a few ideas for a novel. Developing the plot in her head as she helped her sons with such things as swim lessons and potty training, she did not sit down to write each day until her children were in bed for the night and the house was quiet. Her first novel, *Twilight*, was one of 2005's most discussed novels and debuted at #5 on the *New York Times* best seller list within weeks of its release. Named one of the top 10 books for young adults by the American Library Association, it has been translated into 20 languages. With *Twilight* Stephenie became an instant celebrity, not only among teen readers, but also in the publishing world. Sequels followed, each springing quickly to the top of the bestseller list. Stephenie keeps a rather low profile, but her work places her among the top celebrities ever in the world of young adult fiction. Her novels have spawned a series of movies starring Robert Pattinson and Kristen Stewart.

Michael Moore (1954–)

Michael Francis Moore, a filmmaker, actor, and political activist, was born April 23, 1954, in Davison, Michigan, a suburb of Flint. Both his father and grandfather worked for General Motors, a fact that was to figure prominently in Michael's life. He attended parochial school, but transferred to Davison High School when he was 14. He became immediately interested in school politics. At age 18, he ran for the Flint school board and was elected, becoming one of the youngest people in the country to win an election for public office. He enrolled at the University of Michigan-Flint, but dropped out to pursue a career as a social/political activist. After jobs at several newspapers and magazines, Michael considered making a movie about the closure of the General Motors auto plants in Flint; the closures bothered him because the company was highly profitable and there appeared to be no reason to close the plants. He scraped up enough money to begin the film, and when the money ran out, held bingo games to raise money to finish it. The film, *Roger and Me*, featured Moore's repeated attempts to meet with General Motors Chairman Roger Smith to question him about the plant closures and the ultimate effect on Flint's economy. The film was an immediate critical success, making Michael an instant celebrity. Not all of his subsequent films were successful, but several were. *Bowling for Columbine* (2002) won an award at the Cannes Film Festival and an Academy Award for Best Documentary. No question about it now, Michael was a full-fledged celebrity. In 2004, his *Fahrenheit 9/11*, a film critical of George W. Bush and America's war in the Middle East, was a box office hit, becoming the most successful documentary of all time. His most recent films have not experienced the success of his earlier ones, but Michael remains a celebrity, known for his sharp wit and his ability to ask tough questions to the powerful while projecting a regular-guy attitude.

Barack Obama (1961–)

Barack Hussein Obama, born August 4, 1961, in Honolulu, Hawaii, is president of the United States. His father left home when Barack was two; his parents divorced, his mother remarried, and the family moved to Jakarta, Indonesia. Because he had mixed-race parents, he grew up confused about the social differences between the black and white cultures. This confusion may have led to brief experiments with drugs and alcohol. After graduating high school, he did two years at Occidental College in California before enrolling as a political science major at Columbia University in New York City. Barack worked briefly for a financial consulting firm in New York, but was more interested in working as a community organizer. He eventually landed a position with the Developing Community Project in Chicago. He entered Harvard Law School in 1988 and was later named the first African American president (editor) of the *Harvard Law Review*. He met and married Michelle Robinson in 1992. Barack was not yet a celebrity, and there is no evidence that he ever aspired to be one. He was interested in politics and government, however, and was elected to the Illinois State Senate in 1996 where he had few legislative accomplishments. Nevertheless, he was intelligent and a powerful speaker. He delivered the Keynote Address to the 2004 Democratic Convention and just a few months later was elected to the United States Senate. Even in Washington, Barack had few legislative accomplishments. Still, many political insiders considered him a rising star. They were particularly impressed by his book *Dreams from My Father* (1995). His second book, *Audacity of Hope: Thoughts on Reclaiming the American Dream* (2006), vaulted him into the celebrity spotlight. He appeared on *Oprah* and *Larry King Live*. Journalists and media pundits began wondering whether he had his sights set on the presidency. True enough, Barack announced his candidacy for president in early 2007 and faced Hillary Clinton in a battle for his party's nomination. He won the nomination and beat Republican John McCain in the November 2008 general election. Barack became the 45th president of the United States, the first African American to hold that position. Although few politicians can claim celebrity status based on their positive actions, Barack is one who can. He is well spoken, intelligent, and has a sense of humor, but can be overly serious at times. His third book, *Change We Can Believe In: Barack Obama's Plan to Renew America's Promise* (2008), won a Grammy award for spoken recordings.

Conan O'Brien (1963–)

Conan Christopher O'Brien, a television talk show host and writer, was born April 18, 1963, in Brookline, Massachusetts.

He grew up in a large, Irish Catholic family and had an early connection to a limited sort of celebrity—his sister Jane was a scriptwriter and his cousin Denis Leary was an actor and comedian. Conan loved to make people laugh and was known for "goofing off" as a youngster. At Harvard University, he found opportunities to pull pranks and was twice named president of *The Harvard Lampoon,* a humor magazine. By 1988, Conan was writing comedy sketches for NBC's *Saturday Night Live,* but was essentially unknown by the general public. A series of changes in network late-night television programs (11:35 p.m. and later) propelled him into the celebrity spotlight. In 1992, Johnny Carson retired from NBC's *Tonight Show;* Jay Leno was named to replace him. This resulted in David Letterman leaving NBC's *Late Night* (a show that followed Carson's) for a job at CBS. Conan was given the host job on *Late Night,* a move questioned by some critics since he was generally unknown outside of television-writing circles. Nevertheless, after a rough start, Conan eventually established himself in the late-night position with quirky stunts and self-deprecating humor; he became a favorite of college students. However, the late-night television wars were far from over. When NBC failed to renew Leno's contract in 2009, Conan replaced him on the well-known and widely watched *Tonight Show.* Leno was shifted to the 10 p.m. prime time slot where he promptly failed to attract a sizeable audience. NBC announced that Leno would be returning to the 11:35 p.m. *Tonight Show,* but Conan, having occupied the host chair for seven months, declined to step aside. The resulting standoff between Conan and NBC made entertainment news for several weeks and, to some extent, increased his celebrity status. He eventually agreed to a $45 million payoff and left NBC. Rumors circulated about a possible late night show for him on another network. In any case, Conan is a bona fide talk show celebrity from whom we have not heard the last.

Bill O'Reilly (1949–)

Born in New York City on September 10, 1949, Bill O'Reilly grew up in Levittown, New York. He is a radio-television political talk show host and author. At an early age he told everyone he was going to be on television, tell people what to think, and tell them what's right and what's wrong. With such an ambitious goal, perhaps Bill felt destined to be a celebrity. He excelled in sports during his school years, studied history at Marist College where he played quarterback on the football team, and, upon graduation, taught school for two years in Miami, Florida. After a master's degree in broadcast journalism at Boston College, Bill worked as a reporter for several television stations and soon became a correspondent for ABC's *World News Tonight*. He became anchor of the syndicated news/entertainment program *Inside Edition* in 1989. He left that job in 1995 and entered Harvard's Kennedy School of Government, earning a master's in public policy. Bill was immediately hired by the Fox News Channel as host of *The O'Reilly Factor*, described as an alternative to traditional news programs. His combative, outspoken approach allowed him to dismiss the arguments of anyone who challenged him. Bill was little known as a television reporter, but rapidly rose to celebrity status with Fox News. A polarizing figure, he regularly irritates liberals with his conservative stance on most issues.

Danica Patrick (1982–)

Racing star Danica Patrick was born March 25, 1982, in Beloit, Wisconsin, but her younger sister Brooke was the race enthusiast in the family. Brooke raced go-karts and snowmobiles for a while, but gave up racing after crashing four times. Nevertheless, Brooke's influence led to Danica's interest in racing. She felt she could do well—after all, she was two years older than her sister. She began competing in go-kart races sponsored by the World Karting Association, finishing second in overall points in the 1992 season. She won her first Grand National Championship two years later. Racing officials suggested she switch from go-karts to race cars. She did and developed her racing skill on the British racing circuit. In 2002, Bobby Rahall signed her to a racing contract with the Rahal Letterman team. Although she had no first-place finishes in races for Rahal Letterman, Danica was promoted to the Indy Racing League (IRL), becoming the fourth woman to compete in the IRL. In a sport dominated by men, Danica quickly rose to celebrity status. Her celebrity was enhanced when she placed fourth in the Indy 500 in 2005. Described as a "slick, 5 foot-1, 100 pound package of talent and charisma," Danica has a hidden side. As Rahal observed, when she shakes your hand, it's "crunch, like a truck driver . . . The exterior is nice and pretty—and underneath she is as tough as steel." Danica also appears regularly in television commercials for Go-Daddy.com, an Internet domain name service.

Brad Pitt (1963–)

William Bradley Pitt was born December 18, 1963, in Shawnee, Oklahoma, but was raised in Springfield, Missouri. Pitt is an actor, although he was initially interested in a career in advertising. In high school, he enjoyed sports, debating, student government, and school musical productions. He attended the University of Missouri, majoring in journalism with a specialty in advertising. However, near the end of his college career, Brad decided to pursue an acting career. He quit college, just two credits short of his degree. The acting world, however, did not welcome him with open arms. In California, he drove a limousine—transporting strippers from one party to the next—delivered home appliances, and wore a chicken costume to promote a local restaurant. He joined an acting class and eventually landed a few jobs in television. Brad's screen debut came in 1989 with *Cutting Class*, but neither the film nor his performance attracted much attention. Other films followed but none elevated him to celebrity status. His stock rose a bit with his appearance in Robert Redford's 1992 film *A River Runs Through It*. He appeared in other movies with film celebrities Harrison Ford, Tom Cruise, and Anthony Hopkins. However, Brad still lacked that one film, that one performance that would catapult him to film celebrity. He worked in *Fight Club* (1999) with Edward Norton, in *The Mexican* (2000) with Julia Roberts, and in *Spy Game* (2001) with Robert Redford. One might think appearing with all these established celebrities would have some benefit on Brad's own celebrity status; however, for the most part, he was unable to escape the shadows of the more famous. That changed in 2001 when he joined George Clooney and Matt Damon in *Ocean's Eleven*. His performance in that movie was every bit as good as those of his costars and propelled him to A-level celebrity status. Brad's celebrity was further enhanced in 2005 when he appeared opposite Angelina Jolie in the blockbuster *Mr. and Mrs. Smith*. He married Jolie three years later. Brad was nominated for an Academy Award as Best Actor in 2009 for his role in *The Curious Case of Benjamin Button*.

Rachael Ray (1968–)

Rachael Domenica Ray was born August 25, 1968, on Cape Cod, Massachusetts. She is a celebrity chef, television personality, and author. Her parents were employed in the restaurant industry so food was always important in the Ray household. She learned cooking from her mother. After college, Rachael began working for local restaurants and caterers in upstate New York. She held a variety of positions: candy counter clerk, fresh-foods manager, gourmet store manager, and gourmet foods buyer. She soon realized people weren't purchasing a lot of gourmet foods. Thinking it was because they had little time to cook, Rachael started a cooking class—30 minute meals. The class was popular and resulted in her first book, *30 Minute Meals* (1991). Her appearance on NBC's *Today* show in 2001 got the attention of Food Network executives who offered her a show. She accepted; *30 Minute Meals* aired in November 2002. Rachael became one of the most popular figures on the cable network, assuring her celebrity. One of the quickest ways to increase your celebrity is to associate with established celebrities. On *Inside Dish with Rachael Ray* (Food Network, 2004), she regularly interviewed celebrities such as Morgan Freeman and Tony Danza. Another way to increase your celebrity is to work in other media fields. Rachael has published cookbooks and serves as editor for her lifestyle magazine, *Every Day with Rachael Ray*. Personality is perhaps another contributor to celebrity. Rachael has been described as "normal, cute, fun, bubbly, perky, adorable, and chatty." This sort of personality doesn't work for everyone, but it is working for Rachael.

Arnold Schwarzenegger (1947–)

Arnold Alois Schwarzenegger, born July 30, 1947 in Graz, Austria, is governor of California. His family had no indoor plumbing, telephone, or refrigerator until he was 14 years old. He credits a poor childhood environment with his strong desire to succeed. He saw his first movie at age 11, became fascinated with America and believed he was destined for something big. He began a bodybuilding regimen, feeling it was the quickest way to gain entrance to the United States. After a stint in the Austrian army (where he served a year in the brig for being AWOL to compete in a weightlifting competition), Arnold continued building strength and muscle, winning the 1967 Mr. Universe title and becoming a celebrity among those in the bodybuilding/weightlifting field. After competing in Miami Beach in 1968 for a second Mr. Universe title (placing second), he went to Los Angeles hoping to work his way into the film industry. He worked in several B-level movies, including *Hercules Goes to New York* (1970). *Conan the Barbarian* (1982) and *Conan the Destroyer* (1983) utilized his physical assets, and although critics disliked both films, Arnold became a minor film celebrity. He became a U.S. citizen in 1983. He moved to major-celebrity status in 1984, starring in James Cameron's *The Terminator*. A string of movies followed: *Predator* (1987), *Total Recall* (1990), and two more Terminator films, among others. Arnold became interested in politics in the early 1990s. He told friends he hoped one day to seek public office. His chance came in 2003 when he was elected governor of California as a Republican in a special election (occasioned by the recall of Governor Gray Davis). Arnold is married to Maria Shriver, a television journalist and part of the Kennedy family Democratic political dynasty.

Martin Scorsese (1942–)

Martin Luciano Scorsese is a celebrity filmmaker. He was born November 17, 1942, in Flushing, New York, to parents of Italian Sicilian descent. He suffered from asthma as a child and, unable to roughhouse with other children in the neighborhood, play sports, or do odd jobs, became something of an outsider. To take his mind off his poor health, his father took him to movies. He enjoyed the films, but felt he was destined to become a Catholic priest. After a bit of religious training, Martin decided that filmmaking was his true calling. He studied filmmaking at New York University (NYU) where his student films won awards. After earning a graduate degree in film communications, he taught for a while at NYU. Although he made several films before 1976, his big break came in that year with *Taxi Driver*, a film critics deplored for its violence, but a film that won the grand prize at the Cannes Film Festival. Martin was on his way to becoming a celebrity. *Raging Bull* (1980) was praised by critics, but was not a box office success. He continued to battle chronic fatigue and asthma. One doctor told him he was killing himself with work and would have to change his lifestyle if he wanted to live. In the 1980s, he contemplated a change from what he called "personal" films to more market-driven ones. *The Color of Money* (1986), *Goodfellas* (1990), and *Gangs of New York* (2002) firmly established him as a celebrity filmmaker. He worked often with celebrity actor Robert DeNiro. *The Departed* (2006) was hailed by one critic as the "most purely enjoyable movie in years." It won four Academy Awards, including the awards for Best Picture and Best Director.

Britney Spears (1981–)

No list of celebrities destined to be important in the 21st century would be complete without Britney Spears. She is a singer, songwriter, and actress. Love her or hate her, she's been a celebrity most of her life. Britney Jean Spears was born December 2, 1981, in Kentwood, Louisiana. As a child, she took dancing classes, participated in gymnastics, and appeared to know what she was born to do. She once noted that at age seven or eight, she would perform in front of the television set to entertain her parents' guests. At age eight, she auditioned for a role on Disney's *The New Mickey Mouse Club*, but was judged too young for the part. After appearing on *Star Search* (1992) at age 11, she tried out again for *The New Mickey Mouse Club* and was picked for the cast along with Justin Timberlake, Christina Aguilera, and Keri Russell. When the show was cancelled, Britney began focusing on her musical career. Her first hit single, "Baby One More Time," hit the top of the pop music charts in early 1999, but it was probably the song's music video—where Britney wore a skimpy school-girl uniform—that propelled her toward celebrity. As is often the case with celebrities, part of Britney's appeal revolved around her personal life—the full-mouth kiss with singer Madonna at the 2003 Music Video Awards, her two-day marriage to childhood friend Jason Alexander, her involvement with dancer Kevin Federline (his girlfriend was pregnant at the time), her marriage to Federline in 2004, her shaved head and subsequent rehab stint (the first of several), and driving with her infant son in her lap rather than in a child safety seat. Nevertheless, her concerts are well attended and her music continues to be popular. Her album *Blackout* (2007) placed second on the music charts shortly after its release. Britney appears to have settled down a bit in recent years, but she is still a worldwide celebrity.

Steven Spielberg (1946–)

Steven Spielberg is one of the most creative, important filmmakers in the history of the film industry. His work is known and loved worldwide. Steven Allan Spielberg was born December 18, 1946, in Cincinnati, Ohio. Because his family moved often, he had few childhood friends. He was often lonely and dispirited, but found comfort in watching movies. After his parents' divorce in 1965, Steven moved to California where he completed high school. He applied to the University of Southern California film school but was rejected three times. He attended Long Beach State for a time, but dropped out to pursue a career in film. After some early directing experience on several television shows (*Columbo* and *Marcus Welby, M.D.*, among others), he turned his full attention to film. His first film, *The Sugarland Express* (1974), was a box office failure. However, his second film became a classic and vaulted him to celebrity status; *Jaws* (1975) was both a critical and financial success. From there, it was one successful movie after another, each enhancing his reputation as a movie-making genius: *Close Encounters of the Third Kind* (1977), *Raiders of the Lost Ark* (1981), *E.T.: The Extra-Terrestrial* (1982), *Jurassic Park* (1993), *Schindler's List* (a 1993 film that earned seven Oscars, including Best Director and Best Picture), and *Saving Private Ryan* (1998, earning an Oscar for Best Director). Steven has more than a dozen other successful films, and a few not-so-successful ones. He is Hollywood's most successful—and wealthiest—filmmaker. He is a worldwide celebrity.

Jon Stewart (1962–)

Jon Stewart, a comedian and comedy-television-show host, was born Jonathan Stuart Leibowitz in New York City, November 28, 1962. He grew up in Lawrenceville, New Jersey, and graduated from the College of William and Mary in Virginia. Following graduation, he worked a series of jobs back home in New Jersey before moving to New York City in 1986 to pursue a comedy career; he became a familiar figure on the city's comedy club circuit. His minor league celebrity was soon replaced by a more visible sort. Known for his sarcastic, incisive sense of humor, Jon landed a spot on *The Larry Sanders Show* (1992) and served as guest host on *The Late, Late Show with Tom Snyder*. His celebrity status sprang into the television public's consciousness when he was named host of Comedy Central's *The Daily Show* in 1999, which was renamed *The Daily Show with Jon Stewart*. Jon has won Emmy and Peabody awards and was named America's Best Talk Show Host by *Time* magazine. Posing as a fake newsman on *The Daily Show*, his success derives mainly from his entertaining and controversial approach to the news. When asked about his success on the show, Jon said, "Liberal and conservative have lost their meaning in America. I represent the distracted center. When in doubt, I can stare blankly. The rubber face. There's only so many ways you can stare incredulously at the camera and tilt an eyebrow, but that's your old standby."

Taylor Swift (1989–)

Country music singer, songwriter, and musician, Taylor Alison Swift was born December 13, 1989, in Wyomissing, Pennsylvania. Her family owned a Christmas tree farm and that's where she spent her early childhood. However, she had a thin connection to celebrity in those early days—her grandmother had been a professional opera singer. By age 10, Taylor had begun singing at local fairs and civic events. She sang "The Star-Spangled Banner" at age 11 before a professional basketball game and was writing songs and learning to play the guitar a year later. Realizing Taylor's talent and potential, her family moved to Nashville where she could more effectively pursue her interest in music. A performance at Nashville's Bluebird Café caught the attention of a music industry executive who signed her to a recording contract. Her first single, "Tim McGraw" (2006), became a Top 10 hit on the country charts. Her album that same year sold more than 2 million copies. Her celebrity was assured when she won the Academy of Country Music's "Female Vocalist of the Year" award in 2007. Other awards and hit songs followed. In 2009, onstage to accept the MTV award for "Best Female Video," Taylor was interrupted by rapper Kanye West who leaped onstage, took the microphone away from her, and declared that R&B singer Beyoncé should have won the award. Taylor was stunned and unable to make an acceptance speech; West was removed from the stage. Later in the show, Beyoncé, onstage to accept an award for best video, called Taylor to the stage to finish her acceptance speech. West later apologized to her. The incident added to Taylor's celebrity status. Her concerts sell out in just a few minutes; *Forbes* magazine ranked her as the 69th most powerful celebrity. She won four Country Music Association (CMA) awards in 2009 (Album of the Year, Female Vocalist of the Year, Entertainer of the Year, and Music Video of the Year). Onstage to accept the awards, Taylor poked fun at the West incident saying, "I want to thank every single person here tonight for not running up on stage during this speech." No doubt about it, Taylor is a major music celebrity.

Rick Warren (1954–)

Richard Duane "Rick" Warren is an evangelical minister and author. Born January 28, 1954, in San Jose, California, Rick joined a family already committed to a religious life. His father was a minister as was his great-grandfather. After high school, he studied for the ministry, earning bachelor's, master's, and doctoral degrees. After completing his religious education, Rick felt called to start a program to reach people who did not attend church. He organized a small bible study group in his home; the group grew quickly and held its first public service in 1980 for more than 200 people. The Saddleback Valley Community Church, established as a result of that first public service, now has about 20,000 members and is one of the largest mega-churches in America. Rick holds several honorary doctorates, has lectured at Oxford and Cambridge, and has spoken at various United Nations' forums. In religious circles, Rick was now most certainly a celebrity. He was named by *Time* magazine as one of 15 World Leaders Who Mattered Most in 2004 and by *U.S. News and World Report* as one of America's Top 25 Leaders in 2005. Rick is a *New York Times* bestselling author. One of his books, *The Purpose Driven Life*, has sold more than 30 million copies. He hosted the Civil Forum on the Presidency at his church during the 2008 presidential campaign, discussing politics and religion with candidates Barack Obama and John McCain. Obama later asked Rick to deliver the invocation at the presidential inauguration ceremony in January 2009. It is difficult for a religious figure to achieve true celebrity status. The public often feels that religion is a private matter and only a few religious leaders become national or international celebrities. However, Rick's work as a minister, author, and speaker has made him a celebrity, at least in the United States.

Oprah Winfrey (1954–)

Oprah Winfrey, a television personality, actress, and producer, has been called "The Queen of Daytime TV." Oprah Gail Winfrey was born on January 29, 1954, in Kosciusko, a small farming community in Mississippi. Although she learned to read and deliver recitations by age three, her childhood was not happy. She was sexually abused by a number of male relatives and friends of her mother. She moved to Nashville, Tennessee, to live with her father and entered Tennessee State University in 1971, majoring in Speech Communications and Performing Arts. Her broadcast career began almost immediately. She was hired by WVOL radio in Nashville, and two years later landed a job as a reporter/anchor at Nashville's WTVF-TV. Oprah moved to Baltimore, joining WJZ-TV as a news anchor and soon became co-host of the station's "People Are Talking" show. The show became highly popular. Eight years later, she was hired by Chicago's WLS-TV to revitalize its faltering talk show, "AM Chicago." By this time, she had become something of a celebrity in television circles, but was generally unknown to the country at large. That changed in 1986 when *"The Oprah Winfrey Show"* became the number one television talk show in syndication; the following year it received three Daytime Emmy Awards, including Outstanding Host. Oprah was now a national celebrity. For more than 20 years, *The Oprah Winfrey Show*, often called just *Oprah*, has been available in 200 television markets, has dominated daytime television, and enabled her to build a multibillion-dollar media empire. In 2009, *Forbes* magazine listed her as the top-earning celebrity ($275 million). Today, HARPO Productions, her production company, is a powerful and influential force. Her fans were shocked, therefore, when she announced in late 2009 that her show will end its run in 2011. Oprah is involved in several important social causes. In 1993, President Bill Clinton signed the National Child Protection Act, a bill promoted by Oprah establishing a national database of convicted child abusers. Her own Angel Network strives to improve the lives of others.

Mark Zuckerberg (1984–)

Mark Elliot Zuckerberg was born May 14, 1984, in Dobbs Ferry, New York. He is the founder of Facebook, a social networking

Web site. Mark may be the only person in this chapter whose work is better known than he is. His interest in technology began in the sixth grade and by the ninth grade, he was writing software programs. He attended the Phillips Exeter Academy prep school, then enrolled in Harvard in 2002 as a psychology major. However, he continued to write computer programs. One of the programs was called "Facemash," an online directory of Harvard students. By February 2004, the program had morphed into "the facebook.com." Other universities adopted the program for their students; eventually it had more than a million users. The word *the* was dropped in 2005. Facebook began to expand, offering membership not only to students, but also to university faculty and alumni. Since 2006, Facebook has been available to anyone who wishes to join. Facebook statistics are staggering—more than 400 million active users, 5 billion pieces of content shared each week, and more than 3 billion photos uploaded each month. It is the most popular social networking Web site on the Internet. Mark moved to Palo Alto, California, and now operates Facebook full time from four downtown buildings. As suggested earlier in this profile, Facebook may be the real celebrity here, but Mark gets the credit for making it a social and financial success.

6

Data and Documents

This chapter presents facts, figures, and other information relating to celebrities and their work. As you read through the chapter, you will notice much of the information is about individuals in entertainment fields, that is, television, music, and the movies. However, some attention is given to celebrities in other fields, although data in some areas are limited. It is helpful to keep in mind data are accurate only for a short time. In other words, data can be said to be valid immediately after facts are gathered, but the passage of time almost certainly results in changes to some data.

Celebrity Magazines and Television Programs

Television is not as popular as it once was chiefly because consumers have other electronic devices that demand their attention. Many people get news and information from the Internet that can also be used to access television shows and other entertainment programs. This makes computers and smart phones as valuable to consumers as the family television in the living room. While the television news audience may be shrinking, viewership of celebrity television programs, that is, programs *about* celebrities, remains fairly strong. As Table 6.1 shows, overall viewership of celebrity television programs remained steady during the 10-year period 1998–2008. For example, the celebrity show *Extra* had slightly more than 7 million viewers in the 1998–1999

TABLE 6.1
Viewership of Celebrity Television Programs, 1998–2008

Program	Year	Viewers
Access Hollywood	8/98–8/99	2,450,000
Entertainment Tonight	8/98–8/99	4,489,000
Extra	8/98–8/99	7,334,000
Insider	—	—
TMZ	—	—
Access Hollywood	9/00–9/01	3,010,000
Entertainment Tonight	9/00–9/01	7,769,000
Extra	9/00–9/01	3,753,000
Insider	—	—
TMZ	—	—
Access Hollywood	8/05–8/06	3,319,000
Entertainment Tonight	8/05–8/06	6,760,000
Extra	8/05–8/06	2,928,000
Insider	8/05–8/06	3,494,000
TMZ	—	—
Access Hollywood	9/08–12/08	2,588,000
Entertainment Tonight	9/08–12/08	5,951,000
Extra	9/08–12/08	2,233,000
Insider	9/08–12/08	2,573,000
TMZ	9/08–12/08	2,866,000

Adapted from: The Nielsen Company; DeSilva + Phillips

period. By 2005–2006, the program was down to about 3 million viewers. However, the celebrity show *Insider* picked up 3.5 million viewers. During that same period, *Access Hollywood* picked up almost a million viewers. The net result was that there was little overall change. The conclusion most apparent from Table 6.1 is that viewers apparently moved around from one celebrity show to another over the years, but remained rather faithful to these sorts of programs.

Celebrity magazine circulation figures in 2008 (Table 6.2) clearly indicate two longstanding publications dominate the field. *People* and *TV Guide* each had almost double the circulation of the runner-up, *US Weekly*. It could be argued that *TV Guide* is not a real celebrity magazine—its main purpose is providing listings of television program offerings. However, the publication does feature brief articles on celebrities and may, in fact, be the main source of celebrity information for some consumers. Notice that four of the top celebrity magazines in 2008 had circulations of

TABLE 6.2
Celebrity Magazine Circulation, 2008

Magazine Title	Subscriptions	Single Copy	Total
People	2,127,384	1,472,149	3,599,533
TV Guide	2,942,230	155,391	3,097,621
US Weekly	1,011,018	796,669	1,807,687
Entertainment Weekly	1,701,153	50,437	1,751,590
Star Magazine	571,525	617,096	1,188,621
In Touch Weekly	64,419	834,492	898,911
National Enquirer	271,275	620,100	891,375
OK! Weekly	341,759	490,417	832,176
Life & Style Weekly	10,189	461,989	472,178

Adapted from DeSilva + Phillips, LLC

TABLE 6.3
Top Ten Highest-Grossing Films (Worldwide)

Film (year)	Celebrity Stars	Receipts (rounded in millions)
1. Avatar (2009)	Sigourney Weaver, Zoe Saldana	2,249
2. Titanic (1997)	Leonardo DiCaprio, Kate Winslet	1,843
3. Lord of the Rings: Return of the King (2003)	Elijah Wood, Orlando Bloom	1,119
4. Pirates of the Caribbean: Dead Man's Chest (2006)	Johnny Depp, Orlando Bloom	1,066
5. The Dark Knight (2008)	Heath Ledger, Christian Bale	1,002
6. Harry Potter: Philosopher's Stone (2001)	Daniel Radcliffe, Emma Watson	975
7. Pirates of the Caribbean: At World's End (2007)	Johnny Depp, Keira Knightley	961
8. Harry Potter: Order of the Phoenix 2007)	Daniel Radcliffe, Emma Watson	958
9. Harry Potter: Half-Blood Prince (2009)	Daniel Radcliffe, Emma Watson	944
10. Lord of the Rings: The Two Towers (2002)	Elijah Wood, Sean Astin	935

Adapted from: Box Office Mojo; imbd.com

fewer than a million. This may be further evidence of the declining influence of print media in the United States.

Celebrities and the Movies

Movies have been a part of American life since the silent film era of the early 1900s. For actors, actresses, producers, and directors, films have been a quick route to celebrity. The film industry is big business worldwide. Movies draw large audiences. Table 6.3 shows the most popular movies earn millions—and in some cases, billions—of

TABLE 6.4
Movie Celebrities of the 20th Century
(Listed alphabetically with birth and death dates and representative film)

Fred Astaire *Top Hat*	(1899–1987)	Clark Gable *Gone with the Wind*	(1901–1960)
Lucille Ball *The Long, Long Trailer*	(1911–1989)	Cary Grant *North by Northwest*	(1904–1986)
Ingrid Bergman *Murder on the Orient Express*	(1915–1982)	Judy Garland *The Wizard of Oz*	(1922–1969)
Humphrey Bogart *Casablanca*	(1899–1957)	Audrey Hepburn *Breakfast at Tiffany's*	(1929–1993)
Marlon Brando *The Godfather*	(1924–2004)	Boris Karloff *Frankenstein*	(1887–1969)
Richard Burton *Who's Afraid of Virginia Woolf?*	(1925–1984)	Grace Kelly *Rear Window*	(1929–1982)
James Cagney *Yankee Doodle Dandy*	(1899–1986)	Vivian Leigh *Gone with the Wind*	(1913–1967)
Charlie Chaplin *The Great Dictator*	(1889–1977)	Groucho Marx *Duck Soup*	(1890–1997)
Gary Cooper *High Noon*	(1901–1961)	Marilyn Monroe *Some Like It Hot*	(1926–1962)
Bette Davis *All About Eve*	(1908–1989)	Gregory Peck *To Kill a Mockingbird*	(1916–2003)
Marlene Dietrich *Witness for the Prosecution*	(1901–1992)	Edward G. Robinson *Double Indemnity*	(1893-1973)
Bing Crosby *Holiday Inn*	(1903–1977)	Ginger Rogers *Top Hat*	(1911–1995)
Joan Crawford *Mildred Pierce*	(1908–1977)	Spencer Tracy *Judgment at Nuremberg*	(1900–1967)
James Dean *Rebel without a Cause*	(1931–1955)	James Stewart *It's a Wonderful Life*	(1906–1997)
Errol Flynn *The Adventures of Robin Hood*	(1909–1959)	John Wayne *The Green Berets*	(1907–1979)
Henry Fonda *The Grapes of Wrath*	(1905–1982)	Orson Welles *Citizen Kane*	(1915–1985)

dollars. Nine of the top 10 worldwide highest-grossing movies were produced in the 21st century, *Titanic* being the exception in 1997.

Some readers of this book may recognize some of the 20th-century film celebrities and their movies in Table 6.4. It is important to recognize that movies were in large part responsible for the success of many actors and actresses. Although all those listed in Table 6.4 are dead, many of their performances rank as some of

TABLE 6.5
Movie Celebrities of the Early 21st Century
(Listed alphabetically with birth date and representative films)

Jennifer Aniston (b. 1969)	*Marley & Me*	Shia LaBeouf (b. 1986)	*Transformers*
Christian Bale (b. 1974)	*Batman Begins*	Jude Law (b. 1972)	*Sherlock Holmes*
Abigail Breslin (b. 1996)	*Little Miss Sunshine*	Heath Ledger (1979–2008)	*Dark Knight*
Gerard Butler (b. 1969)	*300*	Jennifer Lopez (b. 1969)	*The Wedding Planner*
Jim Carrey (b. 1962)	*The Truman Show*	Rachel McAdams (b. 1978)	*Sherlock Holmes*
Michael Cera (b. 1988)	*Juno*	Toby Maguire (b. 1975)	*Spider-Man*
George Clooney (b. 1961)	*Up in the Air*	Michael Moore (b. 1954)	*Fahrenheit 9/11*
Jennifer Connelly (b. 1970)	*A Beautiful Mind*	Ellen Page (b. 1987)	*Juno*
Bradley Cooper (b. 1975)	*The Hangover*	Dev Patel (b. 1990)	*Slumdog Millionaire*
Daniel Craig (b. 1968)	*Casino Royale*	Robert Pattinson (b. 1986)	The *Twilight Saga*
Russell Crowe (b. 1964)	*Gladiator*	Daniel Radcliffe (b. 1989)	*Harry Potter* films
Tom Cruise (b. 1962)	*Mission Impossible*	Adam Sandler (b. 1966)	*50 First Dates*
Matt Damon (b. 1970)	The *Bourne* films	Will Smith (b. 1968)	*I Am Legend*
Johnny Depp (b. 1963)	*Pirates of the Caribbean*	Kristen Stewart (b. 1990)	The *Twilight Saga*
Cameron Diaz (b. 1972)	*What Happens in Vegas*	Meryl Streep (b. 1949)	*Julie & Julia*
Leonardo DiCaprio (b. 1974)	*The Departed*	Hilary Swank (b. 1974)	*Boys Don't Cry*
Robert Downey Jr. (b. 1965)	*Sherlock Holmes*	John Travolta (b. 1954)	*Taking of Pelham 1 2 3*
Jodie Foster (b. 1962)	*The Brave One*	Vince Vaughn (b. 1970)	*Wedding Crashers*
Megan Fox (b. 1986)	*Transformers*	Denzel Washington (b. 1954)	*The Book of Eli*
Jake Gyllenhaal (b. 1980)	*Brokeback Mountain*	Emma Watson (b. 1990)	*Harry Potter* films
Tom Hanks (b. 1956)	*The Da Vinci Code*	Owen Wilson (b. 1968)	*Wedding Crashers*
Scarlett Johansson (b. 1984)	*Lost in Translation*	Reese Witherspoon (b. 1976)	*Legally Blonde*
Angelina Jolie (b. 1976)	*Mr. & Mrs. Smith*	Elijah Wood (b. 1981)	*Lord of the Rings* films
Nicole Kidman (b. 1967)	*Eyes Wide Shut*		

the all-time best in the movies. For example, Gregory Peck was outstanding in *To Kill a Mockingbird*, Clark Gable was remarkable in *Gone with the Wind*, and Judy Garland was marvelous in *The Wizard of Oz*. But our emphasis in this book is on celebrity in the 21st century. Therefore, Table 6.5 should be of considerable interest to a movie buff. The actors listed there continue to make films and most will be around as film celebrities for some time to come.

Gender Differences in Prime Time Television Celebrity Earnings

There is much talk these days about gender equity in salary and in employment opportunities. While there has been improvement in business, industry, and other fields, there are noticeable differences in earnings of the top male and female celebrities on prime time television.

As Tables 6.6 and 6.7 indicate, male prime time television stars earn considerably more than female prime time stars. The highest-earning female would place fourth on the men's earnings list. Moreover, 7 of the top 10 female earners would not be listed at all on the male top 10.

TABLE 6.6
U.S. Prime Time TV Top-Earning Females

Name	Television Show	Earnings (in millions)
Tyra Banks	The Tyra Banks Show	$30
Katherine Heigl	Grey's Anatomy	$18
Marg Helgenberger	CSI: Crime Scene Investigation	$ 9.5
Eva Longoria Parker	Desperate Housewives	$ 9
Mariska Hargitay	Law & Order	$ 8.5
Julia Louis-Dreyfus	Adventures of Old Christine; Saturday Night Live	$ 8
Maura Tierney	ER; Mercy	$ 8
Tina Fey	30 Rock; Saturday Night Live	$ 7
Marcia Cross	Desperate Housewives	$ 6.2
Jennifer Love Hewitt	Ghost Whisperer	$ 6
Ellen Pompeo	Grey's Anatomy	$ 6

Adapted from Forbes.com, famewatcher.com

TABLE 6.7
U.S. Prime Time TV Top-Earning Males

Name	Television Show	Earnings (in millions)
Simon Cowell	American Idol	$75
Donald Trump	The Apprentice	$50
Ryan Seacrest	American Idol	$38
Charlie Sheen	Two and a Half Men	$21
Steve Carell	The Office	$21
Howie Mandel	Deal or No Deal	$15
Kiefer Sutherland	24	$13
Jeff Foxworthy	Are You Smarter than a Fifth Grader?	$11
Hugh Laurie	House	$10
David Caruso	CSI: Miami	$ 9

Adapted from Forbes.com, famewatcher.com

Highest-Earning Celebrities

In earlier chapters we said that while there are few celebrities in science, medicine, academia, and religion, there are plenty of celebrities in entertainment. Table 6.8 shows this to be true, at least in terms of total earnings. The highest-earning celebrities can be found in music, film, and radio and television. The lone exceptions are novelist James Patterson who ranks 20th and professional golfer Tiger Woods who holds down 5th place on the list of top earners. Woods's earnings represent his earnings from golf and not earnings from endorsements. It is no surprise that television personality Oprah Winfrey is the top-earning entertainment celebrity.

TABLE 6.8
Top 25 Highest-Earning Celebrities

Name	Celebrity Occupation	Earnings (in millions)
Oprah Winfrey	television personality	$275
George Lucas	film producer, writer, director	$170
Steven Spielberg	film producer, writer, director	$150
Madonna	music recording artist	$110
Tiger Woods	professional golfer, advertising spokesperson	$110
Jerry Bruckheimer	film and television producer	$100
Beyoncé Knowles	music recording artist	$ 87
Jerry Seinfeld	actor, comedian	$ 85
Dr. Phil McGraw	television personality, author	$ 80
Simon Cowell	television personality	$ 75
Tyler Perry	actor, writer, producer	$ 75
Bruce Springsteen	music recording artist	$ 70
Coldplay	music recording artist	$ 70
Howard Stern	radio personality	$ 70
Harrison Ford	actor	$ 65
Kenny Chesney	music recording artist	$ 65
Dave Matthews Band	music recording artist	$ 65
Rascal Flatts	music recording artist	$ 65
AC/DC	music recording artist	$ 60
James Patterson	author	$ 60
Adam Sandler	actor	$ 55
Larry David	comedian, television writer	$ 55
Rush Limbaugh	radio talk show host	$ 54
Toby Keith	music recording artist	$ 52
Bon Jovi	music recording artist	$ 50

Adapted from Forbes.com, famewatcher.com

She is one of the most widely recognized and respected celebrities of the early 21st century. A brief biographical profile of Winfrey can be found in Chapter 5. Filmmakers George Lucas and Steven Spielberg have numerous movie successes to their credit and are worthy runners-up to Winfrey. Furthermore, the list of names in Table 6.8 reveals that to make lots of money, one must become a celebrity in an entertainment field such as movies, television, music, and the like.

Top Celebrity Fundraisers

Many celebrities have a strong sense of social responsibility, that is, working for charities or other organizations designed to help the less fortunate of the world. Table 6.9 shows celebrities to be fairly accomplished at raising money for their favorite charity. Celebrity causes are as varied as the celebrities themselves, but the United Nations Children's Fund (UNICEF) appears to be the most popular among the top fundraisers. Singer Justin Timberlake was a surprising first on the 2009 list. Oprah, Bono, and Angelina Jolie have a history of work on behalf of charities and their contributions were significant in 2009. However, Timberlake beat

TABLE 6.9
Top Celebrity Fundraisers, 2009

Name	Profession	Amount	Cause
Justin Timberlake	singer	$9.3 million	Shriners Hospitals for Children
Madonna	singer	5.5 million	Raising Malawi
Pamela Anderson	actress, model	4.8 million	PETA
Oprah	television personality	4.0 million	Oprah's Angel Network
Bono	singer	3.5 million	ONE Campaign
Angelina Jolie	actress	3.0 million	UN Commission for Refugees
Rihanna	singer, model	2.3 million	UNICEF
George Clooney	actor	2.1 million	United Nations
Salma Hayek	actress	1.6 million	UNICEF
Brad Pitt	actor	1.2 million	Not on Our Watch
Shakira	singer	1.2 million	UNICEF
Charlize Theron	actress	1.2 million	PETA
Orlando Bloom	actor	1.1 million	UNICEF
Sharon Stone	actress	950,000	Foundation for AIDS Research
Denzel Washington	actor	900,000	Boys & Girls Clubs of America

Adapted from: www.looktothestars.org; www.thedailybeast.com

second-place Madonna by almost $4 million, Oprah by $5 million, Bono by $5.8 million, and Jolie by more than $6 million.

Celebrities and Religion

We noted in an earlier chapter that religion is a sensitive topic among some people and discussion of religion or religion-related issues makes some people uncomfortable and other people angry. However, for many people—including celebrities—religion is an important part of life. Table 6.10 reveals the religious preferences of some celebrities. Scientology is a popular choice for many celebrities. Although Table 6.10 doesn't show it, there are dozens of celebrities who are either atheists or agnostics.

TABLE 6.10
Religious Preferences of Celebrities*

Celebrity	Profession	Religious Status
Muhammad Ali	professional boxer	Muslim
Woody Allen	actor, director	Atheist
Kirstie Alley	actress	Scientologist
Beck	musician, singer, songwriter	Scientologist
Warren Buffett	businessman	Agnostic
Richard Dreyfus	actor	Agnostic
Jenna Elfman	actress	Scientologist
Larry Flynt	magazine publisher	Atheist
Richard Gere	actor	Tibetan Buddhist
Mel Gibson	actor	Catholic
Katie Holmes	actress	Scientologist
Angelina Jolie	actress	Spiritualist
Nicole Kidman	actress	Catholic
Ben Kingsley	actor	Quaker
Gladys Knight	singer	Mormon
George Lucas	film director, producer	Buddhist Methodist
Lisa Marie Presley	actress	Scientologist
Kelly Preston	actress	Scientologist
Anne Rice	author	Catholic
Jada and Will Smith	actress/actor	Scientologists
Britney Spears	singer	Baptist/Christian Life
Uma Thurman	actress	Buddhist
John Travolta	actor	Scientologist
Serena and Venus Williams	professional tennis players	Jehovah's Witnesses

* List compiled from multiple sources and based on news reports or celebrities' personal statements. Beliefs are subject to change.

TABLE 6.11
Top-Earning Celebrity Chefs

Chef	Earnings (in millions)	Sources of Income
Rachael Ray	$18	Television, magazine, endorsements
Wolfgang Puck	$16	Restaurants, supermarket products
Alain Ducasse	$ 5	International restaurants
Paula Deen	$ 4.5	Television, magazine, cookbooks
Mario Batali	$ 3	Restaurants, television, cookbooks

Adapted from Forbes.com

Celebrity Chefs

Cooking shows are popular television fare. Cookbooks sell well, especially during the holiday season. Almost everyone likes to dine out at a favorite restaurant. In short, we like our food and we want to know how to prepare it; we also enjoy watching others prepare it. Although their earnings are significantly less than the celebrities on the top-earning list, celebrity chefs manage to make a good living. Table 6.11 shows the typical annual earnings of five celebrity chefs. Rachael Ray (profiled in Chapter 5) tops all chefs, but earns only $2 million more than second-place finisher Wolfgang Puck. The "dean" of Southern cooking, Paula Deen, earns a respectable $4.5 million per year.

AKA (Also Known As)

It is widely known that many celebrities do not use their real names in their professional lives. There may be two reasons for this. First, celebrities may wish to preserve the small amount of privacy afforded them by using a "stage name." Second, many celebrities have complicated names that would be difficult for the public to remember. If one wishes to be known and talked about, an easy-to-say-and-remember name—one which might contain a rather common first or last name—goes a long way toward making a celebrity well known. Table 6.12 lists the real names of more than four hundred celebrities, past and present. A close examination of the list reveals celebrities take one of two paths in selecting a professional name. Celebrities may use a variation of their real names. For example, country singer Randy Travis's real

TABLE 6.12
Celebrities' Real Names

Professional Name	Real (Birth) Name
Maud Adams	Maud Solveig Christina Wikstrom
Eddie Albert	Edward Albert Heimberger
Tim Allen	Tim Allen Dick
Woody Allen	Allen Stewart Koningsberg
Tori Amos	Myra Ellen Amos
Don Ameche	Dominic Felix Amici
Julie Andrews	Julia Elizabeth Wells
Jennifer Aniston	Jennifer Anastassakis
Ann-Margret	Ann-Margret Olsson
Adam Ant	Stuart Leslie Goddard
Rosanna Arquette	Rosanna Lauren
Fred Astaire	Frederick Austerlitz
Frankie Avalon	Francis Thomas Avallone
Charles Aznavour	Shahnour Varenagh Aznavourian
Lauren Bacall	Betty Joan Perske
Catherine Bach	Catherine Bachman
Richard Bachman	Stephen Edward King
Lucille Ball	Dianne Belmont
Anne Bancroft	Anna Maria Luisa Italiano
Brigitte Bardot	Camille Javal
Drew Barrymore	Drew Blyth Barrymore
Warren Beatty	Henry Warren Beaty
Bonnie Bedelia	Bonnie Culkin
Pat Benatar	Patricia Andrejewski
Dirk Benedict	Dirk Niewoehner
Tom Berenger	Thomas Michael Moore
Milton Berle	Milton Berlinger
Irving Berlin	Israel Isidore Baline
The Big Bopper	Jiles Perry Richardson
Billy the Kid	Henry McCarty
Robert Blake	Michael Gubitosi
Blondie	Debbie Harry
Dirk Bogarde	Derek Jules Gaspard Ulric Niven van denBogaerde
Michael Bolton	Michale Bolotin
Jon Bon Jovi	John Bongiovi
Bono	Paul Hewson
Victor Borge	Borge Rosenbaum
Ernest Borgnine	Ermes Effron Borgnino
David Bowie	David Robert Hayward Stenton Jones
Edgar Box	Gore Vidal
Beau Bridges	Lloyd Vernet Bridges, III
Morgan Brittany	Suzanne Cupito
Charles Bronson	Charles Buchnisky

(*continued*)

TABLE 6.12 **(continued)**

Albert Brooks	Albert Einstein
Elkie Brooks	Elaine Bookbinder
Geraldine Brooks	Geraldine Stroock
Mel Brooks	Melvin Kaminsky
Yul Brynner	Yuliy Borisovich Bryner
Buffalo Bill	William Frederick Cody
George Burns	Nathan Birnbaum
Ellen Burstyn	Edna Rae Gillooly
Richard Burton	Richard Walter Jenkins Jr.
Red Buttons	Aaron Chwatt
Nicolas Cage	Nicolas Coppola
Michael Caine	Maurice J. Micklewhite
Maria Callas	Maria Ann Sofia Cecelia Kalogeropoulos
Dyan Cannon	Samille Diane Friesen
Eddie Cantor	Israel Itskowitz
Kate Capshaw	Kathleen Sue Nail
Tia Carrere	Althea Janairo
Lewis Carroll	Rev. Charles Lutwidge Dodgson
Butch Cassidy	George Robert LeRoy Parker
Phoebe Cates	Phoebe Katz
Jackie Chan	Chan Kong-Sang
Coco Chanel	Gabrielle Bonheur Chanel
Stockard Channing	Susan Stockard
Cyd Charisse	Tula Ellice Finklea
Leslie Charteris	Leslie Charles Bowyer Lin
Chevy Chase	Cornelius Crane Chase
Chubby Checker	Ernest Evans
Cher	Cherilyn Sarkisian LaPiere
Eric Clapton	Eric Patrick Clap
Jimmy Cliff	James Chambers
Patsy Cline	Virginia Patterson Hensley
Lee J. Cobb	Leo Jacoby
Claudette Colbert	Claudette Lily Chauchoin
Nat King Cole	Nathaniel Adams Coles
Chuck Connors	Kevin Joseph Connors
Mike Connors	Krekor Ohanian
Joseph Conrad	Jozef Teodor Konrad Nalecz Korzeniowski
Alice Cooper	Vincent Damon Furnier
David Copperfield	David Kotkin
Alex Cord	Alexander Viespi
Elvis Costello	Declan Patrick McManus
Lou Costello	Louis Francis Cristillo
Peter Coyote	Peter Cohon
Joan Crawford	Lucille Fay LeSueur
Michael Crawford	Michael Dumbell-Smith
Bing Crosby	Harry Lillis Crosby
Christopher Cross	Christopher Geppert

TABLE 6.12   (continued)

Tom Cruise	Thomas Cruise Mapother IV
Marie Curie	Marja Sklodowska
Tony Curtis	Bernard Schwartz
Rodney Dangerfield	Jacob Cohen
Ted Danson	Edward Bridge Danson III
Tony Danza	Anthony Ladanza
Bette Davis	Ruth Elizabeth Davis
Geena Davis	Virginia Davis
Miles Davis	Dewey Davis III
Doris Day	Doris Mary Ann von Kappelhoff
James Dean	James Byron
Kiki Dee	Pauline Matthews
Delores Del Rio	Lolita Dolores Martinez Asunsolo Lopez
Catherine Deneuve	Catherine Dorleac
John Denver	Henry John Deutschendorf Jr.
Bo Derek	Mary Cathleen Collins
John Derek	Derek Harris
Danny DeVito	Daniel Michaeli
Susan Dey	Susan Smith
Angie Dickinson	Angeline Brown
Bo Diddley	Elias McDaniel
Snoop Doggy Dogg	Calvin Broadus
Fats Domino	Antoine Domino
Diana Dors	Diana Fluck
Kirk Douglas	Issur Danielovitch Demsky
Melvyn Douglas	Melvyn Edouard Hesselberg
Margaret Dumont	Margaret Baker
Bob Dylan	Robert Allen Zimmerman
Sheena Easton	Sheena Shirley Orr
Blake Edwards	William Blake McEdwards
Carmen Electra	Tara Patrick
Duke Ellington	Edward Kennedy Ellington
Gloria Estefan	Gloria Fajardo
Linda Evans	Linda Evanstad
Tom Ewell	S. Yewell Tompkins
Douglas Fairbanks	Douglas Elton Ulman
Morgan Fairchild	Patsy Ann McClenny
Jamie Farr	Jameel Farrah
José Ferrer	Vicente Ferrer De Otero y Cintron
Sally Field	Sally Mahoney
W. C. Fields	William Claude Dukenfield
Linda Fiorentino	Clorinda Fiorentino
Grandmaster Flash	Joseph Saddler
John Forsythe	John Lincoln Freud
Jody Foster	Alicia Christian Foster
Samantha Fox	Stacia Micula
Redd Foxx	John Elroy Sanford
Connie Francis	Concetta Franconero

(*continued*)

TABLE 6.12 (continued)

Kenny G	Kenny Gorelick
Zsa Zsa Gabor	Sari Gabor
Greta Garbo	Greta Lovisa Gustafsson
Andy Garcia	Andres Arturo Garci-Menendez
Vincent Gardenia	Vincente Scognamiglio
Ava Gardner	Lucy Johnson
Judy Garland	Frances Ethel Gumm
James Garner	James Scott Baumgarner
Ben Gazzara	Biago Anthony Gazzara
Boy George	B. George Alan O'Dowd
George Gershwin	Jacob Gerhvin
Stan Getz	Stanley Gayetzsky
Barry Gibb	Douglas Gibb
Dizzy Gillespie	John Birks Gillespie
Lillian Gish	Lillian de Guiche
Paulette Goddard	Pauline Marion Goddard Levy
Whoopi Goldberg	Caryn Johnson
Samuel Goldwyn	Schmuel Gelbfisz
Elliott Gould	Elliott Goldstein
Stewart Granger	James Leblanche Stewart
Cary Grant	Archibald Alexander Leach
Peter Graves	Peter Aurness
Rocky Graziano	Thomas Rocco Barbella
Joel Grey	Joel Katz
D. W. Griffith	David Lewelyn Ward Griffith
Che Guevara	Ernesto Guevara
Alex Guinness	Alec Guinness de Cuffe
Buddy Hackett	Leonard Hacker
Gene Hackman	Eugene Alden Hackman
Arsenio Hall	Chuckton Arthur Hall
M. C. Hammer	Stanley Kirk Burrell
Mata Hari	Margaretha Geetruida Zelle
Renny Harlin	Lauri Harjola
Jean Harlow	Harlean Carpenter
Rex Harrison	Reginald Carey Harrison
P. J. Harvey	Polly Jean Harvey
Goldie Hawn	Goldie Jean Studlendgehawn
Rita Hayworth	Margarita Carmen Cansino
Tippi Hedren	Natalie Kay Hedren
Hugh Hefner	Larry Douglas Hefner
Jimi Hendrix	James Marshall Hendrix
Buck Henry	Buck Henry Zuckerman
Audrey Hepburn	Edda van Heemstra Hepburn-Ruston
Pee Wee Herman	Paul Rubenfield
James Herriot	James Alfred Wight
Barbara Hershey	Barbara Herzstein
Charlton Heston	John Charles Carter

TABLE 6.12   (continued)

Hulk Hogan	Terry Bollea
Hal Holbrook	Harold Rowe Holbrook Jr.
William Holden	William Franklin Beedle Jr.
Billie Holiday	Eleanora Fagan
Buddy Holly	Charles Hardin Holley
Bob Hope	Leslie Townes Hope
Harry Houdini	Ehrich Weiss
John Houseman	Jacques Haussmann
Rock Hudson	Roy Harold Scherer Jr.
Engelbert Humperdinck	Arnold George Gerry Dorsey
Lauren Hutton	Mary Laurence Hutton
Lee Iacocca	Lido Anthony Iacocca
Janis Ian	Janis Eddy Fink
Ice Cube	O'shea Jackson
Ice-T	Tracy Marrow
Vanilla Ice	Robert Van Winkle
Billy Idol	William Michael Albert Broad
Burl Ives	Icle Ivanhoe Ives
L. L. Cool J.	James Todd Smith
Kareen Abdul-Jabbar	Ferdinand Lewis Alcindor Jr.
Wolfman Jack	Robert Weston Smith
Tito Jackson	Toriano Adaryll Jackson
Bianca Jagger	Bianca Perez Morena de Macias
Mick Jagger	Michael Philip Jagger
Etta James	Jamesetta Hawkins
Rick James	James Johnson
David Janssen	David Harold Meyer
Jose Jimenez	Bill Dana
Elton John	Reginald Kenneth Dwight
Don Johnson	Donnie Wayne Johnson
Al Jolson	Asa Yoelson
Brian Jones	Lewis Brian Hopkins Jones
Jennifer Jones	Phylis Isley
Spike Jones	Lindley Armstrong Jones
Tom Jones	Thomas Jones Woodward
Louis Jourdan	Louis Gendre
Raul Julia	Raul Rafael Carlos Julia y Arcelay
Boris Karloff	William Henry Pratt
Danny Kaye	David Daniel Kominski
Elia Kazan	Elia Kazanjoglou
Buster Keaton	Joseph Francis Keaton
Diane Keaton	Diane Hall
Michael Keaton	Michael Douglas
Howard Keel	Harold Clifford Leek
Gene Kelly	Eugene Curran Kelly
Chaka Khan	Carole Yvette Marie Stevens
B. B. King	Riley B. King
Carole King	Carole Klein

(*continued*)

TABLE 6.12 **(continued)**

Larry King	Lawrence Harvey Zeiger
Ben Kingsley	Krishna Banji
Rudyard Kipling	Richard Kipling
Calvin Klein	Richard Klein
Evel Knievel	Robert Craig Knievel
Cheryl Ladd	Cheryl Jean Stoppelmoor
Diane Ladd	Rose Diane Ladner
Frankie Laine	Frank Paul LoVecchio
Jimmy Lane	Abel Ferrara
Veronica Lake	Constance Frances Marie Ockelman
Hedy Lamarr	Hedwig Eva Maria Kiesler
Dorothy Lamour	Mary Leta Dorothy Kaumeyer
Burt Lancaster	Stephen Burton
Audrey Landers	Audrey Hamburg
Judy Landers	Judy Hamburg
Michael Landon	Eugene Maurice Orowitz
K. D. Lang	Katherine Dawn Lang
Jessica Lange	Mary MacGregor
John Lange	Michael Crichton
Mario Lanza	Alfredo Arnold Cocozza
Stan Laurel	Arthur Stanley Jefferson
Ralph Lauren	Ralph Lifshitz
Piper Laurie	Rosetta Jacobs
John Le Carre	David John Moore Cornwell
Bruce Lee	Lee Jun Fan
Peggy Lee	Norma Engstrom
Spike Lee	Shelton Jackson Lee
Janet Leigh	Jeanette Helen Morrison
Jennifer Jason Leigh	Jennifer Lee Morrow
Vivien Leigh	Vivian Mary Hartley
Jack Lemmon	John Uhler Lemmon III
Julian Lennon	John Charles Lennon
Jay Leno	James Douglas Muir Leno
Tea Leoni	Tea Pantleoni
Huey Lewis	Hugh Cregg
Jerry Lewis	Joseph Joey Levitch
Liberace	Wladziu Lee Valentino
Virna Lisi	Virna Pierlisi
Tone Loc	Anthony Terrell Smith
Herbert Lom	C. Angelo Kuchacevich
Carole Lombard	Jane Alice Peters
Traci Lords	Nora Louise Kuzma
Sophia Loren	Sofie Villani Scicolone
Peter Lorre	Ladislav Loewenstein
Joe Louis	Joe Barrow
Courtney Love	Love Michelle Harrison
Myrna Loy	Myrna Williams

TABLE 6.12 (continued)

Bela Lugosi	Bela Ferenc Blasko
Dolph Lundgren	Hans Lundgren
Loretta Lynn	Loretta Webb
Andie McDowell	Rosalie Anderson Qualley
Ali McGraw	Alice MacGraw
Elle Macpherson	Eleanor Nancy Gow
Madonna	Louise Veronica Ciccone
Lee Majors	Harvey Lee Yeary II
Karl Malden	Malden Sekulovich
Anthony Mann	Emil Anton Bundsmann
Jayne Mansfield	Vera Jayne Palmer
Marilyn Manson	Brian Warner
Sophie Marceau	Sophie Maupu
Frederic March	Frederick Ernest McIntyre Bickel
Teena Marie	Mary Christine Brockert
E. G. Marshall	Edda Gunnar Marshall
Dean Martin	Dina Paul Crocetti
Chico Marx	Leonard Marx
Groucho Marx	Julius Henry Marx
Gummo Marx	Milton Marx
Harpo Marx	Adolph Arthur Marz
Zeppo Marx	Herbert Marx
Walter Matthau	Walter Matuschanskatasky
Elaine May	Elaine Berlin
John McEnroe	Patrick John McEnroe Jr.
Kristy McNichol	Christina Ann McNichol
Meat Loaf	Marvin Lee Aday
Ethel Merman	Ethel Zimmerman
George Michael	Georgios Kyriacos Panayiotou
Vera Miles	Vera Ralston
Ray Milland	Reginald Alfred Truscott-Jones
Carmen Miranda	Maria do Carmo Miranda Da Cunha
Joni Mitchell	Roberta Joan Anderson
Marilyn Monroe	Norma Jean Mortenson (Baker)
Yves Montand	Ivo Montand Livi
Chris Montez	Christopher Montanaez
Demi Moore	Demetria Guynes
Rita Moreno	Rosita Dolores Alverio
Pat Morita	Noriyuki Morita
Zero Mostel	Samuel Joel Mostel
Mother Teresa	Agnes Gonxha Bojaxhiu
Liam Neeson	William Neeson
Sam Neill	Nigel John Dermot Neill
Mike Nichols	Michael Igor Peschkowsky
Stevie Nicks	Stephanie Nicks
Harry Nilsson	Edward Nilsson III
Chuck Norris	Carlos Ray Norris
Nostradamus	Michel de Notredame

(continued)

TABLE 6.12   **(continued)**

Billy Ocean	Leslie Sebastian Charles
Warner Oland	Johan Verner Olund
Ryan O'Neal	Patrick Ryan O'Neal
George Orwell	Eric Arthur Blair
Ozzy Osbourne	John Osbourne
Marie Osmond	Olive Osmond
Frank Oz	Frank Richard Oznowicz
Al Pacino	Alfredo James Pacino
Jack Palance	Walter Jack Palanuik
Robert Palmer	Alan Palmer
Col. Thomas A. Parker	Andreas van Kuijk
Mandy Patinkin	Mandel Patinkin
Gregory Peck	Eldred Gregory Peck
Sam Peckinpah	David Samuel Peckinpah
Pele	Edson Arantes do Nascimento
Pepa	Sandra Denton
Isabel Peron	Maria Estela Martinez Cartas
Luke Perry	Coy Luther Perry III
Bernadette Peters	Bernadette Lazzara
Michelle Phillips	Holly Graham Gilliam
Edith Piaf	Edith Giovanna Gassion
Slim Pickens	Louis Bert Lindley Jr.
Mary Pickford	Gladys Mary Smith
Brad Pitt	William Bradley Pitt
Pocahontas	Matoaka Rebecca Rolfe
Iggy Pop	James Newell Osterberg
Stephanie Powers	Stefina Zofia Frederkiewcz
Paula Prentiss	Paula Ragusa
Priscilla Presley	Priscilla Beaulieu
Prince	Prince Rogers Nelson
Claude Rains	Williams Rains
Anne Rampling	Anne Rice
Tony Randall	Leonard Rosenberg
Robert Redford	Charles Robert Redford Jr.
Paul Reubens	Paul Reubenfeld
Fernando Rey	Fernando Casado Arambillet
Burt Reynolds	Burton Leon Reynolds Jr.
Debbie Reynolds	Marie Frances Reynolds
Little Richard	Richard Penniman
Joan Rivers	Joan Sandra Molinsky
Edward G. Robinson	Emmanuel Goldenberg
Sugar Ray Robinson	Walter Smith Jr.
Smokey Robinson	William Robinson Jr.
Gene Roddenberry	Wesley Eugene Roddenberry
Ginger Rogers	Virginia Katherine McMath
Roy Rogers	Leonard Franklin Slye
Henry Rollins	Henry Garfield

TABLE 6.12 (continued)

Mickey Rooney	Joe Yule Jr.
Axl Rose	William Rose Bailey
Diana Ross	Diane Ross Earle
Katherine Ross	Dorothy Walter
Johnny Rotten	John Lydon
Mickey Rourke	Philip Andrew Rourke Jr.
Jack Ruby	Jacob Rubenstein
Jane Russell	Ernestine Russell
Theresa Russell	Theresa Paup
Babe Ruth	George Herman Ruth
Meg Ryan	Margaret Mary Emily Anne Hyra
Bobby Rydel	Robert Luigi Ridarelli
Winona Ryder	Winona Laura Horowitz
Yves Saint-Laurent	Henri Donat Mathieu
Susan St. James	Susan Jane Miller
Jill St. John	Jill Oppenheim
Salt	Cheryl James
Susan Sarandon	Susan Abigail Tomalin
Telly Savalas	Aristoteles Harris Savalas
Leo Sayer	Gerald Hugh Sayer
Romy Schneider	Rosemarie Albach-Retty
Seal	Sealhenry Samuel
Peter Sellers	Richard Henry Sellers
Jane Seymour	Joyce Penelope Wilhelmina Frankenberg
Del Shannon	Charles Weeden Westover
Omar Sharif	Michael Shalhoub Prizhivago
Ally Sheedy	Alexandra Elizabeth Sheedy
Charlie Sheen	Carlos Irwin Estevez
Martin Sheen	Ramon Estevez
Sam Shepard	Samuel Shepard Rogers VII
Talia Shire	Talia Rose Coppola
Simone Signoret	Simone Henriette Charlotte Kaminker
Gene Simmons	Chaim Whitz
Nina Simone	Eunice Kathleen Waymon
O. J. Simpson	Orenthal James Simpson
Frank Sinatra	Francis Albert Sinatra
Sinbad	David Adkins
The Singing Nun	Jeanine Deckers
Slash	Saul Hudson
Christian Slater	Christian Hawkins
Suzanne Somers	Suzanne Mahoney
Elke Sommer	Elke Schletz
David Soul	David Solberg
Sissy Spacek	Mary Elizabeth Spacek
Mickey Spillane	Frank Morrison Spillane
Dusty Springfield	Mary Isobel Catherine Bernadette O'Brien
Robert Stack	Robert Langford Modini
Sylvester Stallone	Michael Sylvester Stallone

(continued)

TABLE 6.12   (continued)

Barbara Stanwyck	Ruby Stevens
Ringo Starr	Richard Starkey
Cat Stevens	Steven Georgiou
Stella Stevens	Estelle Egglestone
Rod Stewart	Roderick David Stewart III
Sting	Gordon Matthew Sumner
Lee Strasberg	Israel Strassberg
Dorothy Stratten	Dorothy Hoogstratten
Meryl Streep	Mary Louise Streep
Barbra Streisand	Barbara Joan Streisand
Donna Summer	LaDonna Andrea Gaines
Gloria Swanson	Gloria May Josephine Svensson
D. B. Sweeney	Daniel Barnard Sweeney
Booker T	Booker T. Jones
Mr. T	Lawrence Tureaud
Terry-Thomas	Thomas Terry Hoar Stevens
Lily Tomlin	Mary Jean Tomlin
Rip Torn	Elmore Rual Torn Jr.
Peter Tosh	Winston Hubert McIntosh
Randy Travis	Randy Bruce Traywick
Lana Turner	Julia Jean Mildred Frances Turner
Ted Turner	Robert Edward Turner III
Mark Twain	Samuel Langhorne Clemens
Twiggy	Leslie Hornby
Liv Tyler	Liv Rundgren
Roger Vadim	Roger Vadim Plemiannikov
Ritchie Valens	Richard Steven Valenzuela
Frankie Valli	Frank Castelluccio
Jean-Claude Van Damme	Jean-Claude Van Varenberg
Vangelis	Evangelos Papathanassiou
Vanity	Denise Katrina Smith
Eddie Vedder	Edward Louis Severson III
Sid Vicious	John Simon Ritchie
Gore Vidal	Eugene Luther Vidal Jr.
Gene Vincent	Eugene Vincent Craddock
Bobby Vinton	Stanley Robert Vinton
Diane Von Furstenburg	Diane Michelle Halfin
Max Von Sydow	Carl Adolph Von Sydow
Christopher Walken	Ronald Walken
Andy Warhol	Andrew Warhola
Dinah Washington	Ruth Jones
Muddy Waters	McKinley Morganfield
John Wayne	Marion Michael Morrison
Sigourney Weaver	Susan Alexandra Weaver
Raquel Welch	Raquel Tejada
Tuesday Weld	Susan Ker Weld
H. G. Wells	Herbert George Wells
Oskar Werner	Oskar Josef Schliessmayer

TABLE 6.12 **(continued)**

Dr. Ruth Westheimer	Karola Ruth Siegel
Vanna White	Vanna Marie Rosich
Oscar Wilde	Fingal O'Flahertie Wills
Billy Wilder	Samuel Wilder
Gene Wilder	Jerome Silberman
Tennessee Williams	Thomas Lanier Williams
Bruce Willis	Walter Bruce Willis
Shelly Winters	Shirley Schrift
Tom Wolfe	Thomas Kennerley
Stevie Wonder	Steveland Morris Hardaway
John Woo	Wu Yusen
Natalie Wood	Natasha Nikolaevna Zacharenko-Gurdin
Jane Wyman	Sarah Jane Fulks
Tammy Wynette	Virginia Wynette Pugh
Malcolm X	Malcolm Little
Susannah York	Susannah Yolande Fletcher
Sean Young	Mary Sean Young
Pia Zadora	Pia Schipani

Source: www.netogram.com

name is Randy Bruce Traywick. He kept the common first name "Randy," but morphed Traywick into "Travis." Actress Goldie Hawn kept her first name but uses only the last four letters of her real last name, Studlendgehawn. On the other hand, some celebrities select a professional name that bears no relationship to their real name. Thus, actor-singer Marvin Lee Aday became Meat Loaf, actor-rapper James Todd Smith became L. L. Cool J., singer Louise Veronica Ciccone became Madonna, and wrestler-actor Terry Bollea became Hulk Hogan.

Celebrities and Music

Americans love their music. They spend millions of dollars purchasing music for their iPods or other electronic listening devices. Some music is sold on CDs, but the old-time 45 rpm and 33 1/3 rpm vinyl records are long gone, as are 8-track and cassette tapes. Table 6.13 shows the top-selling music artists as of 2008. Ironically, two of the top three have not recorded anything new in more than 30 years. The Beatles top the list with 170,000,000 units sold. The Beatles' last album was recorded and released in 1970. Since then, two of the Beatles have died. Elvis Presley, who died in 1977, ranks third with 120,000,000 units sold.

TABLE 6.13
Top-Selling Music Artists (as of 2008)

Artist	Units Sold (in millions)	Artist	Units Sold (in millions)
The Beatles	170	Celine Dion	50
Garth Brooks	128	Neil Diamond	48.5
Elvis Presley	120	Fleetwood Mac	48.5
Led Zeppelin	111.5	Kenny G	48
The Eagles	100	Shania Twain	48
Billy Joel	79.5	Journey	47
Pink Floyd	74.5	Alabama	46
Barbra Streisand	71.5	Guns 'N Roses	43.5
AC/DC	71	Santana	43
Elton John	70	Alan Jackson	42.5
Michael Jackson	69.5	Eric Clapton	42.5
George Strait	68.5	Bob Seger/Silver Bullet Band	41
Aerosmith	66.5	Reba McIntire	40.5
The Rolling Stones	66	Prince	39.5
Madonna	64	Chicago	38.5
Bruce Springsteen	64	Simon & Garfunkel	38.5
Mariah Carey	63	Foreigner	37.5
Metallica	59	2 PAC	37.5
Van Halen	56.5	Bob Dylan	37
Whitney Houston	55	Backstreet Boys	37
U2	51.5	Rod Stewart	37
Kenny Rogers	51	Tim McGraw	35.5

Source: Recording Industry Association of America (RIAA)

It is interesting to note the public's music-purchasing habits (see Table 6.14). Rock music continues to be the most popular, averaging about 30 percent of sales in recent years. Rap/Hip Hop, R&B/Urban, and Country compete for second place, each averaging about 11 percent of sales. Other music types sell only in the single-digit percentages, some even less than 1 percent in 2008 (Oldies, New Age, and Soundtracks). Table 6.14 also shows the format in which music is acquired. Full-length CDs captured most of the sales through 2008, with digital downloads becoming increasingly popular. With the widespread use of the iPod and easily downloadable music from the iTunes store, digital downloads are likely to become more popular as we move along into the 21st century and will overtake CDs as the primary music delivery format.

Who purchases all this music? Good question. Table 6.15 breaks down music purchases for 2000–2008 by age group, gender, and purchase method. We should take the data on purchase method/location lightly because the data report behavior only

TABLE 6.14
Consumer Music-Purchasing Profile by Genre and Format, 2000–2008

Category	(percent of total sales)								
	2000	2001	2002	2003	2004	2005	2006	2007	2008
Genre									
Rock	24.8	24.4	24.7	25.2	23.9	31.5	34.0	32.4	31.8
Rap/Hip-Hop	12.9	11.4	13.8	13.3	12.1	13.3	11.4	10.8	10.7
R&B/Urban	9.7	10.6	11.2	10.6	11.3	10.2	11.0	11.8	10.2
Country	10.7	10.5	10.4	10.4	13.0	12.5	13.0	11.5	11.9
Pop	11.0	12.1	9.0	8.9	10.0	8.1	7.1	10.7	9.1
Religious	4.8	6.7	6.7	5.8	6.0	5.3	5.5	3.9	6.5
Classical	2.7	3.2	3.1	3.0	2.0	2.4	1.9	2.3	1.9
Jazz	2.9	3.4	3.2	2.9	2.7	1.8	2.0	2.6	1.1
Soundtracks	0.7	1.4	1.1	1.4	1.1	0.9	0.8	0.8	0.8
Oldies	0.9	0.8	0.9	1.3	1.4	1.1	1.1	0.4	0.7
New Age	0.5	1.0	0.5	0.5	1.0	0.4	0.3	0.3	0.6
Children's	0.6	0.5	0.4	0.6	2.8	2.3	2.9	2.9	3.0
Other	8.3	7.9	8.1	7.6	8.9	8.5	7.3	7.1	9.1
Format									
Full-length CDs	89.3	89.2	90.5	87.8	90.3	87.0	85.6	82.6	77.8
Full-length cassettes	4.9	3.4	2.4	2.2	1.7	1.1	0.8	0.3	0.4
Singles (all types)	2.5	2.4	1.9	2.4	2.4	2.7	3.4	2.4	3.8
Music videos/Video DVDs	0.8	1.1	0.7	0.6	1.0	0.7	1.1	0.4	0.8
DVD audio	NA	1.1	1.3	2.7	1.7	0.8	1.3	1.2	1.0
Digital download	NA	0.2	0.5	1.3	0.9	5.7	6.7	11.2	12.8
Other	0.5	0.6	0.7	1.0	1.7	1.9	0.6	1.3	2.1

Source: Recording Industry Association of America (RIAA)

through 2008. Music purchase at retail stores accounted for more than 87 percent of sales in 2002, but only 58 percent of sales in 2008. Digital downloads were not available until 2005, but since then have become increasingly popular (more than 13 percent in 2008). One would expect that figure to grow—and the retail store purchases to decline—as we move forward in the 21st century.

The data on gender and age are more revealing. More females than males purchased music between 2000 and 2008, but not by much. As a rule, 51 percent of music purchasers were female, 49 percent male. In terms of the age of music purchasers, one might expect younger people to purchase the lion's share of music. However, as late as 2008, the 45-plus age group accounted for almost 34 percent of sales. The 24-and-under group accounted for about 28 percent of sales. Thirty-nine percent of sales went to the 25 to 44 age group. These differences are interesting, but mainly reveal that all age groups purchase music in a generally consistent fashion.

TABLE 6.15
Consumer Music-Purchasing Profile by Gender, Age, and Purchase Method, 2000–2008

Category	\(percent of total sales\)								
	2000	2001	2002	2003	2004	2005	2006	2007	2008
Age									
10–14 Years	8.9	8.5	8.9	8.6	9.4	8.6	7.6	11.5	7.3
15–19 Years	12.9	13.0	13.3	11.4	11.9	11.9	12.8	12.3	10.9
20–24 Years	12.5	12.2	11.5	10.0	9.2	12.7	9.8	11.3	10.1
25–29 Years	10.6	10.9	9.4	10.9	10.0	12.1	12.7	9.2	8.3
30–34 Years	9.8	10.3	10.8	10.1	10.4	11.3	10.2	11.3	8.9
35–39 Years	10.6	10.2	9.8	11.2	10.7	8.8	10.6	11.9	9.8
40–44 Years	9.6	10.3	9.9	10.0	10.9	9.2	9.0	7.9	11.0
45–plus Years	23.8	23.7	25.5	26.6	26.4	25.5	26.1	24.8	33.7
Purchase Method/Location									
Record Store	42.4	42.5	36.8	33.2	32.5	39.4	35.4	31.1	30.0
Other Store	40.8	42.4	50.7	52.8	53.8	32.0	32.7	29.7	28.4
Record Club	7.6	6.1	4.0	4.1	4.4	8.5	10.5	12.6	7.2
Media Ad/800 Number	2.4	3.0	2.0	1.5	1.7	2.4	2.4	1.7	1.8
Internet	3.2	2.9	3.4	5.0	5.9	8.2	9.1	10.9	14.6
Digital Download	NA	NA	NA	NA	NA	6.0	6.8	12.0	13.5
Concert	NA	NA	N	NA	1.6	2.7	2.0	1.5	3.0
Gender									
Female	49.4	51.2	50.6	50.9	50.5	48.2	49.6	50.8	51.5
Male	50.6	48.8	49.4	49.1	49.5	51.8	50.4	49.2	48.5

Source: Recording Industry Association of America (RIAA)

Specialized Celebrities

We noted several times many of today's celebrities come from entertainment fields, that is, television, movies, music, and sports. We also observed that while many other fields have well-known or famous people, they are less likely to become celebrities due primarily to the absence of regular media exposure, although the public's lack of knowledge or interest in their accomplishments may also play a role in their failure to become celebrities. Table 6.16 illustrates this point.

The Nobel Prize is an international award given annually to individuals for their outstanding achievements in physics, chemistry, physiology/medicine, economics, literature, and peace. The award consists of a gold medal, a diploma, and a cash award, usually $1 million. If more than one person wins a specific award, the cash is divided. Most of the names in Table 6.16

TABLE 6.16
Nobel Prize Winners, 2001–2009

Name(s)	Field	Year
Eric A. Cornell, Wolfgang Ketterie, Carl E. Wieman	Physics	2001
William S. Knowles, Ryoji Noyori, K. Barry Sharpless	Chemistry	2001
Leland H. Hartwell, Tim Hunt, Sir Paul Nurse	Physiology/Medicine	2001
Sir Vidiadhar Surajprasad Naipaul	Literature	2001
George A. Akerlof, A. Michael Spence, Joseph Stiglitz	Economics	2001
Kofi Annan	Peace	2001
Raymond Davis Jr., Masatoshi Koshiba, Riccardo Giacconi	Physics	2002
John B. Fenn, Koichi Tanaka, Kurt Wuthrich	Chemistry	2002
Sydney Brenner, H. Robert Horvitz, John E. Sulston	Physiology/Medicine	2002
Imre Kertesz	Literature	2002
Daniel Kahneman, Vernon L. Smith	Economics	2002
Jimmy Carter	Peace	2002
Alexei A. Abrikosov, Vitaly L. Ginzburg, Anthony J. Leggett	Physics	2003
Peter Agre, Roderick MacKinnon	Chemistry	2003
Paul C. Lauterbur, Sir Peter Mansfield	Physiology/Medicine	2003
John M. Coetzee	Literature	2003
Robert F. Engle III, Clive W. J. Granger	Economics	2003
Shirin Ebadi	Peace	2003
David J. Gross, H. David Politzer, Frank Wilczek	Physics	2004
Aaron Ciechanover, Avram Hershko, Irwin Rose	Chemistry	2004
Richard Axel, Linda B. Buck	Physiology/Medicine	2004
Elfride Jelinek	Literature	2004
Finn E. Kydland, Edward C. Prescott	Economics	2004
Wangari Muta Maathai	Peace	2004
Roy J. Glauber, John L. Hall, Theodor W. Hansch	Physics	2005
Yves Chauvin, Robert H. Grubbs, Richard R. Schrock	Chemistry	2005
Barry J. Marshall, J. Robin Warren	Physiology/Medicine	2005
Harold Pinter	Literature	2005
Robert J. Aumann, Thomas C. Schelling	Economics	2005
Mohamed ElBaradei	Peace	2005
John C. Mather, George F. Smoot	Physics	2006
Roger D. Kornberg	Chemistry	2006
Andrew Z. Fire, Craig C. Mello	Physiology/Medicine	2006
Orhan Pamuk	Literature	2006
Edmund S. Phelps	Economics	2006
Muhammad Yunus, Grameen Bank	Peace	2006
Albert Fert, Peter Grunberg	Physics	2007
Gerhard Erti	Chemistry	2007
Mario R. Capecchi, Sir Martin J. Evans, Oliver Smithies	Physiology/Medicine	2007
Doris Lessing	Literature	2007
Leonid Hurwicz, Eric S. Maskin, Roger B. Myerson	Economics	2007
Albert Arnold (Al) Gore	Peace	2007
Yoichiro Nambu, Makoto Kobayashi, Toshihide Maskawa	Physics	2008
Osamu Shimomura, Martin Chalfie, Roger Y. Tsien	Chemistry	2008

(continued)

TABLE 6.16 (continued)

Harald zur Hausen, Francoise Barre-Sinoussi, Luc Montagnier	Physiology/Medicine	2008
Jean-Marie Gustave Le Clezio	Literature	2008
Paul Krugman	Economics	2008
Martii Ahtisaari	Peace	2008
Charles K. Kao, Willard S. Boyle, George E. Smith	Physics	2009
Venkatraman Ramakrishnan, Thomas A. Steitz, Ada E. Yonath	Chemistry	2009
Elizabeth H. Blackburn, Carol W. Greider, Jack W. Szostak	Physiology/Medicine	2009
Herta Muller	Literature	2009
Elinor Ostrom, Oliver E. Williamson	Economics	2009
Barack H. Obama	Peace	2009

Adapted from http://nobelprize.org

are unfamiliar to most people. However, these individuals are likely well known, perhaps even famous, within their specific disciplines. For example, Charles K. Kao, Willard S. Boyle, and George E. Smith won the 2009 Nobel Prize in Physics. These are men of significant achievement. Their work involves "the transmission of light in fibers for optical communication," and "semiconductor circuits." It is safe to say most of us could not explain either of these accomplishments or what they mean to life. These men are likely to be known, perhaps even well known, in the world of physics, but they are not household names and are not likely to be profiled on television or asked to star in movies. They may be celebrities within the physics world but are not celebrities beyond that world.

There are, of course, exceptions. A careful, well-informed reader will find a few recognizable names in Table 6.16. The United Nations' Kofi Annan won the 2001 Nobel Peace Prize. Former president Jimmy Carter won the 2002 Nobel Peace Prize. British poet and playwright Harold Pinter was awarded the 2005 Nobel Prize in Literature. Former Vice President Al Gore received the 2007 Nobel Peace Prize. Economist Paul Krugman was awarded the 2008 Nobel Prize in Economics. President Barack Obama won the 2009 Nobel Peace Prize. These men are known worldwide and are considered celebrities in many parts of the world.

Celebrity Families

Does celebrity run in families? It would seem so. Table 6.17 reveals several things. First, celebrity siblings seem to be

TABLE 6.17
Keeping Celebrity in the Family

Names	Birth Year	Celebrity Profession (s)
Affleck brothers		
Ben	1972	actor
Casey	1975	actor
Dillon brothers		
Matt	1964	actor
Kevin	1965	actor
Astin brothers		
Sean	1971	actor, director, producer
Mackenzie	1973	actor
Belushi brothers		
John	1949 (d. 1982)	actor, comedian, musician
Jim	1954	actor, comedian musician
Phoenix brothers		
River	1970 (d. 1993)	actor
Joaquin	1974	actor, musician
Connery brothers		
Sean	1930	actor, producer
Neil	1938	actor
Howard brothers		
Ron	1954	actor, director, producer
Clint	1959	actor
Bridges brothers		
Beau	1941	actor
Jeff	1949	actor, musician
Quaid brothers		
Randy	1950	actor, comedian
Dennis	1954	actor
Savage brothers		
Fred	1976	actor, producer, director
Ben	1980	actor
Wahlberg brothers		
Donnie	1969	singer, actor, producer
Mark	1971	actor, producer
Arquette siblings		
Rosanna	1959	actress, director, producer
Patricia	1968	actress
Alexis (born Robert)	1969	transwoman, actress, musician
David	1971	actor, director, producer
Duff sisters		
Haylie	1985	actress, singer
Hillary	1987	actress, singer
Tilly sisters		
Jennifer	1958	actress, poker player
Meg	1960	actress, dancer, writer

(continued)

TABLE 6.17   (continued)

Bateman siblings		
Justine	1966	actress
Jason	1969	actor
Gyllenhaal siblings		
Maggie	1977	actress
Jake	1980	actor
Fonda family		
Henry	1905 (d. 1982)	actor
Jane	1937	actress, political activist
Peter	1940	actor
Bridget	1964	actress
Cusack siblings		
Joan	1962	actress, comedienne
John	1966	actor, screenwriter
Madsen siblings		
Michael	1957	actor, poet, photographer
Virginia	1961	actress, documentary producer
Roberts family		
Eric	1956	actor
Emma	1991	actress, singer
Lisa (Gillan)	1965	actress
Julia	1967	actress
Baldwin brothers		
Alec	1958	actor
Daniel	1960	actor, producer, director
William (Billy)	1963	actor
Stephen	1966	actor, writer, producer
Judd family		
Naomi	1946	singer, songwriter
Wynonna	1964	singer
Ashley	1968	actress
Simpson sisters		
Jessica	1980	singer, actress, TV personality
Ashley	1984	singer, songwriter
Carter brothers		
Nick	1980	singer, musician, actor
Aaron	1987	singer
Bacon brothers		
Michael	1949	singer, musician, composer
Kevin	1958	actor, musician, singer
Deschanel sisters		
Emily	1976	actress
Zooey	1980	actress, singer, musician

commonplace: Ron and Clint Howard, Beau and Jeff Bridges, Maggie and Jake Gyllenhaal, and Jessica and Ashley Simpson, for example. In some cases, however, one sibling is quite well known, the other less so. Take the Connery brothers. Sean Connery is famous for his role in the James Bond films. His brother Neil is not well known in America, but is a well known actor in Great Britain. Another good example is the Bacon brothers. Kevin is an established Hollywood celebrity, having appeared in numerous films. His older brother Michael is not an actor and is known only as one-half of the Bacon Brothers band, younger brother Kevin being the other half. Second, a few families' celebrity runs more than one generation. The family of actor Henry Fonda is a good example. Fonda's children Jane and Peter are celebrities, as is granddaughter Bridget. A third observation about siblings (and families) as celebrities is the consistency of profession within a family. In other words, most of them are singers, actors, actresses, or musicians, with a few going on to produce or direct. No sibling has become a nuclear engineer, or a grade-school teacher, or a customer service representative. What this means, of course, is what we have said several times thus far in this book: celebrities, highly visible in media, come primarily from entertainment fields; accomplishments by individuals in other fields are not media noteworthy and are routinely ignored. This is neither bad nor good; it's simply the way things are.

Early Celebrity Jobs

Not all celebrities come from famous families. Some had to earn their way to stardom. Table 6.18 shows a few of the jobs a dozen celebrities had before they became famous and well known. It is not all that difficult to envision Clint Eastwood as a lumberjack or Paula Abdul as a cheerleader, but it stretches the imagination to think of Whoopi Goldberg as a garbage collector or Matthew McConaughey as a dishwasher.

Early Celebrity Deaths

More than a few members of the public wish they could be celebrities. Fame, wealth, and a lavish lifestyle seem to be the

TABLE 6.18
Before They Were Celebrities

Name	Early Jobs	Celebrity Job
Paula Abdul	cheerleader (L.A. Lakers)	singer; dancer
Marlon Brando	ditch digger; night watchman	actor
Sean Connery	milkman; lifeguard	actor
Clint Eastwood	lumberjack; steel mill worker	actor; director
Dennis Farina	police officer	actor
Whoopi Goldberg	bricklayer; garbage collector	actress; television host
Mick Jagger	hospital porter	singer; songwriter
Jason Lee	fast food employee	actor
David Letterman	television weatherman	television talk show host
Matthew McConaughey	dishwasher; manure remover	actor
Madonna	donut shop worker	singer; actress
Ozzy Osbourne	slaughterhouse worker	singer; songwriter

Adapted from http://howstuffworks.com

height of accomplishment and perfection. However, celebrity often has a high price: an early death. Table 6.19 lists celebrities who died before age 40. More troubling is the cause of death for many on the list. Plane crashes and drug overdoses appear to be the main cause of early death among celebrities. Although we cannot hold celebrities responsible for plane crashes, we can hold them responsible for drug overdoses. The common explanation for drug deaths is that the life of a celebrity is so controlled, so intense, and so public that some turn to drugs to escape the stress. Society appears to understand rather than condemn this. To be fair, we should note that some celebrities died early from causes not related to their famous lives: actress Heather O'Rourke from a bowel obstruction and musician Bob Marley from lung and brain cancer.

Celebrity Writers

A common joke among some people who are retiring is this one: When asked the question about what he or she plans to do in the golden years, the answer is "write The Great American Novel." Literature has been a part of culture as far back as the early civilizations. Contemporary American culture is no different. Getting a book on the *New York Times* bestseller list is a sure way to

TABLE 6.19
Celebrities Who Died Young

Name	Age	Profession	Apparent Cause of Death
Heather O"Rourke	12	actress	bowel obstruction
Ritchie Valens	17	singer	plane crash
Aaliyah	22	singer	plane crash
Buddy Holly	22	singer	plane crash
Freddie Prinze	22	actor	suicide
River Phoenix	23	actor	drug overdose
Selena	23	singer	homicide
James Dean	24	actor	auto accident
Otis Redding	26	singer	plane crash
Janis Joplin	27	singer	drug overdose
Jim Morrison	27	singer	heart attack; drug overdose
Jimi Hendrix	27	singer; musician	drug overdose
Kurt Cobain	27	singer; musician	suicide (?)
Brandon Lee	28	actor	accidental shooting
Hank Williams	29	singer	heart attack; drug overdose
Andy Gibb	30	singer	heart failure; drug abuse
Jim Croce	30	singer	plane crash
Patsy Cline	30	singer	plane crash
Bruce Lee	32	actor	allergic reaction (?)
Cass Elliott	32	singer	heart attack
Karen Carpenter	32	singer	cardiac arrest
Keith Moon	32	musician	medication overdose
Chris Farley	33	actor; comedian	drug overdose
John Belushi	33	actor	drug overdose
Andy Kaufman	35	actor; comedian	lung cancer
Stevie Ray Vaughan	35	musician	helicopter crash
Bob Marley	36	musician	lung and brain cancer
Princess Diana	36	British royal	auto accident
Marilyn Monroe	36	actress	drug overdose
Lou Gehrig	37	baseball player	ALS
Florence Joyner	38	Olympic runner	seizure
Harry Chapin	38	singer	auto accident
John F. Kennedy, Jr.	38	journalist/publisher	plane crash
Roberto Clemente	38	baseball player	plane crash
Sam Kinison	38	comedian	auto accident
Anna Nicole Smith	39	actress; model	medication overdose
Martin Luther King, Jr.	39	minister; activist	assassination

Adapted from http://howstuffworks.com

fame—and maybe fortune. Even if we don't plan to write the great novel, many of us do keep journals, daily diaries, or blogs. It is no surprise, then, that some celebrities turn to writing, either to earn extra income or to tell a story important to them. Table 6.20

TABLE 6.20
Celebrity Authors

Name	Celebrity Profession	Book Title
Woody Allen	actor; director	*Mere Anarchy*
Pamela Anderson	actress	*Star Struck: A Novel*
Julie Andrews	actress	*Last of the Really Great Whangdoodles* (c)
Alan Arkin	actor	*The Lemming Condition* (c)
Victoria Beckham	singer; actress	*Learning to Fly*
Jimmy Buffett	singer; actor	*A Salty Piece of Land*
Naomi Campbell	model	*Swan*
Kim Cattrall	actress	*Satisfaction: The Art of the Female Orgasm*
Lynne Cheney	author; scholar	*Sisters*
Stephen Colbert	comedian	*I Am America (And So Can You!)*
Lauren Conrad	TV personality; author	*L. A. Candy*
Bill Cosby	actor; comedian	*Fatherhood*
Katie Couric	television news anchor	*The Blue Ribbon Day* (c)
Billy Crystal	actor	*700 Sundays*
Macaulay Culkin	actor	*Junior*
Miley Cyrus	actress; singer	*Miles to Go* (p)
Fabio	model	*Wild*
Jane Fonda	actress; political activist	*My Life So Far*
Whoopi Goldberg	actress; TV personality	*Sugar Plum Ballerinas* (c)
Amy Grant	singer	*Mosaic: Pieces of My Life So Far*
David Hasselhoff	actor	*Making Waves*
George Hamilton	actor	*Don't Mind if I Do*
Teri Hatcher	actress	*Burnt Toast & Other Philosophies of Life*
Ethan Hawke	actor	*Ash Wednesday*
Paris Hilton	actress; socialite	*Confessions of an Heiress*
Larry the Cable Guy	actor; comedian	*Git-R-Done*
Hugh Laurie	actor	*The Gun Seller*
Jay Leno	TV talk show host	*If Roast Beef Could Fly* (c)
Danica McKellar	actress	*Math Doesn't Suck* (t)
Madonna	singer; actress	*Mr. Peabody's Apples* (c)
Steve Martin	actor; comedian	*Born Standing Up: A Comic's Life*
Bette Midler	singer; actress	*The Saga of Baby Divine* (c)
Julianne Moore	actress	*Freckleface Strawberry* (c)
Deborah Norville	TV host	*The Power of Respect*
Rosie O'Donnell	actress; comedienne	*Celebrity Detox*
Sarah Palin	politician	*Going Rogue*
Dolly Parton	singer; actress	*Coat of Many Colors* (c)
Jada Pinkett-Smith	actress	*Girls Hold Up This World* (c)
Paulina Porizkova	model; actress	*A Model Summer* (t)
Carrie Prejean	model	*Still Standing*
LeAnn Rimes	singer	*What I Cannot Change*
Nicole Ritchie	actress; socialite	*The Truth about Diamonds*
Jerry Seinfeld	actor; comedian	*SeinLanguage*
Jane Seymour	actress	*Making Yourself at Home*
William Shatner	actor	*Tek Power*

TABLE 6.20 (continued)

Ally Sheedy	actress	Yesterday I Saw the Sun: Poems
Will Smith	actor	Just the Two of Us (c)
Britney Spears	singer; actress	Heart to Heart
Jon Stewart	comedian	Naked Pictures of Famous People
Elizabeth Taylor	actress	My Love Affair with Jewelry
Shirley Temple	actress	Child Star
Tila Tequila	singer; model	Hooking Up with Tila Tequila
John Travolta	actor	Propeller: One-Way Night Coach
Henry Winkler	actor	Hank Zipzer: Niagara Falls — or Does It? (c)

(c) = children's book; (t) = teen; (p) = preteen

lists some celebrities and their books. You will note that many of those on the list are actors or actresses, but there is a smattering of individuals from other celebrity fields. There seem to be a lot of children's books on the list. Are they easier to write? Perhaps. Some books have a clear connection to their authors' lives. For example, country singer Dolly Parton's children's book *Coat of Many Colors* bears the same title as one of her hit songs. Actor John Travolta is also a pilot, so it is reasonable for him to write *Propeller: One-Way Night Coach.* Just looking at their titles, some of these books appear to be worthwhile reads: Bill Cosby's *Fatherhood,* Danica McKellar's *Math Doesn't Suck,* and Deborah Norville's *The Power of Respect.* On the other hand, several books—by their titles—do not encourage us to read them: Elizabeth Taylor's *My Love Affair with Jewelry,* Nicole Ritchie's *The Truth about Diamonds,* and Teri Hatcher's *Burnt Toast and Other Philosophies of Life.* With all due respect to Ms. Hatcher, burnt toast is not a philosophy of life; it is a breakfast mistake. However, we should not judge these celebrities too harshly. There is usually something to be learned from reading any book; some celebrities have a large number of fans who would be willing to read anything their favorite celebrities write.

Celebrity Business Criminals

Lawbreakers can be found in all professions. Some individuals have drawn considerable media attention, due in large part to the magnitude of their illegal activities. Media exposure and their often lengthy trials make celebrities of many of these lawbreakers. Members of the public are usually willing to forgive and forget a charge of "driving under the influence" but are less forgiving when their money is involved. Table 6.21 lists 10 celebrity criminals in American business. The list is not exhaustive, but it does contain the most egregious violations of the law in the late 20th and early 21st centuries. The lone exception dates to the early 20th century when Charles Ponzi was involved in a pyramid-type scam, an illegal practice that bears his name even today. When one hears the term "Ponzi scheme," it means large profits are promised to early investors but the money is never invested; profits are paid from the money of later investors. Eventually, the

TABLE 6.21
Ten Celebrity Criminals in American Business

Year	Name	Description of Criminal Activity/Resulting Punishment
1920	Charles Ponzi	Established the pyramid-style scam by promising investors 50% or better profit, then paying them off with money from new investors; ruined 5 banks; sentenced to 5 years in prison and then another 7 on a related scam; deported upon release and died poor in South America.
1969	Frank W. Abagnale	Con man, forger, swindler famous for passing bad checks; made more than $2.5 million; served less than 5 years and was released in 1974 to become a government contact in fraud and scam cases.
1987	Barry Minkow	Ran an apparently successful carpet-cleaning empire, but company collapsed due to financial fraud; investors lost $100 million; sentenced to 25 years in prison where he was converted to Christianity and became a minister.
2002	Martin Frankel	Involved in insurance fraud, racketeering, and money laundering; famous for ripping off small-town insurance companies; collected $208 million; sentenced to 16 years in prison.
2003	James Lewis	Collected more than $311 million by swindling the elderly in California using a Ponzi scheme; used most of the money to fund his high lifestyle; sentenced to 30 years in prison.
2005	Bernie Ebbers	Cofounder of Worldcom; investors lost $11 billion due to false financial reporting; sentenced to 25 years in prison.
2005	Dennis Kozlowski	Former CEO of Tyco; convicted of misappropriation of more than $400 million of the company's money to support his lavish lifestyle; sentenced to 8 years, 4 months in prison.
2006	Kenneth Lay	Involved in fraud, corruption, and illegal bookkeeping as chairman of ENRON, an energy company; investors lost millions; company went bankrupt; died of a heart attack before he was sentenced for securities fraud.
2008	Lou Pearlman	Another Ponzi scheme artist; created "paper" companies and convinced high-profile people to invest in them; he pocketed the cash, valued at an estimated at $300 million; sentenced to 25 years in prison.
2009	Bernard Madoff	Used a Ponzi scheme to cheat more than a thousand investors, including some Hollywood stars, out of $65 billion; sentenced to 150 years in prison.

Adapted from http://business.rediff.com

practice collapses when money from new investors is insufficient to pay older investors. That's something of an oversimplification, but it serves our purpose here because more than a few business criminals have used it to enrich themselves; James Lewis in 2003 and Bernard Madoff in 2009 are good examples.

Celebrities and Controversial Issues

Most celebrities have never been shy about expressing their views on important social and political issues from time to time. Table 6.22 lists celebrities who have commented positively about,

TABLE 6.22
Celebrities Who Have Shown Support for Gay, Lesbian, and Transgender Causes

Name	Profession	Name	Profession
Brad Pitt	actor	Melissa Ethridge	singer
Madonna	singer; actress	Rosie O'Donnell	actress, comedienne
Elton John	singer; songwriter	Mary J. Blige	singer
Ben Affleck	actor	Jake Gyllenhaal	actor
Katherine Heigl	actress	Quincy Jones	musician; composer
Sharon Stone	actress	Janet Jackson	singer
Antonio Banderas	actor	Jennifer Aniston	actress
Cher	singer; actress	Rosario Dawson	actress; singer
Charlize Theron	actress	Liza Minnelli	singer; actress
Whoopi Goldberg	actress; TV host	Sigourney Weaver	actress
Pink	singer	Hillary Duff	actress
Gillian Anderson	actress	Debra Messing	actress
Megan Mullally	actress	Brittany Snow	actress
Roseanne Barr	actress; comedienne	Joan Jett	singer
Margaret Cho	comedienne	George Michael	singer
Anne Hathaway	actress	Hillary Clinton	politician
Jorja Fox	actress	Nathan Lane	actor
Alan Cumming	actor	Carmen Electra	actress; model
Cyndi Lauper	singer	Pauley Perrette	actress
Bridget Fonda	actress	Gus Van Sant	director
George Takei	actor	Barbra Streisand	singer; actress
David Hyde Pierce	actor	Rob Reiner	actor; director
Wanda Sykes	actress; comedienne	Lance Bass	singer; actor
Rose McGowan	actress	James Cromwell	actor
Patricia Clarkson	actress	Anjelica Huston	actress
Sean Penn	actor	Portia de Rossi	actress
Ellen DeGeneres	TV host	Samantha Ronson	disc jockey
Antonio Villaraigosa	politician	Bruce Cohen	producer

TABLE 6.23
Celebrities Who Have Spoken Out on Abortion

Name	Profession	Apparent Stand on Abortion
Matthew Broderick	actor	pro-choice
Margaret Colin	actress	pro-life
Jonathan Demme	director	pro-choice
Jane Fonda	actress; political activist	pro-choice
Joel Grey	actor	pro-choice
Mel Gibson	actor; producer; director	pro-life
Deborah Harry	singer	pro-choice
Patricia Heaton	actress	pro-life
Kathy Ireland	model	pro-life
Michelle Malkin	journalist	pro-life
Mary Stuart Masterson	actress	pro-choice
Kate Mulgrew	actress	pro-life
Sarah Jessica Parker	actress	pro-choice
Brooke Shields	actress	pro-life
Ron Silver	actor	pro-choice
Gloria Steinem	writer; editor	pro-choice
Blair Underwood	actor	pro-choice

made appearances on behalf of, or donated money to various gay, lesbian, and transgender causes. The list is not exhaustive; there are likely other celebrities who have similar views but are not mentioned. Remember, also, that views change. The table reflects celebrity opinion over the last several years. Their views may be different today.

The same subject-to-change qualifications apply to the celebrities presented in Table 6.23. Abortion has been a sensitive issue in America for several years. Strong opinions exist on both sides. Those who are pro-choice appear to outnumber those who are pro-life, but the table does not represent any scientific study of the issue among celebrities. The table does reflect the views of *some* celebrities who have spoken out forcefully on the issue.

America's war on terrorism, and specifically the War in Iraq, has generated much comment among celebrities. As Table 6.24 shows, more celebrities appear to be against the war effort than celebrities who support it. Remember the table does not list every celebrity who has an opinion on war. Nevertheless, entertainment celebrities appear to almost always reject war as a solution to political problems. During the administration of President George

TABLE 6.24
Celebrity Views on the War in Iraq/War on Terrorism

Support War in Iraq/On Terrorism

Robert Duvall	actor
Kelsey Grammer	actor
Jason Priestley	actor
Kid Rock	rapper
Ron Silver	actor
Fred Thompson	actor; former senator
Bruce Willis	actor

Do Not Support War in Iraq/On Terrorism

Robert Altman	director
Ed Asner	actor
Sandra Bernhard	actress; comedienne
David Clennon	actor
George Clooney	actor
Sheryl Crow	singer
Janeane Garofalo	actress
Danny Glover	actor
Woody Harrelson	actor
Avril Lavigne	singer
Spike Lee	actor; producer; director
Natalie Maines	singer
Dave Matthews	singer; musician
Michael Moore	filmmaker
Susan Sarandon	actress
Shakira	singer

W. Bush, 104 celebrities signed a letter to the president calling on him to reconsider declaring war on Iraq. The list of those who signed is not reprinted here, but may be viewed at www.celebrity-websites.com/celebritypetition.htm.

Celebrities and the Public

As noted earlier in this book, celebrity requires, among other things, a connection to the public. Ideally, a celebrity embodies the dreams and desires of the public and is highly visible in or on media. The public, however, does not play a passive role in this relationship. In the same way a celebrity must seek to maintain a high profile, the public must seek the latest information about celebrities, attend events featuring celebrities, or in some other way be engaged as a member of the celebrities' audience.

Table 6.25
Participation in Two Celebrity-Related Leisure Activities, 2008

		Rounded in Percent	
Category (number participating)		Movie Attendance	Sports Attendance
Gender:	Female (116,300,000)	54	27
	Male (108,500,000)	53	35
Age:	18–24 years (28,900,000)	74	37
	25–34 years (39,900,000)	65	37
	35–44 years (41,800,000)	60	37
	45–54 years (43,900,000)	53	31
	55–64 years (33,300,000)	46	26
	65–74 years (19,900,000)	32	18
	75 years & older (17,100,000)	19	10
Education:	Grade school (11,200,000)	17	07
	High school grad (68,300,000)	43	23
	Some college (61,400,000)	61	34
	College grad (41,300,000)	69	45
	Graduate school (20,500,000)	72	44

Adapted from U.S. Census Bureau's *2010 Statistical Abstract*.

Two Celebrity-Related Leisure Activities

Americans have many options when it comes to enjoying leisure time. Two of the most popular ways to relax and be entertained are the movies and sports events. Table 6.25 clearly indicates the widespread popularity of movies and sports. Many celebrities come from the movie or professional sports industries. In terms of the public, more males than females attend sports events, but about the same percentage of males and females attend movies. Both movie and sports attendance appear to be more popular among the young. However, the more education you have the more likely you are to attend movies or sports contests.

A closer look at attendance at sports events is more revealing. Table 6.26 shows attendance figures for some major sports events for the 1990–2008 period. During that time, the popularity of major league baseball has increased, particularly since 2000. Attendance at NCAA men's and women's basketball games increased markedly in 2004 and has held steady since. The National Hockey League has also shown increased attendance since 2000.

TABLE 6.26
Attendance at Selected Spectator Sports, 1990–2008

Sport	(in thousands)							
	1990	1995	2000	2004	2005	2006	2007	2008
Major League Baseball	55,512	51,288	74,339	74,822	76,286	77,524	80,803	79,975
NCAA Men's Basketball	28,741	28,548	29,025	30,761	30,569	30,940	32,836	33,396
NCAA Women's Basketball	2,777	4,962	8,698	10,016	9,940	9,903	10,878	11,121
National Hockey League	13,936	10,563	20,325	22.065	—	22,384	22.359	23,828

Adapted from U.S. Census Bureau's *2010 Statistical Almanac.*

TABLE 6.27
Selected Individual Expenditures for Recreation 1990–2007

Type of Purchase Activity	(rounded in billions of dollars)						
	1990	2000	2003	2004	2005	2006	2007
Books and maps	16	34	39	40	42	44	46
Magazines, newspapers, sheet music	22	35	36	39	42	45	49
Audio/video products, computers	53	116	123	133	142	154	161
Television/radio repair	3	4	4	5	5	5	5
Admission to spectator amusements	15	30	36	38	38	41	44

Adapted from U.S. Census Bureau's *2010 Statistical Abstract.*

Recreational Expenditures

Table 6.27 presents financial data relating to the public's expenses for other sorts of recreational activities. Celebrities can be found multiple places in the culture and the public appears willing to spend some money to follow their interests. Since 1990, the greatest growth has been in money spent on audio/video products and computers. This is not surprising, given the technological advancements of recent years. Since 2000, however, expenditures for items like books, maps, magazines, radio/TV repair, and the like have generally remained stable. Still, since figures in the table are reported in the billions of dollars, these expenditures represent significant activity.

Table 6.28 shows 2008 attendance and demographic information related to two other leisure time activities: music concerts and plays. In general, more people attended plays than concerts. Percentage wise, those who attended both plays and concerts were more often individuals with advanced education and greater

TABLE 6.28
Attendance and Demographics: Selected Arts Activities, 2008

Category	Adult Population	(in percent)	
		Jazz/Classical Concert	Plays (incl. musicals)
Gender:			
Male	108.5 million	16.2	22.6
Female	116.3 million	17.9	29.5
Age:			
18–14	28.9 million	14.2	22.7
25–34	39.9 million	14.7	25.2
35–44	41.8 million	16.1	27.1
45–54	43.9 million	20.0	26.1
55–64	33.3 million	21.3	31.8
65–74	19.9 million	18.3	29.0
75–plus	17.1 million	13.7	17.4
Race/Ethnicity:			
White	154.5 million	20.1	31.4
African American	25.6 million	12.9	14.1
Hispanic	30.4 million	7.7	12.4
Other	14.3 million	12.8	19.5
Education:			
Grade school	11.2 million	3.3	2.4
Some high school	22.1 million	4.7	8.0
High school grad	68.3 million	7.0	12.1
Some college	61.4 million	17.2	26.1
College grad	41.3 million	30.4	47.6
Grad school	20.5 million	44.5	62.2
Income:			
Less than $10,000	11.6 million	8.3	10.6
$10,000–19,999	19.3 million	7.5	10.0
$20,000–29,999	23.4 million	8.5	11.8
$30,000–39,999	22.6 million	13.9	17.7
$40,000–49,999	18.8 million	17.6	22.8
$50,000–74,999	40.7 million	17.1	24.0
$75,000–99,999	27.2 million	20.4	35.2
$100,000–149,999	21.4 million	28.2	46.1
$150,000 & over	16.0 million	38.2	64.3

Adapted from U. S. Census Bureau's *2010 Statistical Abstract.*

annual income. The age and gender distributions for these activities were fairly stable across all categories.

Internet Use

We get a lot of information about celebrities from the Internet, particularly the celebrities' own Web sites as well as the well-known

TABLE 6.29
Daily Internet Activities, Adults 18 and Older, November 2008–April 2009

Activity	(percent by age group)			
	18–29	30–49	50–64	65 & Older
Read/send e-mail	57	62	53	46
Use search engine	56	56	41	30
Get news	35	44	37	28
Watch a video	36	17	10	10
Use a social networking site	51	28	10	04
Send instant messages	20	12	04	03
Purchase a product online	09	08	07	06
Create or work on a blog	05	03	02	02
Rate a product, service, person	03	02	03	05
Download a podcast for later use	06	03	02	01

Survey sample size ranged from 2,254 in November 2008 to 2,253 in April 2009.
Adapted from U.S. Census Bureau's *2010 Statistical Abstract*, Pew Internet & American Life Survey

gossip Web sites. We are able to communicate with others using Internet social media; we can purchase products or watch a video online. Table 6.29 lists some daily Internet activities and reports on their use by individuals in various age groups. Reading and sending e-mail and using a search engine appeared to be the most popular Internet uses for the November 2008–April 2009 period among the more than 2,000 people polled. Social networking (Facebook, MySpace, and the like) was popular among those 18–29. Individuals 30–49 used the Internet to get news to a greater degree than any other age group.

Letters to Celebrities

For many celebrities, getting and reading fan mail is an enjoyable experience. Celebrities have almost always received letters, birthday cards, and the like from their adoring fans. For the most part, these communications are harmless. However, from time to time, celebrities receive some letters that are not only bizarre but also threatening. Table 6.30 presents excerpts from some letters to celebrities. To call these letters "bizarre" might be an understatement. The table shows letters with the wording exactly as received. It is obvious the writers have little concern for grammar, punctuation, and spelling. All four examples seem to suggest the writer feels he is important to the celebrity and that his suggestions or wishes will be seriously considered. Of course, nothing

TABLE 6.30
Bizarre Letters to Celebrities

Example: A middle-aged man wrote to a young singer:
I am afraid I made a mistake when I told you I was your father. Some guy showed me a picture of you and your father standing together when you got your award. I was so proud when I thought I was your pop. I guess that means my daughter aint your sister either . . . I asked your manager to borrow $10,000 I hope she lets me have it. Before I go I just want to say that the only reason I thought I was your pop was because I used to go with a person that looked like you. Love forever

Example: A man wrote to a female celebrity:
hello darling this is youre New friend . . . we will be soon together for our love honey. I will write and mail a lovely photo of myself okay. I will write to you Soon, have a lovely Easter time hoping to correspond. . . . here is a postcard for you . . . honey how are you doing . . . wishing to correspond with you Soon . . . hoping we do some camping and Barbecueing Soon okay.

Example: A woman sent a Christmas card to an actor:
I know that Jason is my beautiful baby and that [you are] the daddy. I never been in love and I always been a queen . . . I don't know much of anything other than the fact that I love my son and [you] very much. I don't know very much about life I was never told about life or how to love or be loved . . . I know I don't deserve a man like [you] . . . come get Jason and take him Home with you and the boys.

Thanks, love, . . .

Example: A young man wrote to an actress:
. . . I hate to trouble you with my problems, but I have a few. You see, I'm being harassed by this wall that . . . controls [most of the state]. Myself, I am a *cat*, yes really. Believe it or not, this wall is trying to frame me and put me in jail. You see I'm just a helpless image, and I control more than one wall. Nine I think. Please get in touch with me, because I know who L-7 is.

Sincerely	Tommy, alias — the LINE	
	P. S. I am Round	
	But I don't know how long	
	I can last. — H.E.L.P	

could be further from the truth. It is difficult to see how any of the four writers could be considered as having a grasp on reality. For example, no one with a firm understanding of the real world would ask for or expect to get $10,000 from a singer's manager. Another writer thinks he is a cat. That's bad enough, but he also thinks he knows who L-7 is. These letter writers don't appear to be evil, just out of touch with real life.

Some researchers have studied the sorts of communications and items sent to celebrities. The results of one such research project are presented in Table 6.31. This table categorizes the objects sent to celebrities. One has to wonder whether those who

TABLE 6.31
Enclosures Sent to Hollywood Celebrities

Enclosure	N (%)
Subject's creative efforts*	50 (23)
Photograph of subject	38 (18)
Other apparently homemade photographs**	22 (10)
Bizarre materials***	18 (08)
Religious or mystical materials	14 (07)
Media clippings and photographs	13 (06)
Commercial pictures****	13 (06)
Valuables and commercial materials	12 (06)
Business cards	17 (08)
Other business-like enclosures*****	24 (11)
Other	41 (20)

* includes drawings, poems, tape recordings, and literary works
** includes only those that could have been taken by the subject; excludes photographs of the subject or the celebrity
*** includes biological materials (blood, semen, hair, coyote head), personal documents (Social Security card, driver's license, birth certificate), drugs, pebbles, dirt, seeds, and similar objects
**** includes commercial drawings, stickers, seals
***** includes literature explaining businesses and self-addressed replies

Reprinted, with permission, from *The Journal of Forensic Sciences* 36(1), January 1991, Copyright ASTM International, 100 Barr Harbor Drive, West Conshohocken, PA 19428, www.astm.org.

mailed poems, blood, semen, dirt, seeds, and the like to celebrities expected the celebrities to do something with the objects. Did the writers think this was the way to establish a connection with the celebrity? It seems those who enclosed items, like those who wrote the letters in Table 6.30, were not in touch with the real world, or at least had a warped sense of how reality works. Table 6.32 lists specific items some fans sent celebrities.

One again has to wonder what use the fans expected celebrities to make of the items sent. Why would you send a pencil to a celebrity? A half-eaten candy bar? A bed pan? A shampoo coupon? It is beyond the ability of most of us to understand what they were thinking when they stuffed these (and other useless items) in a letter or package and sent it to their favorite celebrity. However, threats are the most troubling of all the things sent to celebrities. Table 6.33 presents the precise wording of eight threats celebrities received. Researchers found many more, of course, but the eight found in Table 6.33 are typical. One person writes, "I am not a nut." Most people reading the first part of that communication might disagree: "I realize that you aren't going to come

TABLE 6.32
Specific Items Sent to Celebrities

dog teeth	2 sleeping pills	a bed pan
a syringe of dried blood	animal feces	a toy submarine
a facsimile bomb	2150 A.D. (a science fiction novel)	a disposable lighter
a driver's license	U.S. currency	a half-eaten candy bar
a tape of the subject speaking to the celebrity in a halting manner with music in the background	5 one-cent stamps	a disposable razor
copies of Texas Monthly magazine		
57 Ohio State lottery tickets	a pad of blank paper	a motorcycle
8 tubes of red lipstick from various manufacturers	a pack of cigarettes	a deposit slip and three personal checks—one made out to the celebrity for $1.00; 2 blank
3 ballpoint pens	a small stone	a pencil
A Rubik's Cube key chain	4 $100 bills of play money	a shampoo coupon
6 comic books	3 playing cards	blood-smeared paper
a map of the subject's home town	a photograph of the celebrity's home	25 drawings and water color paintings, mostly of faces or eyes
a tape of the subject singing along with a record, interspersed with comments to the celebrity	medical photographs of corpses with the celebrity's face pasted on the corpses' torsos	a book inscribed to the celebrity: "I'm still stuck on you . . . Still believe I'm your Husband!!!"

Reprinted, with permission, from *The Journal of Forensic Sciences* 36(1), January 1991, Copyright ASTM International, 100 Barr Harbor Drive, West Conshohocken, PA 19428, www.astm.org.

TABLE 6.33
Threats Made in Letters to Celebrities

- I don't know what else to tell you. I've warned you. Repent and accept Christ before the hour of God's Wrath upon the world arrives. It will be a Holocaust like the world has never seen.
- You better not get your hair cut because if you do—Jupiter will collide with Mars.
- I feel that you are in danger with you new boyfriend . . . if he has brown eyes. I lost my only brother whom was married to a brown eyed girl.
- May the veins in your legs get darker, bluer, and uglier; and bigger; and hideous—like your repulsive body.
- Write that letter to me God Damn It or else I'll have you all fornicating with Ubangies before I'm through with you—and I mean it!!
- My People are out to kill all Gays & Lesbian Women all over the world all Gay men who Do Not Work In Show Bussiness & also Lesbian Women who Do Not Work In Show Bussiness will also Be Killed.
- I realize that you aren't going to come looking for me. So, I'm going to have to go looking for you. Please don't be frightened. I am not a nut.
- I saw your movie you looked at me at the last of the picture, now I am going to do something else with my time. This was not in this letter last time! You will see.

Reprinted, with permission, from *The Journal of Forensic Sciences* 36(1), January 1991, Copyright ASTM International, 100 Barr Harbor Drive, West Conshohocken, PA 19428, www.astm.org.

looking for me. So, I'm going to have to go looking for you." That seems pretty nutty. It suggests the individual is a stalker. That sort of behavior is clearly illegal and dangerous. Another writer wants to kill all the gays and lesbians in show business. That, too, is both illegal and dangerous, not to mention immoral.

Thus, it is obvious not all celebrity followers are well-meaning, rational individuals, although most are. It is those who appear to be out-of-touch with reality and those who clearly wish to do a celebrity harm who cause the most concern.

7

Directory of Celebrity Organizations and Web Sites

There are many organizations, associations, and agencies connected in some way to celebrities. This chapter presents brief profiles of some of the better-known ones. Celebrity-sponsored charities are presented first. These are listed in alphabetical order by a celebrity's last name if the name appears as part of the charity's official name. If the charity has some other name, the organization takes its alphabetical place among all the others. The second section profiles charities with celebrity affiliations, that is, celebrity volunteers or spokespersons; none of these carries a celebrity's name; they are also listed alphabetically. A description of important and well-known professional organizations and associations follows in the third chapter section. For-profit organizations with celebrity connections are presented in the fourth chapter section. Speakers' bureaus and celebrity look-alike companies follow in the fifth and sixth sections. It is, however, the seventh section—celebrity news and gossip Web sites—that many readers will find most useful if they are interested in specific, current celebrity information and photos. The final section in this chapter suggests ways a reader can go about accessing information about a specific celebrity. A Web site address is provided for each profiled organization in this chapter. Individuals who wish specific contact information such as e-mail addresses, telephone numbers, or postal mailing addresses can usually get that information by logging on to the Web site and clicking on the "contact us" button.

Celebrity-Sponsored Charities

The charities in this section usually bear the name of the sponsoring celebrity. The celebrity appears to be quite active in the on-going work of the charity. Having a charity carry the name of a famous, well-known individual is often an important way to gain attention and attract resources.

Lance Armstrong Foundation

http://www.livestrong.org

Tour de France bicycle race champion Lance Armstrong developed testicular cancer at the height of his career. Untreated, the cancer spread to other locations in his body. Armstrong, however, decided to be a survivor, not a victim. He undertook a strong program of physical conditioning and medical treatment. This aggressive approach enabled him to beat the disease. The Lance Armstrong Foundation was founded in 1997 by Armstrong, well before he knew he would survive the disease. The foundation seeks to inspire and empower people with cancer. It provides practical information and tools people living with cancer need to fight their disease. Like Armstrong, the foundation believes strength, knowledge, and attitude are of primary importance in fighting cancer. The foundation emphasizes prevention, of course, but has been quite successful in giving people access to screening and care and in funding cancer research.

Children's Health Fund

http://www.childrenshealthfund.org

Celebrity singer-songwriter Paul Simon and pediatrician Irwin Redlener established the Children's Health Fund in 1987. Its purpose is to provide health care to America's most underserved children. This may involve primary medical care, responses to public health crises, or educational programs. One of the fund's first efforts was to launch the New York Children's Health Project, a state-of-the-art mobile medical clinic that brought medical care directly to children who had no other way to get care. Down through the years, the fund has replicated this program across the country. Each program is affiliated with a local health institution and delivers medical care through mobile medical clinics. Since it began, the national network of mobile clinics has served more than 200,000 children, all underserved and many in disadvantaged rural and urban communities. The fund has a number of celebrity supporters, including singer-songwriters Billy Joel and Bruce Springsteen, *American Idol*'s Simon Cowell, actor-comedian Robin Williams, and former Secretary of State Colin Powell, among others.

William J. Clinton Foundation

http://www.clintonfoundation.org

The William J. Clinton Foundation is interested in issues requiring significant and immediate action. The foundation is worldwide in scope and emphasizes solutions to problems, especially solutions with measurable results. Founded by President Bill Clinton after he left office, the foundation's primary purpose is to act in ways that make a significant difference in the lives of people around the world. The foundation is particularly interested in issues such as global climate change, health among peoples in the developing world, and economic development in Third World Countries. The foundation is composed of seven initiatives ranging from the Alliance for a Healthier Generation to the Clinton HIV/AIDS Initiative.

The Michael J. Fox Foundation for Parkinson's Research

http://www.michaeljfox.org

The Michael J. Fox Foundation's main purpose is finding a cure for Parkinson's disease. Celebrity actor Michael J. Fox has the disease and devotes considerable time to raising money for his foundation. He has testified before Congress in an attempt to raise awareness and generate financial support for more research. The foundation funds a research agenda that focuses not only on finding a cure but also on improving life for those living with Parkinson's. TeamFox encourages individuals and organizations to sponsor fundraising events by holding breakfasts, marathons, bicycle competitions, and the like to benefit Parkinson's research.

The Hole in the Wall Gang Camp

http://holeinthewallgang.org

Actor Paul Newman founded The Hole in the Wall Gang Camp in 1988. The camp was named for the secret hideout in Newman's film *Butch Cassidy and the Sundance Kid*. It has been serving seriously ill children for more than 20 years. It provides year-around programs, but the summer camp experience is the most popular. The summer camp often serves more than 1,000 children, stressing safety, respect, and love and engaging children in a variety of activities, including archery, swimming, boating, fishing, horseback riding, sports, and arts and crafts, among others. The events are managed so that every child experiences success. One camper summed it up pretty well saying, "I love it here. Sometimes you think being so sick gives you limits, but the camp helps you try everything." Weekend programs during the fall and spring serve another 3,000 seriously ill children. Under its Hospital Outreach Program, the camp provides services to more than 10,000 children in major hospitals from New York to Boston. The program has many friends and supporters and provides all its services free of charge.

The Elton John AIDS Foundation

http://www.ejaf.org

Established in 1992 by celebrity singer-songwriter-musician Elton John, the Elton John AIDS Foundation has two separate grant-awarding offices: the United States office is in New York City; the United Kingdom office is in London. The mission of these two offices, however, is the same—to support important HIV prevention programs and to provide direct care and support services for people living with HIV/AIDS. Together, the two offices have raised more than $175 million to support projects in 55 countries around the world. The United States office emphasizes projects in the Americas and the Caribbean, while the United Kingdom office focuses on programs in Africa, Asia, and Europe.

The Larry King Cardiac Foundation

http://www.lkcf.org

The Larry King Cardiac Foundation (LKCF) was established in 1988 to provide funding for individuals who would otherwise be unable to afford treatment for heart disease. These individuals usually have limited means or no insurance. In partnership with hospitals throughout the nation, the foundation works to ensure that proper medical attention is rendered and that doctors perform necessary surgery at no charge; however, hospitals are compensated for the materials used in the operating procedures. Named for television talk-show host Larry King, the foundation is funded primarily by the royalties from King's books, the honoraria from his speaking engagements, and from entertainment parties in major American cities. More than 60 million Americans suffer from heart disease; King is, of course, one of them. To assist him in the work of the foundation, King has recruited his celebrity friends who have had heart problems; they tell their stories in an effort to educate the public about this growing problem. The foundation also has the financial support of such well-known institutions as the Cleveland Clinic and the St. Jude Medical Foundation.

McCarty Cancer Foundation

http://mccartycancerfoundation,org

National Hockey League star Darren McCarty (of the Calgary Flames) established the McCarty Cancer Foundation in 1997 as a Father's Day gift to his father Craig who had been diagnosed with multiple myeloma a couple of years earlier. Craig died in 1999. The foundation is dedicated to raising awareness of multiple myeloma, improving the lives of those with the disease, and working to find a cure. It finances forward-looking research, particularly projects that show significant promise in finding a cure for cancer. The foundation's board of directors is advised by a panel of scientists and physicians who help guide the project's funding decisions.

New York Restoration Project

http://www.nyrp.org

Founded by actress-singer Bette Midler in 1995, the New York Restoration Project (NYRP) is a nonprofit organization whose purpose is to reclaim and restore New York's city parks, community gardens, and open space. In cooperation with the City of New York, NYRP is leading the effort—called MillionTreesNYC—to plant one million trees throughout the city's five boroughs by 2017. The project has a number of significant accomplishments.

Working with other organizations, NYRP has already planted thousands of trees, shrubs, and flowers in city parks and has removed almost 2,000 tons of garbage from the city's open space. Additionally, NYRP has saved more than 100 community gardens from commercial development and established a trust fund to ensure these gardens will always be available for public use. Other projects include the transformation of a Harlem dumping ground into a park and the development of environmental education programs.

The Christopher and Dana Reeve Foundation

http://www.christopherreeve.org

The Christopher and Dana Reeve Foundation is dedicated to curing spinal cord injury. Named for paralyzed actor Christopher Reeve and his wife Dana (both now deceased), the foundation funds aggressive research and works to improve the lives of people with paralysis. Through its Quality of Life program, the foundation awards grants to nonprofit organizations that provide important, caring service to paralyzed individuals. The foundation has a resource center that provides information and referral services. Charity Navigator, an online charity watchdog, (www.charitynavigator.org) gave the Christopher and Dana Reeve Foundation an overall rating of 2 out of 4 for its operating efficiency, somewhat lower than other charities performing similar types of work.

Rock Bottom Remainders

http://rockbottomremainders.com

The Rock Bottom Remainders is not a typical charity organization. Members of the group meet only once a year. The group is composed of well-known, celebrity authors who, together with a supporting entourage (including groupies), tour the country raising money for charitable causes. The group's members include Stephen King, Amy Tan, Dave Barry, and Ridley Pearson, among others. In 2010, The Rock Bottom Remainders raised money in Washington, New York, and Boston on behalf of Haiti earthquake relief and in Philadelphia in support of the Free Library of Philadelphia. America's Promise and Jumpstart, organizations working to improve the lives of children, have also received support from the group. The group's music is available on CD and Rock Bottom Remainder T-shirts are also available.

Charlize Theron Africa Outreach Project

http://www.charlizeafricaoutreach.org

Partnered with the Entertainment Industry Foundation, Academy Award–winning actress Charlize Theron has established the Charlize Theron Africa Outreach Project. Its goal is to improve the lives of poor children and their families in South Africa, especially those children and families suffering from HIV/AIDS. The project looks for unique, creative ways to raise funds for its work. In a recent promotion, TOMS Shoes joined the project to create a limited edition shoe for men and women. For every pair of these shoes purchased, TOMS donated a pair of shoes to a child in need. Ten thousand pairs of shoes were given to children living in remote parts of South Africa. The project has also created mobile health units that travel throughout South Africa providing educational information about health and social issues.

The Mike Utley Foundation

http://www.mikeutley.org

Former National Football League (NFL) offensive guard Mike Utley has founded the Mike Utley Foundation whose mission is to provide financial support for activities designed to improve functioning for individuals with spinal cord injuries. Utley, who played for the Detroit Lions, was paralyzed in an NFL game in 1991. As he was carried from the field, he gave his teammates and fans a "thumbs up" signal, a gesture that symbolized his fighting spirit; he believes those with spinal cord injuries can improve their quality of life and expand their full potential through rehabilitation, education, and a positive attitude. The Mike Utley Foundation supports research, patient and family assistance programs, rehabilitation and therapy equipment, and education programs.

The V Foundation for Cancer Research

http://www.jimmyv.org

Founded by North Carolina State basketball coach Jim Valvano and cable sports giant ESPN, the V Foundation for Cancer Research has raised more than $90 million, awarding cancer research grants in 38 states and the District of Columbia. As he battled cancer, Valvano often dreamed of a foundation that would further research into finding a cure for the disease. He decided to turn his dream into reality and recruited family and friends to lead an effort to eradicate the disease. The foundation's advisory board consists of some of the top physicians and research scientists in the country. Only projects with the most potential are funded. Nevertheless, the foundation has been successful in finding brilliant, young research-ers who have made progress in learning about the disease and find-ing ways to fight it. The foundation prides itself on spending 100 percent of all new cash donations on research and related projects. This wise financial management earned the foundation a rating of 4 out of 4 by Charity Navigator, the online charity watchdog. The foundation has received a four-star rating multiple times.

The Montel Williams MS Foundation

http://montelms.org

The Montel Williams MS Foundation was established to further the scientific study of multiple sclerosis (MS). It provides finan-cial assistance to certain organizations and institutions who are conducting innovative research. In addition, the foundation seeks to raise national awareness about multiple sclerosis and to work for an increase in research allocations from the federal govern-ment. More than $1.5 million in grants have been awarded. The foundation is named for television personality Montel Williams who has MS. When Williams was diagnosed with the disease, he said "it hit me like a brick. "I thought the diagnosis was a death sentence. I'd heard of multiple sclerosis, but I really didn't know what it was." Williams realized that, as host of a nationally syn-dicated television show, he had the platform to raise awareness and launch a fight against the disease. The foundation has made grants to research centers at Johns Hopkins, Yale University, and Harvard's Brigham and Women's Hospital, among others.

Oprah Winfrey's Angel Network

http://www.oprahsangelnetwork.org

Oprah's Angel Network has a simple mission: to encourage people to make a difference in the lives of others. The idea began in 1997 on *The Oprah Winfrey Show* when Oprah asked viewers to join her in helping improve the lives of others. One of the first efforts involved partnering with the Boys and Girls Clubs of America to raise money for 150 scholarships and build homes for the needy through Habitat for Humanity International. In all, the Angel Network has received more than $80 million in public donations and has built more than 55 schools in 12 countries. In one year alone, more than $1 million worth of school supplies and school clothes were given to poor children in South Africa. A number of subsidiary charities operate under the Oprah's Angel Network banner. These include Free the Children and OAmbassadors.

YUM-O!

http://www.yum-o.org

Celebrity chef Rachael Ray established Yum-O! in 2006. This nonprofit organization is designed to educate kids and their families about food and cooking. It also works to feed hungry American kids and provides education and scholarships in partnership with the National Restaurant Association Educational Foundation and the Alliance for a Healthier Generation. Ray believes that today's kids and their families are so active and busy they may not take the time (or even know how) to cook basic nutritious meals, settling instead for prepackaged food with low nutritional value. Yum-O! hopes to inspire kids and their parents to make better food choices. Another important function of the organization is the feeding of hungry children. A startling number of Americans go hungry each year and one in five of those is a child. In cooperation with Share our Strength, Yum-O! contributes to the fight against hunger and works to raise awareness of the problem.

Celebrity-Affiliated Charities

The charity organizations in this section are affiliated with one or more celebrities, but the celebrities were not the "founders." Celebrities often serve as honorary chairpersons or spokespersons for the charity and give generously of their time to support worthy causes.

Celebrities Fore Kids, Inc.

http://www.celebritiesforekids.org

Celebrities Fore Kids (CFK) is a specialized charity providing financial assistance to children with cancer and their families living on Florida's Treasure Coast. Established in 1997, CFK works closely with physicians, schools, hospitals, and pediatric care centers to offer financial, emotional, and social support. The organization's annual fundraiser is a golf tournament that draws a number of celebrities, most from the sports world. Celebrities who have participated in past events include baseball's Whitey Ford, Gary Carter, Jim Palmer, and Mike Schmidt, baseball umpire Paul Runge, hockey's Bobby Orr, and well-known world athlete Jim Thorpe.

Make-A-Wish Foundation

http://wish.org

The Make-A-Wish Foundation is well known for granting the wishes of children with life-threatening medical conditions. It seeks to enrich the lives of these children with hope, strength, and joy. Celebrities of one sort or another are often a part of a child's wish; the foundation has worked with many celebrities as well as members of the general public to make a child's wish come true. Established in 1980, the foundation has served more than 174,000 children around the world. The foundation utilizes a network of volunteers as wish granters, fundraisers, and special events workers.

Mickelson ExxonMobil Teachers Academy

http://mickelson.nsta.org

The Mickelson ExxonMobil Teachers Academy was established for teachers in grades three through five and is designed to assist teachers in providing learning experiences for children to advance their knowledge of math and science. As teachers gain content knowledge, they can couple this knowledge with innovative instructional strategies to better serve their students. The academy conducts one-week seminars around the country. Each seminar is highly structured for maximum impact. Teachers are given the opportunity to network with others as a way to improve both communication and instruction. The academy carries the name of professional golfer Phil Mickelson who provides some financial support. However, it is unclear whether Mickelson founded the academy, whether it was jointly decided upon by Mickelson and ExxonMobil, or whether it was ExxonMobil's idea. Regardless of how it began, the academy has drawn interest from elementary school teachers around the country. Mickelson's wife, Amy, produces a bimonthly blog in support of education and the academy.

National Stroke Foundation

http://www.stroke.org

Established in 1984, the National Stroke Foundation focuses all of its efforts on stroke. Its goal is to lower the incidence and impact of stroke by developing forward-thinking community outreach programs. It also emphasizes improving the care of stroke patients and educating both health care professionals and the general public about stroke, particularly prevention, symptom recognition, and treatment options. The National Stroke Association is not celebrity sponsored, but works with celebrities who support the mission. Often this support is financial, but publicity is important, too. Among the celebrities who have supported the association are actresses Marcia Cross, Courtney Cox, Eva Longoria, Felicity Huffman, and Nicollette Sheridan, guitarist Carlos Santana, and professional boxer Laila Ali, daughter of famed boxer Muhammad Ali.

Professional Organizations

Professional organizations serve the needs of individuals employed in a particular profession. Almost every area of work has a supporting professional organization. For example, teachers have the National Education Association, truckers have the Teamsters Union, scientists and engineers have the National Academy of Sciences, and so on. When it comes to celebrities, professional organizations in the entertainment field seem to dominate. This is not to say organizations do not exist for celebrities in politics, medicine, religion, and the like. They do. However, a typical member of the general public is more likely to have heard of organizations that support celebrities in the various entertainment fields. This section presents brief profiles of some professional organizations well known in the entertainment world. Membership lists for these organizations are closely guarded. Therefore, it is not possible to know the names of the celebrities who are members.

Academy of Motion Picture Arts and Sciences

http://www.oscars.org

The Academy of Motion Picture Arts and Sciences is the world's best-known professional movie organization. Its membership totals more than 6,000 individuals working in the film industry. In addition to its annual Oscar telecast (where outstanding performances and accomplishments are recognized), the organization sponsors education and research activities, supporting libraries, museums, and other outreach programs.

Academy of Television Arts and Sciences

http://www.emmys.org

The Academy of Television Arts and Sciences recognizes outstanding prime-time television programming. Twenty-six peer groups who have specific areas of expertise examine all areas of television work, both in front of and behind the cameras. Based in Los Angeles, the Academy awards Emmys for significant and important prime-time television programming. A related organization, the National Academy of Television Arts and Sciences, is based in New York and determines awards for daytime, news, and sports programming.

Actors Fund

http://www.actorsfund.org

Founded in 1882, the Actors Fund serves all performing professionals, including individuals in film, theater, television, music, opera, and dance. The organization works with more than 11,000 performing artists across the country. The fund understands that the life of a performer is unpredictable. Economic, political, and social concerns often rob performers of job security. Moving from job to job is not the easiest way to make a living. When problems arise, the fund can assist with financial support, health care, housing, and social services.

American Federation of Musicians of the United States and Canada

http://afm.org

The American Federation of Musicians of the United States and Canada is the largest organization in the world representing the interests of professional musicians. Services include negotiating agreements, protecting ownership of music, securing health care and pension benefits, as well as lobbying efforts.

American Federation of Television and Radio Artists (AFTRA)

http://aftra.org

AFTRA is a national labor union with a membership of more than 70,000 performers, journalists, and others working in the entertainment and news industries. The organization's reach is broad, drawing members from broadcast, public, and cable television, talk and variety shows, reality shows, children's programming, radio, sound recordings, Broadway shows, and Internet and digital programming. AFTRA negotiates and enforces more than 300 collective bargaining agreements that deal with a wide range of employment issues.

American Society of Composers, Authors and Publishers (ASCAP)

http://www.ascap.org

ASCAP claims more than 380,000 members who work primarily in the music industry. Individuals may be composers, songwriters, lyricists, or publishers. This performing rights organization assists its members in securing copyrights and performance royalties. Its members include Duke Ellington, George Gershwin, and Leonard Bernstein from the past and Dave Matthews, Stevie Wonder, Beyoncé, and Alan Jackson, among others, from the present.

Country Music Association (CMA)

http://www.countrymusic.org

The Country Music Association is dedicated to promoting country music worldwide. CMA's annual televised awards ceremony recognizes excellence in the country music industry. The organization publishes the CMA Directory, which contains contact information for a wide range of country music artists, promoters, agents, and other professionals. Membership is available only to those working in the country music industry.

International Society for the Performing Arts (ISPA)

http://www.ispa.org

ISPA is an international network of performing arts professionals whose goal is to strengthen the arts worldwide by stressing leadership and excellence. With a membership of more than 350 individuals and organizations, ISPA works in more than 40 countries around the world. The society believes that much can be accomplished by connecting with other cultures and by understanding the interconnectedness that exists among performers. The organization's goal is to provide the best possible support for cultural exchange resulting in positive outcomes for those involved.

National Academy of Recording Arts and Sciences

http://www2.grammy.com

The National Academy of Recording Arts and Sciences is often called The Recording Academy. It is best known for its televised Grammy awards ceremony where outstanding performances in music and recording are recognized. Awards are given for technical proficiency, artistic achievement, and overall excellence. The Academy's overall goal is to positively impact the lives of musicians, those who work throughout the industry, and those who enjoy music and musical performances.

Recording Industry Association of America (RIAA)

http://www.riaa.com

RIAA is a trade organization supporting and promoting the creative and financial health of the major music companies.

Membership includes companies whose music labels comprise about 85 percent of all legitimate music produced and sold in the United States. Protecting intellectual property and advocating First Amendment rights are two important functions of the association. Additionally, the organization funds research related to the music industry, as well as monitoring all laws, regulations, and policies relating to music. RIAA is responsible for certifying album sales as Gold, Platinum, Multi-Platinum, or Diamond.

Songwriters Hall of Fame

http://www.songwritershalloffame.org

The Songwriters Hall of Fame was established in 1969. It honors those whose songs are among the most recognized and most popular. The Hall believes music is the soundtrack of American life and that songwriters are part of the country's rich history. Each year songwriters are inducted into the Hall after being approved by membership vote. The list of those honored in the Hall is impressive: John Fogerty, Isaac Hayes, Carole King, Paul Simon, Bob Dylan, Billy Joel, Elton John, James Taylor, James Brown, Bruce Springsteen, Phil Collins, Van Morrison, and Dolly Parton, among others. The Hall is also involved in the development of programs to develop new songwriting talent through workshops, seminars, and scholarships. Its digital initiative has resulted in an online museum (www.songhall.org).

Multi-Service Organizations

The organizations profiled in this section are for-profit businesses that regularly recruit and employ celebrities to serve publicity or other client needs. The organizations usually provide a variety of other services for their clients; many services are related to media.

Burns Entertainment

http://www.burnsent.com

Burns Entertainment offers a variety of celebrity services, including advertising, public relations, and celebrity appearances at special events. The company is especially proud of its expertise in the sports world, providing sports celebrities for product endorsement or for participation in marketing campaigns. The company has recruited and worked with many celebrities, including Joe Montana, Jada Pinkett-Smith, Paula Abdul, Carmen Electra, Paris Hilton, Stevie Wonder, Madonna, and Cindy Crawford, among others.

Celebrity Connections

http://celebrityconnections.net

"How can we get our message out to the public?" This is a question many charities, social organizations, or community groups often ask. Celebrity Connections says it has the answer. A division of Tailored Marketing, Celebrity Connections was created to link advocacy groups or charity organizations with a commanding celebrity voice. Messages using celebrities often stand out in a world bombarded daily by thousands of media communications. The organization has used celebrities such as the NFL's Peyton Manning, PGA golfer Vijay Singh, and actress Julianne Moore, among others, to raise the visibility of and promote fundraising for its clients. Celebrity Connections offers a variety of creative services, including graphic design, copywriting, audio and video production, and Web development.

Celebrity Talent Agency

http://celebritytalentagency.com

Celebrity Talent Agency is an entertainment and talent organization providing a variety of entertainment activities, usually related to music. The company specializes in hip-hop, jazz, and R&B musician celebrities and has placed many throughout America and Europe. Over the years, the agency has worked with superstars such as Prince, Eddie Murphy, Grandmaster Flash, and Ice-T. The company is open to developing and promoting emerging artists.

Executive Vision, Inc.

http://www.executivevisions.com

Executive Vision, Inc. (EVI) produces corporate communication and brand-linked events. The company offers a variety of services including celebrity entertainment concerts and events, the staging of corporate meetings, product launchings, marketing consulting, and training/education programs. Celebrities often figure prominently in these activities. EVI emphasizes activities that inform, entertain, motivate, and sell products and services. Celebrities often appear in promotions for such clients as Coca-Cola, McDonalds, IBM, and Holiday Inn Worldwide, among others.

Speakers Bureaus

Need a celebrity speaker for your organization's annual conference or other event? Speakers Bureaus specialize in providing celebrity speakers for all sorts of events and special occasions. The organizations profiled in this section are for-profit companies that regularly recruit celebrities for special speaking engagements.

AEI Speakers Bureau

http://www.aeispeakers.com

AEI Speakers Bureau has recruited motivational and inspirational speakers from the world of sports, business, and politics. Their roster of celebrities also includes individuals who can speak on literature, popular culture, technology, and the media. The company accepts all types of clients, including corporations and nonprofit organizations as well as educational and civic groups. The goal is to provide an entertaining and inspiring speaker who is specific to a client's needs. The company has utilized celebrities such as Donald Trump, Olivia Newton-John, Jamie Lee Curtis, and Diahann Carroll, among others.

All-American Speakers Bureau and Celebrity Network

http://allamerianspeakers.com

The All-American Speakers Bureau and Celebrity Network maintains a database of speakers and high-profile talent from almost every walk of life. The company considers itself one of the premier professional bureaus and claims it has the most comprehensive list of celebrity speakers. Celebrities are often in highest demand as motivational and inspirational speakers, but the company also offers celebrities for autograph and book signings, cooking demonstrations, "meet and greets," and trade shows, among other events. All-American has placed celebrities such as Kareem Abdul-Jabbar, Hector Elizondo, Spike Lee, George Lopez, and Billie Jean King, among others, at various events.

The Allen Agency

http://www.speakerbooking.com

The Allen Agency provides professional speakers, celebrities, and entertainers for private parties, charity fundraising activities, and corporate events. The agency has arranged for celebrities such as Jay Leno, Naomi Judd, and Pat Riley to appear, speak, or entertain at events worldwide. Stressing client satisfaction, The Allen Agency is willing to work small events.

BigSpeak

http://www.bigspeak.com

Like almost all the other organizations of its type, BigSpeak offers celebrity motivational or keynote speakers for a variety of meetings and events. Some speakers serve as consultants or trainers and are dedicated to getting a positive response from employees, stockholders, or others in attendance at specified meetings. The company offers assistance in planning meetings as well as in providing speakers for the meetings. Lance Armstrong, Donald Trump, Deepak Chopra, and John Wooden are among the celebrities placed by the company at conventions, retreats, or other corporate events.

The Lighthouse Agency

http://www,lighthouseagency.co.uk

The Lighthouse Agency works with churches in Great Britain to organize and conduct special events. Speakers and entertainers are willing to share their Christian faith and to lead or participate in church breakfasts, conferences, evangelistic outreach, or special dinners. The agency is willing to work with all age groups, from children to senior citizens, and to participate in events for any specialized segment of a congregation. The agency's celebrities are likely to be well known to religious communities and organizations, but perhaps not so well known to the general public. The agency's roster includes Bill Legend, the drummer of the famous rock band T-Rex, as well as John Gaughan, a member of Herman's Hermits and a songwriter for The Drifters.

NOPACTalent

http://www.nopactalent.com

The National Organization of Professional Athletes and Celebrities Talent Agency (NOPACTalent) was founded in 1998 and specializes in booking celebrity sports figures, but books entertainers and musicians, too. The agency claims access to more than 15,000 celebrities. Celebrities often serve as motivational speakers, product endorsers, or VIPs for "meet and greet." Celebrities come from every area of sports. Stand-up comedians, celebrity chefs, famous models, journalists, authors, politicians, and reality TV stars are popular choices for celebrity appearances. Sports celebrities Isiah Thomas, Jason Elam, and Darrell Green are joined by actors Billy Crystal and Joe Pesci, and by entertainers Patti LaBelle, Sister Sledge, and Mark Knopfler on the agency's roster.

Millionaire's Concierge

http://millionairesconcierge.com

Millionaire's Concierge offers an "individual" experience with a celebrity. Advertising "celebrities for hire," the company can provide a celebrity for a special event or simply for an individual experience. Dinner with actor Woody Harrelson? Boating with pro wrestler Hulk Hogan? Comedians Chris Rock and Roseanne as well as the Beach Boys, blink-182, and Julio Iglesias are also apparently available. The company does not reveal much on its Web site, noting that "some celebrity names cannot be displayed for security reasons." The Web site does, however, provide a reservation form and an e-mail address, but stresses it wants "serious inquiries only."

Celebrity Look-Alikes

Event planners for charity fundraisers, corporate meetings, annual conventions, and the like are often unable to afford bringing a real celebrity to their special event. Sometimes they must settle for the next best thing: a celebrity impersonator or a celebrity look-alike. The companies profiled in this section make these types of individuals available for less money than it would take to bring in a real celebrity.

Celebrity Management

http://www.celebritymgr.com

Celebrity Management provides celebrity look-alikes and celebrity impersonators for clients throughout the United States and abroad. The company claims its talent is among the best in the industry. Experience, reliability, and professionalism are company trademarks. Celebrity look-alikes available include Barbra Streisand, Cher, Dolly Parton, Elton John, Frank Sinatra, and George W. Bush, among others.

Lookalike-USA

http://lookalikes-usa.com

Lookalike-USA is a full-service entertainment company, specializing in celebrity look-alikes, impersonators, and doubles. The company also offers professional disc jockeys, models, musicians, and other services. With more than 900 look-alikes, doubles, and impersonators available, the company believes it has the personnel to meet any need. Conventions, trade shows, and commercial placement are popular venues for the company's talent. Look-alikes are available for celebrities such as Sarah Palin, Hillary Clinton, John McCain, Johnny Depp, Paris Hilton, Tom Cruise, Angelina Jolie, Al Gore, and even fictional superspy James Bond. The company has placed talent in the United States, Europe, Asia, Australia, South America, and Canada.

Talent Plan, LLC

http://www.lookalikes.net

Talent Plan, LLC is the parent company of Mulligan Management. Mulligan Management was established in 1987 by Brian Mulligan, who is an internationally recognized Charlie Chaplin impersonator. The company says it is the country's leading look-alike talent management agency. The company provides talent and production assistance to a variety of corporations, including such well-known companies as IBM, Toshiba, Disney, and Warner Brothers, among others. The company's impersonators have appeared in advertising for *Esquire* magazine, Cherokee Clothing, and Chanel fragrances. In 2005, the company expanded services to include musicians, bands, comedians, and other specialty acts.

Celebrity News and Gossip Web Sites

Web sites specializing in celebrity news, information, and other items of celebrity interest are briefly profiled in this section. In many cases, visitors to these Web sites can get some information free, but to get in-depth information, special photos, interviews, and access to chat rooms or discussion forums, visitors usually must register with the Web site. In some cases, a subscription is necessary to access special or unusual features. One does not usually think of Web sites as organizations; however, in a world where social media have an increasing influence, celebrity Web sites are essentially "electronic, virtual-world organizations."

Absolute Celebrities

http://www.absolutecelebrities.com

Celebrity news and photos are featured on this Web site. Links are provided to celebrity photo galleries. Two of the most interesting links will send users to information on celebrity heights and celebrity mug shots.

Access Hollywood

http://accesshollywood.com

The Top 5 celebrity news stories of the day lead on this Web site's home page. Other celebrity news and photos are also available. Celebrity fashion information, television, and music links are provided.

Anything Hollywood

http://anythinghollywood.com

The usual mixture of celebrity news, photos, and gossip is available on this Web site. The site provides dozens of celebrity bios and links to "blogs we like."

Ayyyy

http://ayyyy.com

This Web site says it is "where fashion and celebrity collide." Admitting that its purpose is "gently making fun of the famous," this site does, in fact, poke fun at celebrities and their clothing choices. There are links to information and photos on dozens of celebrities. The site appears to be sponsored by Manolo Blanhnik footwear. The Manolo name is everywhere on the site; the site's publisher is listed as "Manolo the Shoeblogger."

Celebrities Zone

http://www.celebritieszone.com

This Web site contains photos of the "hottest" celebrities (all women). A user can browse by category, such as actors, musicians, athletes, models, and so forth. This Web site does not emphasize celebrity news or other bits of celebrity information.

Celebrity Café

http://thecelebritycafe.com

This is a typical Web site offering celebrity news, photos, and information on music, movies, travel, and contests. The site reviews music, television programs, and books relating to celebrities.

Celebrity-Gossip

http://www.celebrity-gossip.net

This Web site says it has the "hottest" celebrity news stories and photos. Information on celebrity videos, awards, signings, couples, scandals, television, and music, weddings, pregnancies, and fashion is available.

Celebrity Palace

http://www.celebritypalace.com

Brief profiles of celebrities past and present appear on this Web site. There are few photos; however, links are provided to celebrity news, gossip, jokes, and the like.

Celebrity Wallpaper

http://www.go4celebrity.com

Free celebrity wallpapers are available from this Web site. All the celebrities are female and listed alphabetically by first name.

Celebrity Wonder

http://www.celebritywonder.com

This Web site appears to emphasize celebrities and the movies. Celebrity news and photos are provided and so are celebrity videos and movie trailers. Links take users to photo galleries, wallpaper, and games.

Celebuzz

http://www.celebuzz.com

This site contains celebrity news and photos and is packed with links to other stories, photos, and gossip. Photos and features appear to number in the hundreds. Movie information is available. User comments are frequently displayed.

dlisted

http://www.dlisted.com

This Web site warns users to "be very afraid." That's probably because the celebrity photos here are less appealing than those on other sites. Not all celebrities have beautiful moments, as some of the photos on this site clearly show. There are links to other celebrity sites, discussion forums, and sites where dlisted merchandise may be purchased.

E!

http://www.eonline.com

Celebrity news, photos, and videos populate this Web site's home page. It provides links to celebrity-award events and programs as well as information about celebrities and the latest movies. A user can access a directory of E! television shows or access celebrity message boards.

Gabby Babble

http://gabbybabble.celebuzz.com

This Web site contains the latest celebrity news, photos, and gossip. The site proclaims, "We've got the juicy juice." The site is fond of labeling its information. For example, a user will find "babblicious pictures" of celebrities and "babblicious comments" about them. There's the "Gabber Quote of the Day." Links are provided to dozens of "gabber categories," such as actors, arrests, and so on. However, some information and many photos are archival in nature, that is to say, out-of-date, in some of the categories.

Gawker

http://gawker.com

The latest celebrity news and photos can be found on this Web site's home page. Links are available to other celebrity information sites, including Deadspin (sports), Kotaku (gaming), Jezebel (women and fashion), io9 (the future), and Lifehacker (tips for getting things done). Other unique sites that can be accessed from gawker.com include Jalopnik (automobiles) and Gizmodo (gadgets).

Hollyscoop

http://www.hollyscoop.com

The word *scoop* in this Web site's name suggests it has information or features others do not. However, the Web site is not particularly unique. Like many of the others, it provides celebrity news and photos, celebrity videos and photo galleries, and current information on movies, music, television, and fashion.

Hollywood.com

http://www.hollywood.com

This Web site is all about movies and the celebrities who star in them. The site was rated a "Top 10 Film Site" by the *London Times*. Photo galleries of film stars are available as well as movie trailers. Links are provided to some fan sites.

Hollywood Gossip

http://www.thehollywoodgossip.com

This Web site is typical of many. The latest celebrity news is provided in addition to celebrity photos and videos. Information on celebrity scandals, hairstyles, fashion, and babies is available.

Lemondrop

http://www.lemondrop.com

This Web site says it is "sweet, tasty, tart." The content here is generally about sex and relationships and appears to be mostly of interest to women. There are few photos. Hot features include dating/love, dudes, animals, booze, humor, and weird news.

Maxim

http://www.maxim.com

This Web site appears to be designed primarily for men. There are lots of scantily clad girls on this site; a few of them are celebrities, but most appear to be celebrity wannabees. A section named "Hometown Hotties" allows a user to browse photos of girls by city and state. Links are provided for information on the best places to meet women, as well as information on games, sports, movies, music, and television.

Omg!

http://www.omg.yahoo.com

This Web site delivers celebrity news, the latest celebrity photos, and some celebrity videos. A search box enables a user to look for information on a specific celebrity. Links are provided to celebrity blogs.

People

http://www.people.com

This Web site appears to be an online version of *People* magazine. The home page features a "top story," as well as celebrity news, photos, and videos. A visitor can find information on celebrity babies, television stars, and the latest fashions. A user can access new "games" and get a free trial play, but the connection of the games to celebrities is unclear. *People* magazine archives may also be accessed from this Web site.

PerezHilton

http://perezhilton.com

This Web site features celebrity news and photos. The home page requires a user to move through several screens to see all the information. Most stories on the site lack a date; therefore, a reader can never be sure if a story is current or out-of-date. It is a popular Web site, perhaps because some of the information presented is quite detailed.

PopCrunch

http://popcrunch.com

There is some celebrity news and information on this Web site, but its primary focus is on celebrity photos. Dozens of celebrity photo galleries are available. A user can page through numerous celebrity photos, some of which date back several years.

PopEater

http://www.popeater.com

This Web site's home page presents the latest celebrity news and photos. A user can access celebrity information relating to movies, television, music, and videos. An unusual feature provides information on how to get a PopEater iPhone or iPad app. Another special feature delivers the latest Latino celebrity news and photos. This Web site is one of the few (and maybe the only one) to provide pictures and information about the site's editorial staff.

Pop on the Pop

http://poponthepop.com

This site provides the usual celebrity news and photos, together with user comment. Links are available to celebrity videos, as well as information about and photos of celebrities who are not currently in the news, but who are well-known and of continuing interest. A link to "Exclusives" takes a user to special celebrity news and information, some of which may include celebrity interviews.

PopSugar

http://popsugar.com

This Web site advertises itself as "insanely addictive." In addition to the latest celebrity news and photos, the site provides information on fashion, home décor, health, food, money, technology, pets, and games. However, very little of the information is connected to celebrities. Once a user gets past the home page, the information is rarely tied to a specific celebrity.

Radar

http://www.radaronline.com

The usual celebrity news and photos are available on this Web site. Special features include pop culture information, beauty tips, fashion tips, and giveaways (free merchandise and event tickets). Links provided to Popeater, Huff Post, and other celebrity sites.

Socialite Life

http://socialitelife.celebuzz.com

"Gossip is served" on this Web site. There is some celebrity news and a few photos, but the information on the site is heavy on gossip (as promised). Users can explore dozens of celebrity categories (A to Z) ranging, for example, from Adam Lambert to Zac Efron.

Starlink

http://starlink.com

There is nothing fancy about this Web site. Its home page is simply a list of celebrities, presented alphabetically by first name. Clicking on a celebrity name will send a user to another Web site (www.the-alist.org). There a user will find the celebrity's photo as well as news and other information relating to the celebrity.

Star Pages

http://starpages.net

Celebrity news is featured here. Links are provided to celebrity Web sites by category (actors, actresses, impressionists, dancers, and so on). A user can link to Web sites offering merchandise and tickets to concerts or sports events.

Starpulse

http://www.starpulse.com

This Web site is similar to many others, offering celebrity news and photos on the home page, as well as celebrity information from music, movies, and television. Links are provided to sites offering ringtones, celebrity event tickets, shopping, contests, and chat rooms. This site also has links to other celebrity Web sites, including Popeater, Fark, and the Frisky.

SuperiorPics

http://www.superiorpics.com

This Web site specializes in celebrity photos. Celebrity news and some videos are also available. Visitors to this site can register and enter one of several discussion forums, most relating in some way to celebrities.

Teen Hollywood

http://www.teenhollywood.com

Although apparently for teens, this Web site differs little from some of the others in terms of its home page. Celebrity news and photos are presented. Movie news, celebrity videos, and information on contests and horoscopes are available. However, clicking on the "profiles" button will send a user to a Web site where teens are allowed to establish a profile (and photo) of themselves. Other teens may sign up as "friends" of those profiled.

theFrisky

http://thefrisky.com

This Web site says it's about "love, life, stars, style." A user will find the latest celebrity news and a few photos here as well as a smattering of world and national news. The site identifies what it considers to be "hot" in the celebrity world and provides information on relationships, sex, and movies.

The Popeye

http://thepopeye.blogspsot.com

This Web site describes itself as "steaming plates of useless junk . . . served daily." The news here tends to be a bit bizarre and often titillating. News from the television program *American Idol* seems to dominate the site, but there are links to other celebrity gossip sites. There is little reason for a user to disagree with the site's description of itself.

The Superficial

http://www.thesuperficial.com

This Web site is somewhat different from many of the others. There is little news on this site, but plenty of photos—many of them somewhat revealing. The language is less restrained on this site than elsewhere. Links are provided to the latest celebrity gossip and to current movies.

The Wrap

http://thewrap.com

Touting itself as a site that provides "entertainment industry analysis" and "breaking Hollywood news," this site won the

LA Press Club's National Entertainment Journalism Award for Online News in 2009. On the home page a user will find links to as many as 20 news stories, most with photos. Movie and television news and information is provided. Links are available to the blogs of some Hollywood personalities, but few of them appear to be well known outside the movie-television industry.

TMZ

http://www.tmz.com

TMZ is one of the most popular Web sites. It is known for breaking celebrity news, in most cases before the television and cable news networks report the story. The death of Michael Jackson in 2009 is a good example. TMZ had information well before any of the other news outlets. The Web site prides itself on its investigative journalism, particularly when it comes to celebrities. The Web site has lots of information—the home page usually requires a user to move through several screens. The site provides photos, videos, celebrity sports news, celebrity games, and clips from TMZ's syndicated celebrity television program.

US

http://www.usmagazine.com

This Web site appears to be related to *US Magazine*. A user will find the latest celebrity news and photos, along with information on style and beauty. Celebrity moms and their babies may be seen. Information is also available on movies, television, and music. Some celebrities offer lifestyle tips. A celebrity directory allows a user to browse all the celebrities available on the Web site.

Wonderwall

http://www.wonderwall.msn.com

This Web site provides entertainment news and photos. There are links to sports, financial matters, and other topics; however, these links usually lead to other MSN Web sites that have news of general interest and importance, but which may or may not have news, information, or photos about celebrities.

Your Tango

http://www.yourtango.com

"Smart talk about love" can be found on this Web site. There is, indeed, much talk about love here, but whether the information is smart depends on one's point of view. Celebrity news and photos are available, but much space is given to tips about relationships, dating, and the like. Links are provided to other celebrity news Web sites and blogs.

Connections to Celebrity Fan Clubs and Web Sites

Some people may want to avoid celebrity news and gossip Web sites in favor of a celebrity's own personal Web site. Finding that site may not be as easy as one might think. Some celebrities prefer Facebook interactions; others have an official Web site. This section should help a user searching for information directly connected to a celebrity.

A General Approach

Fans using a general search engine such as Google or Bing to find a celebrity's Web site will likely be disappointed with the search results. General searches do not lead directly—or quickly—to celebrity Web sites or fan clubs. A few Web sites offer tips and links to a limited number of celebrities. For example, Fan Source (http://fansource.com) has a short list of celebrity mailing addresses and fan club information. The list contains older celebrities such as Ann-Margaret, Barbara Eden, and Lindsay Wagner. The addresses provided are mostly post office boxes. Another Web site (http://picturetrail.com) invites users to join existing fan clubs or create their own. An assortment of fan clubs is listed, but most have fewer than 200 members. A general search will also yield Web sites providing information about celebrities in other countries such as India or Australia. A number of Web sites that turn up in a general search sell celebrity merchandise of one sort or another.

A Specific Approach

Taking a more specific approach to finding celebrity fan clubs and Web sites is not without problems. Celebrity Base (http://celebritybase.net) provides a celebrity search engine some users might find useful. Enter a celebrity's name in the search box, click on the "search" button, and you may or may not get information. The database's coverage of celebrity sites is spotty. For example, inquiries about Megan Fox, Angelina Jolie, and Lady Gaga returned no results. However, inquiries about Jennifer Lopez, Tom Cruise, and Brad Pitt did return results. Unfortunately, results are often little more than links to celebrity bios, movie trailers, photos, and the like. An occasional fan club or official celebrity Web site will appear, but not often.

Much the same thing can be said of the Big Celebrity Directory (http://www.bigcelebritydirectory.com). Hundreds of celebrities are listed alphabetically, each linking a user to information. Fan club and Web site information is rare. More often, the information is general. Moreover, many of the celebrities listed have been dead many years. Can Fatty Arbuckle or Bing Crosby still be considered celebrities? Arbuckle, a silent film actor and comedian, died in 1933. Crosby, a singer and actor, died in 1977. Few "modern" celebrities are listed in the big celebrity directory. However, links are provided to a variety of other celebrity information sites, ranging from celebrity icons to celebrity trivia.

Celebrity watchers may find Celebrity Websites (http://websites.celebritypro.com) more informative. The main celebrity Web sites directory asks a user to first select a celebrity's profession (actor, actress, band, model, singer, athlete, and the like). Clicking on the profession link will result in an alphabetized list (by first name) of celebrities in that profession. Click again on a specific celebrity name and the information appears. Touted as the celebrity's "home on the Internet," it is unclear whether the information is celebrity-sanctioned or simply aggregated by the Web site owners—more likely the latter. Additional links are provided for each celebrity. These range from celebrity pictures, posters, blogs, and screensavers to YouTube videos.

Celebrity Link (http://www.celebrity-link.com) is a directory of links to Web sites dedicated to celebrities. A user can browse by celebrity first name, category, or nationality. The site claims a database of more than 26,000 celebrities and links to more than 42,000 Web sites.

8

Selected Print and Nonprint Resources

This chapter provides a list of books, journals, journal articles, general articles, and nonprint resources important to an understanding of celebrity. The list ranges from books fundamental to the concept of celebrity to academic articles exploring various aspects of celebrity to audio and video products offering unique celebrity perspectives. The overall goal of this chapter is to demonstrate the range and depth of the resources available for further study.

Print Resources

Books with Historical Perspectives

Barbas, Samantha. 2001. *Movie Crazy*. New York: Palgrave. 218 pages.

This book is subtitled "Fans, Stars, and the Cult of Celebrity." It explores America's fascination with film and film stars after World War I. It argues that film significantly influenced moviegoers' ideas about stardom, celebrity, reality, and life.

Boorstin, Daniel. 1962. *The Image, or What Happened to the American Dream*. New York: Atheneum. 315 pages.

Although this book is more than 40 years old, it is a seminal work on celebrity, but celebrity as seen in the larger context of our failure to see the realities of life—preferring instead to believe the images we are presented. This conflict between image and reality was further developed by postmodernist philosopher Jean Baudrillard in the late 20th century. Thus, this book is slightly ahead of its time in exploring the image-reality issue. There is quite a bit of history here, but gems of insight about fame and celebrity are scattered throughout.

Braudy, Leo. 1986. *The Frenzy of Renown: Fame and Its History.* New York: Oxford University Press. 649 pages.

This book is more than 25 years old, but has been influential in helping us understand fame's historical roots. The author suggests that those who seek fame do so out of a desire to be unique, but also take pleasure in pleasing the audience. Historical references range from Caesar and Jesus to P. T. Barnum. There is much historical detail here and not all of it is tied directly to fame and celebrity; however, the book reveals the social and political complexities of fame.

Burns, Eric. 2007. *Virtue, Valor, and Vanity: The Founding Fathers and the Pursuit of Fame.* New York: Arcade Publishing. 239 pages.

In the 21st century almost all politicians are celebrities of one sort or another. However, in America's early days, celebrity was not automatically awarded to those who held public office or engaged in public service. This book examines the founding fathers and the reasons why they were celebrities. The author discusses six qualities of fame possessed by those early leaders: ambition, vanity, modesty, jealousy, image, and myth. He shows how these qualities played a role in the rise of some early American politicians and public figures to fame. The book focuses on 13 early personalities, ranging from well-known individuals such as Benjamin Franklin and Thomas Jefferson to less well-known Americans such as James Wilson and Benjamin Rush.

Cashmore, Ellis. 2006. *Celebrity/Culture.* New York: Routledge. 311 pages.

This book examines the origins, meaning, and global influence of celebrity. It suggests celebrities may be commodities, that is, products to be marketed to a consumer culture. This may explain why we have become so interested, perhaps even addicted, to celebrities. The author draws examples from the early Hollywood film industry, the music industry, television, and new media on his way to answering the question of why we are so absorbed in the lives of people who essentially have no material impact on our rather ordinary lives.

Law, Lisa. 2000. *Interviews with Icons.* **Santa Fe, NM: Lumen. 286 pages.**

Subtitled "Flashing on the Sixties," this book is composed of celebrity interview transcripts. Interviews were conducted by the author who is a photographer and documentary producer. Interview subjects were famous personalities during the turbulent 1960s in America. Most interviews date from the late 1980s and ask the subjects to recall their lives in the 1960s. Among those interviewed are poet Allen Ginsberg, Woodstock's Wavy Gravy, musician/singer Graham Nash, and actors Peter Fonda and Dennis Hopper.

Ponce de Leon, Charles L. 2002. *Self-Exposure: Human-Interest Journalism and the Emergence of Celebrity in America, 1890–1940.* **Chapel Hill, NC: University of North Carolina Press. 325 pages.**

Acknowledging that contemporary America is obsessed with celebrity, the author of this book initially set out to write a book critical of celebrity, but as the writing progressed, he found that celebrity is more complex than generally thought and full of ambiguities and contradictions. This book is not without critical comment; however, it makes a positive contribution to the literature by tracing the development of celebrity journalism and its consumption by audiences. The author advocates a sort of media literacy when it comes to celebrity: read (or watch) carefully and be skeptical; understand how images are produced and readers manipulated; and appreciate the contributions celebrity makes to the culture.

Schickel, Richard. 1985. *Intimate Strangers: The Culture of Celebrity.* **Garden City, NY: Doubleday & Company. 299 pages.**

Considered by many to be the most important early work on the subject, this book is critical to an understanding of the history and significance of celebrity. Although the book is more than 25 years old, one does not get that impression when reading it. The author's comments and observations seem to fit today's celebrity world as well as they fit the 1980s. Especially important in this book are the connections the author makes between celebrity and the power inherent in our social and political cultures. This book has no table of contents and no index, so specific information is hard to find, but it is intelligently written and a must read for celebrity researchers.

Books with Special Perspectives

Breitbart, Andrew, and Mark C. Ebner. 2004. *Hollywood, Interrupted: Insanity Chic in Babylon—The Case against Celebrity.* New York: Wiley. 394 pages.

Many Hollywood celebrities have been known to act up from time to time: drunken driving, infidelity, spouse abuse, and the like. This book reveals some of the closely guarded secrets held by celebrities. The authors suggest that instances of negative or inappropriate behavior are pathological in nature and contribute to ruined relationships, broken families, and regular visits to rehab centers. Drawing on examples from the lives of Tom Cruise, Anne Heche, Eddie Murphy, Courtney Love, Robert Downey Jr., and others, the authors expose a side of Hollywood that may be shocking to outsiders, but is not all that unusual for Hollywood types.

Burns, Kelli. 2009. *Celeb 2.0: How Social Media Foster Our Fascination with Popular Culture.* Santa Barbara, CA: ABC-CLIO. 212 pages.

Social media are almost as important to celebrities as they are to many members of the general public. Facebook, MySpace, Twitter, and all the rest are discussed in this book in terms of their importance to and primary role in popular culture. Special attention is given to the impact of social media on television, film, popular fiction, and advertising. One particularly useful chapter explores how celebrities engage fans by maintaining blogs that give fans an inside look at celebrity life.

Cowen, Tyler. 2000. *What Price Fame?* Cambridge, MA: Harvard University Press. 248 pages.

This book explores some of the less positive aspects of fame and celebrity life. While many fans love and adore celebrities, celebrities can also face hostility, ridicule, and failure. For some celebrities, fame is a burden. However, fame can be addictive and can give celebrities an inflated view of their worth. Many celebrities, past and present, are discussed in this book. Examples include a broad range of personalities, from Plato to baseball's Babe Ruth to singer Michael Jackson.

DeAngelis, Michael. 2001. *Gay Fandom and Crossover Stardom.* **Durham, NC: Duke University Press. 285 pages.**

Gay and lesbian characters have been a part of television programming for several years. Their appearance in movies has been somewhat less noticeable. This book examines aspects of the complex dynamic between gay male audiences and Hollywood stars. The focus is on three well-known film stars: James Dean, Mel Gibson, and Keanu Reeves. None of the three stars is presented as gay, but there may be certain facets of their performances that are potentially important to gay male moviegoers. The three featured actors' performances and personas are viewed for: (1) shifts in perceptions of male sexuality, (2) a star's physical and emotional vulnerability, (3) the degree to which a star has the potential to be gay, (4) ambiguities in the cultural interpretation of a performance, and (5) the role of identity and fantasy in the perception of a star.

Dezenhall, Eric. 2003. *Nail 'em! Confronting High-Profile Attacks on Celebrities and Businesses.* **Amherst, NY: Prometheus Books. 341 pages.**

A business may be targeted for an attack by a competitor, an individual, even the public. The attack is often vicious and may or may not be backed up by facts. For a business under attack, the goal is survival. This is increasingly difficult because, as this book argues, many attacks really work. Moreover, the techniques used to attack businesses are also often used to attack celebrities of one sort or another. There is usually a victim, a villain, a vindicator, a void, a vehicle (usually the media), and a value in any successful attack. Drawing examples from the business world (including Prozac, ValuJet, and General Motors) and examples from the celebrity world (designer Tommy Hilfiger, former president Bill Clinton, and television personality Kathie Lee Gifford), the author discusses how the attack process works and why it is often successful.

Dyer, Richard. 1998. *Stars.* **London: British Film Institute. 217 pages.**

This book is primarily about celebrities in the film industry. The author calls them "film stars." Beginning with an examination of the sociological aspects of film and film stars, this book further examines semiotic aspects (signs and symbols) present in film. Film is essentially a text that can be closely examined to reveal that stars merely signify something. We do not see them as real people, but as individuals who represent a type of social reality. This book is heavy on theory but is important to readers who are especially interested in film studies.

Espejo, Roman (ed.) 2009. *Can Celebrities Change the World?* **Detroit: Greenhaven Press. 97 pages.**

This slim volume is a collection of essays presenting arguments both for and against specific propositions involving celebrities and their activism on behalf of worthy causes. For example, many celebrities undertake fundraising or other work on behalf of poor nations and poverty-stricken people in parts of Africa. This book presents two essays on celebrity activism in Africa: one essay argues that the work of celebrities benefits Africa; the other presents the counterargument that the work of celebrities *does not* benefit Africa. Other essays examine celebrity activism in international affairs, in philanthropy, and as role models, among other topics.

Giles, David. 2000. *Illusions of Immortality: A Psychology of Fame and Celebrity.* **New York: St. Martin's Press. 187 pages.**

What is it like to be famous? What role does society play in the lives of the famous? This book examines these and other questions relating to celebrity, and discusses the psychology involved in the relationship between celebrities and their fans. The author identifies different types of fame, noting that our concept of *fame* has changed down through the years, and ultimately suggests it might be time to retire the word in favor of the word *celebrity*, given the influence of media in today's world.

Herwitz, Daniel. 2008. *The Star as Icon.* **New York: Columbia University Press. 157 pages.**

This book examines what the author calls "the star icon," an endlessly talked about but little understood individual who somehow captures our attention and garners our adoration. What is it about television, film, and consumer culture that singles out some individuals to go beyond stardom to iconic status? The author attempts to answer this question, drawing primarily on the lives of Princess Diana, Jackie Onassis, Marilyn Monroe, and Grace Kelly.

Holmes, Su, and Sean Redmond (eds.). 2006. *Framing Celebrity: New Directions in Celebrity Culture.* **New York: Routledge. 369 pages.**

This book is a collection of essays from 20 scholars. When the book speaks of fame, it essentially means celebrity. The two terms are used interchangeably here. Fame (or celebrity) is presented in four different frames, or contexts. Each frame is designed to help us understand something about the complex nature of the celebrity/fame phenomenon. For example, one contributor, in a frame titled "fame damage," examines mental illness in celebrity culture. Another frame, titled "fame now," looks at celebrity politicians.

McCutcheon, Lynn E., John Maltby, James Houran, and Diane D. Ashe. 2004. *Celebrity Worshippers: Inside the Minds of Star-gazers.* **Baltimore: PublishAmerica. 184 pages.**

This is an academic book, written by scholars and full of information on their various research projects, projects designed to explore the psychology behind celebrity worship. Following a rather exhaustive review of the literature on the subject of celebrity worship, the authors explain in detail their attempts to measure attitudes about celebrities. Examples of questionnaires and measurement scales are presented. Tables show some statistical analyses of the data. A casual reader can simply glide over the research methodology explanation and take the word of these experienced researchers as to what it all means. What the researchers found is not all that surprising: celebrity worship exists and usually for a variety of (or multiple) reasons. The book also suggests ways to reduce celebrity worship.

Moran, Joe. 2000. *Star Authors: Literary Celebrity in America.* **Sterling, VA: Pluto Press. 187 pages.**

Although some people may not think of authors, that is, writers of books, as celebrities, they can be if certain conditions are met. In fact, authors are highly visible—in media and elsewhere. Newspapers and magazines regularly review their work; they appear on television programs promoting their work; they often tour the country to appear at signings and book fairs. Theirs is a special breed of celebrity. Nevertheless, as this book argues, authors are often thrown in with all the other entertainment celebrities. This often trivializes their work and marginalizes the serious, intellectual aspects of literature. The book gives in-depth attention to four popular authors: John Updike, Philip Roth, Don DeLillo, and Kathy Acker.

Newton, Michael. 2008. *Celebrities and Crime.* **New York: Chelsea House. 112 pages.**

There can be little doubt that Americans love their celebrities. Fans enjoy watching singers, actors, athletes, fashion models, and others as they rise to fame. To some degree, fans live vicariously through the lives of their favorite celebrities. However, quite often fans also enjoy media reports of celebrity divorce, disgrace, or other misfortunes. This book's 10 chapters do a rather thorough job of examining some celebrities and their problems with crime. In most cases, the fact that a celebrity is involved in some sort of wrongdoing affects the justice system to one degree or another. Among the book's chapters are ones on the 1969 Manson Family murders, the still-unsolved murder of actor Bob Crane (of *Hogan's Heroes* fame), the mysterious murder of the wife of actor Robert Blake, and the issues between rival rap stars Tupac Shakur and Notorious B.I.G. and the death of both men.

Orth, Maureen. 2004. *The Importance of Being Famous.* **New York: Henry Holt & Company. 372 pages.**

This book presents profiles of the famous. Some individuals are well known; others are not. The more well known include singers Madonna and Tina Turner, as well as Russia's Vladimir Putin, among others. The less well known include personalities such as Sinn Fein's Gerry Adams and fashion designer Karl Lagerfeld. Most of the profiles provide information from the mid-to-late 1900s. The book presents itself as a behind-the-scenes look at the celebrity-industrial complex, which the author defines as "the media monster that creates the reality we think we see, and the people who thrive or perish there."

Schmid, David. 2005. *Natural Born Celebrities: Serial Killers in American Culture.* **Chicago: University of Chicago Press. 327 pages.**

Most people have heard of Jack the Ripper, the famous serial killer of the Victorian era. In the past several decades or so, America has had its share of serial killers: Jeffrey Dahmer, Ted Bundy, John Wayne Gacy. The American media machine and the public's compelling interest have made these men celebrities. They are the subjects of made-for-TV movies; their deeds are chronicled in books. Why do we find these men so fascinating? This book considers this and other questions and examines why we can't look away from these men and their deeds.

Weber, Brenda R. 2009. *Makeover TV: Selfhood, Citizenship, and Celebrity.* **Durham, NC: Duke University Press. 324 pages.**

At the end of the 20th century, there was much discussion and some research on the prevalence of "perfect" models in television and magazine advertising. Some argued this was appropriate; others argued that such representations were not congruent with real life. The arguments have cooled somewhat as America entered the 21st century. However, the issue of what might be called "body image" remains important to many. This book examines the various makeover TV shows, including those involving makeovers of finances, trucks, and homes. Viewers are often told to uncover their true self, or reinvent themselves, or become empowered, or take the advice of experts. The ultimate message appears to be this: to be special, you must look and act like everyone else. The author discusses this notion and contends that makeover television shows are complicated texts that tell us much about our culture and our fears.

Academic Journal Articles

Alperstein, Neil M. 1991. "Imaginary Social Relationships with Celebrities Appearing in Television Commercials." *Journal of Broadcasting and Electronic Media* **35(1): 43–58.**

There is much academic literature exploring the practice and impact of celebrity endorsement. This study reports the results of interviews with 21 individuals who were professionals or homemakers living in Columbia, Maryland, and 39 college students also living in Columbia, Maryland. The author was interested in determining the degree to which these subjects established social relationships with celebrities who appeared in television commercials as well as the nature of those relationships. The study assumed the relationships would be imaginary, since it was highly unlikely any real-world relationship existed between the subjects and the celebrities. Results revealed the subjects were quite aware that celebrity use in commercials was an advertising technique and that this knowledge may lead to an adjustment of their beliefs about celebrities. Nevertheless, the subjects were attracted to the celebrities and incorporated the knowledge and impressions they gained from the celebrities' appearances into their overall social perception of the celebrity.

Basil, Michael D. 1996. "Identification as a Mediator of Celebrity Effects." *Journal of Broadcasting and Electronic Media* **40(4): 476–495.**

This is yet another study among the many on the effect of celebrity endorsement on consumer behavior. One hundred forty-seven Hawaiian college students were surveyed. The research project was conducted after basketball star Magic Johnson revealed he tested positive for HIV. The author hypothesized that Johnson's announcement may determine the degree to which students who identify with him modify their AIDS-related beliefs, attitudes, and behaviors. The hypothesis was only partially supported. The study revealed that the issue was complex and that some differences occurred when it came to issues of personal concern, perceived risk, and sexual behavior.

Boon, Susan D., and Christine D. Lomore. 2001. "Admirer-Celebrity Relationships among Young Adults: Explaining Perceptions of Celebrity Influence on Identity." *Human Communication Research* **27(3): 432–465.**

This study investigated the judgments young adults make regarding the degree to which their relationships with celebrities influenced the young people's sense of identity and self-worth. Seventy-five participants completed a survey questionnaire. Responses indicated the young adults were moderately to strongly attracted to celebrities they identified as life idols. The study examined the celebrities identified as idols and identified some of the characteristics of the respondents that may have led them to use a celebrity in forming their identities or their sense of self-worth.

Bush, Alan J., Craig A. Martin, and Victoria D. Bush. 2004. "Sports Celebrity Influence on the Behavioral Intentions of Generation Y." *Journal of Advertising Research* **44: 108–118.**

This is an academic study examining the effects of athlete role models on teenagers' intentions and purchase behavior. A survey of 218 adolescents revealed that celebrity sports figures have a positive influence on word-of-mouth advertising and brand loyalty. When celebrities made brand choices and said positive things about a product, survey respondents were influenced to adopt the celebrities' views. Additionally, females were more likely than males to engage in word-of-mouth advertising. The study suggests using athletes as spokespersons for products or brand names is usually a wise strategy.

Dietz, Park Elliott, Daryl B. Matthews, Cindy Van Duyne, Daniel Allen Martell, Charles D. H. Parry, Tracy Stewart, Janet Warren, and J. Douglas Crowder. 1991. "Threatening and Otherwise Inappropriate Letters to Hollywood Celebrities." *Journal of Forensic Sciences* 36(1): 185–209.

Although this study is at least 20 years old, it remains compelling reading. The authors examined the characteristics of approximately 1,800 threatening and inappropriate letters sent to Hollywood celebrities. The 214 letter writers whose work was examined mailed an average of eight letters apiece. The article quotes from some of the letters and provides interesting tidbits of information from the others. In some instances, the letters were harmless, if somewhat bizarre. In other cases, the letter writers appear to be interested in pursuing encounters with their favorite celebrity and could, therefore, be considered a possible threat to the celebrity's safety.

Ferris, Kerry O. 2001. "Through a Glass Darkly: The Dynamics of Fan-Celebrity Encounters." *Symbolic Interaction* 24(1): 25–47.

This study examines the activities through which some fans seek face-to-face encounters with the celebrities they admire. The article discusses some of the problems that result from these encounters. Through participant observation and personal interviews, the author gathered data from groups of *Star Trek* fans and fans of soap operas. The study found that encounters can come in any one of several ways: (1) at public events that are usually highly controlled and often in a question-and-answer format; (2) celebrity sightings, particularly in large cities such as New York or Los Angeles, and often at airports, supermarkets, or theaters; or (3) active pursuit, defined as fans gathering addresses and other personal information about celebrities and attempting to stage a meeting; this approach can develop into stalking behavior. The study concludes that fan-celebrity interaction can be pleasant or problematic, depending on the circumstances.

Fraser, Benson P., and William J. Brown. 2002. "Media, Celebrities, and Social Influence: Identification with Elvis Presley." *Mass Communication and Society* **5(2): 183–206.**

In a media-saturated world, celebrity is no longer restricted to one country or one region. Celebrity can be international. This study looks at the powerful influence celebrities have on those who closely identify with a celebrity's media image. Researchers interviewed 35 Elvis Presley fans, including some who were Elvis impersonators. Results indicate that both fans and impersonators identify strongly with Elvis and consciously model his values by changing their own lifestyles to more closely resemble his.

Gamson, Joshua. 2001. "Jessica Hahn, Media Whore: Sex Scandals and Female Publicity." *Critical Studies in Media Communication* **18(2): 157–173.**

This essay examines the 1980s sex scandal involving televangelist Jim Bakker and occasional television performer Jessica Hahn. It is fairly common for politicians and other public figures to become involved in sex scandals of one sort or another. The author focuses on the whole Bakker-Hahn saga, with particular emphasis on events in 1987. The encounter between Bakker and Hahn, apparently in a Florida hotel room, led to the collapse of Bakker's PTL television empire, but vaulted Hahn to media fame. Both *Playboy* and *Penthouse*, well-known "men's magazines," competed for interviews and photos. Was she an innocent victim? Was she promiscuous and experienced before the encounter? The media's treatment of Hahn appeared to be uneven; sometimes positive, sometimes negative. The article suggests that media coverage of the scandal probably confused the truth rather than revealing it. This finding may hold true for today's media coverage of sex scandals.

Gamson, Joshua. 1992. "The Assembly Line of Greatness: Celebrity in the Twentieth Century." *Critical Studies in Media Communication* **9(1): 1–24.**

Two intertwining textual narratives are discussed in this essay that examines the relationship of celebrity to the development of publicity techniques. The first narrative, said to be typical of the first part of the twentieth century, suggests those who are deserving naturally rise to the top, that is, to celebrity status. The second narrative, typical of the latter part of the twentieth century, suggests celebrities are artificially manufactured, that is, made famous by a variety of sophisticated publicity techniques that enable them to become more highly visible. The author questions the role of publicity and the dynamics of public image making in a democracy.

Greene, A. L., and Carolyn Adams-Price. 1990. "Adolescents' Secondary Attachments to Celebrity Figures." *Sex Roles* **23(7/8): 335–347.**

This is an academic study of the influence of age, gender, and physical development on the qualities adolescents see in celebrities their own age. Sixty students, both males and females from the fifth, eighth, and eleventh grades, completed questionnaires assessing the maturity, attractiveness, and personality of six young male and six young female celebrities. Results indicated that, for the most part, students preferred opposite-sex celebrities rather than same-sex celebrities (no surprise). However, the study also found that as females approach puberty, they have a greater need for attachment to or identification with a same-age celebrity, sometimes even a same-sex celebrity. Interestingly, a number of students in the survey reported they preferred androgynous celebrities.

Gwenllian-Jones, Sara. 2000. "Starring Lucy Lawless?" *Continuum: Journal of Media and Cultural Studies* **14(1): 9–22.**

This is a case study examining the ways in which the star image of the fictional television character Xena (of *Xena, Warrior Princess*) is related to Lucy Lawless, the actress who played the part. Interviews were conducted with the show's fans. Results revealed that the fictional Xena was of more interest to fans than Lawless herself. One explanation suggested that the fictional character was more accessible (via the television show) than the actress was in real life. In other words, access to the fictional character was essentially unlimited, while access to the actress who played the part was strictly controlled. Anecdotally, some fans reported being dissatisfied with some of the show's episodes and vowed to stop watching.

Laurens, R. H. 2001. "Year of the Living Dead: California Breathes New Life into Celebrity Publicity Rights." *Hastings Communications and Entertainment Law Journal* **24(1): 109–147.**

The use of images of deceased actors in films (and more recently in commercials) is highly controversial. Digital imaging technology has made it possible to insert these images into contemporary films or other video material. The heirs of deceased actors often object to this practice for a number of reasons, including economic and privacy concerns. A law was passed in California in 1999, and although it failed to extend full protection to deceased celebrities, it did strengthen a few existing protection rules. This article traces the development of the law and comments on the legal, economic, and public policy issues involved.

McRobbie, Angela. 1986. "Postmodernism and Popular Culture." *Journal of Communication Inquiry* **10(2): 108–116.**

This article is written for an informed academic audience. However, it makes several important points about the relationship between postmodern thinking and popular culture. The author suggests postmodern theory can be useful in analyzing various aspects of popular culture. For example, postmodernism rejects a singular explanation of almost everything in favor of multiple explanations for the events, phenomena, and situations we see or are involved in. Moreover, media have considerable influence in presenting an image of a celebrity, for example. The image is quite likely to be different from reality, postmodernists say. The essay uses numerous examples from popular culture, including television shows *Dynasty* and *Dallas*, as well as celebrity music groups from the 1980s (Frankie Goes to Hollywood and Culture Club). The author suggests that if more young people knew about postmodern thinking, they'd probably like it because it can offer explanations and points of view about celebrities and popular culture that fit their worldview.

Mittelstaedt, John D., Peter C. Riesz, and William J. Brown. 2000. "Why Are Endorsements Effective?" *Journal of Current Issues in Research in Advertising* **22(1): 55–65.**

This study examines three different explanations of the relationship between celebrity endorsers and the products they endorse. The authors evaluated the endorsement potential of three Olympic athletes for three different products. Three hundred sixty-seven individuals were contacted by telephone. Results indicated that the most effective matches between endorser and product were not based on either the product itself or the endorser alone, but on the perceived connection between the product and the endorser.

Ross, Rhonda, Toni Campbell, John C. Wright, Aletha C. Huston, Mabel L. Rice, and Peter Turk. 1984. "When Celebrities

Talk, Children Listen: An Experimental Analysis of Children's Responses to TV Ads with Celebrity Endorsement." *Journal of Applied Developmental Psychology* 5(3): 185–202.

This study is one of the early ones exploring the effects of television ads with celebrity endorsement on the product preference of 8- to 14-year-old boys. The study also examined the subjects' understanding of advertising intent and techniques. Results showed that celebrity endorsement led to increased preference for a toy (a brand of model racer) chiefly because the boys believed that the celebrities were experts. Furthermore, 8- to 10-year old boys appeared to be highly influenced by the glamour of the celebrity and were thus more likely to take the celebrity's advice than were the 11- to 14-year olds. There was no evidence that the boys understood the complexities of advertising techniques and applied them in critically looking at the product.

Stack, Steven. 1987. "Celebrities and Suicide: A Taxonomy and Analysis, 1948–1983." *American Sociological Review* 52(3): 401–412.

Suicide is a sensitive topic. Many people find it difficult to discuss suicide or even to hear about someone—whom they may or may not know—who has been a victim of suicide. This study focuses on celebrity suicides, categorizing them according to two sociological theories: the laws of imitation and the concept of the elite. The imitation effect applies to American entertainers and political celebrities, but not to artists, villains, and the economic elite. Although suicides are often highly publicized, the reasons for suicides are not: divorce, illness, mental impairment, and the like. The problems that give rise to suicide are often problems shared by both celebrities and the general public.

Stafford, Maria Royne, Nancy E. Spears, and Chung-kue Hsu. 2003. "Celebrity Images in Magazine Advertisements: An Application of the Visual Rhetoric Model." *Journal of Current Issues and Research in Advertising* 25(2): 13–20.

Although the title of this article suggests it is complex, the article, in fact, is rather straightforward. Researchers analyzed the content of 207 advertisements containing celebrity endorsers. Results showed male celebrities are associated with both the verbal and the visual presentation. However, female celebrities are associated with a visual-only presentation. These results are not particularly surprising, given what other researchers have discovered about the nature of celebrity endorsement.

Street, John. 2004. "Celebrity Politicians: Popular Culture and Political Representation." *British Journal of Politics and International Relations* 6(4): 435–452.

Many studies have noted almost all politicians are considered celebrities. This article explains the general notion that there are two main types of celebrity politicians. The first is the politician who uses his/her celebrity status to establish a claim (whether true or not) to represent a particular group or cause. The second is the individual who uses his/her popularity to speak (often without justification) for public opinion. Some scholars feel that the claims these two types of celebrity politicians make are damaging to the democratic process and to honest political representation. This article, however, rejects that argument, suggesting instead that while the claims made by celebrity politicians may or may not be legitimate, they are in fact fairly consistent with normal political representation.

Till, Brian D., and Terence A. Shimp. 1998. "Endorsers in Advertising: The Case of Negative Celebrity Information." *Journal of Advertising* 27(1): 67–82.

The authors conducted three experimental studies. They were interested in examining how negative information about a celebrity can impact the brand the celebrity endorses. The first two studies used fictitious celebrities; the third used an actual celebrity. Results showed negative information about the celebrity resulted in a decline in a subject's attitude toward the brands endorsed only by the fictitious celebrities. There was little or no attitude change recorded as a result of negative information about the real celebrity. Important factors in this study include the timing of the negative information and the strength of the connection between the celebrity and the brand.

Academic Journals

Americana: The Journal of American Popular Culture, 1900 to Present

http://www.americanpopularculture.com

Frequency of publication: Quarterly

This journal is one of three periodicals published by Americana: The Institute for the Study of American Popular Culture, headquartered in Hollywood, California. *Americana: The Journal of*

American Popular Culture features peer-reviewed scholarly research papers written for an academic audience; papers are typically on some aspect of popular culture. Recent issues contain articles on the films *Basic Instinct* and *Silence of the Lambs,* television's *The West Wing,* and *Batman.* The organization is eco-friendly and, as such, does not print hard copies of its publications; its journals are available online only. The organization does, however, have a book division that publishes paperbacks through its Press Americana division. The two other periodicals published by the organization are *Review Americana: A Literary Journal* and *Magazine Americana.* Individuals wishing to submit papers for review can find links to submission guidelines and additional information on the organization's Web site.

Images: A Journal of Film and Popular Culture

http://www.imagesjournal.com

Frequency of publication: Quarterly

This journal is available online only. It features articles that examine visual media as primary material. Articles about movie directors, film genres, comic books, television programs and television stars, and the like are encouraged. However, the editors look specifically for strong images and concrete examples in a written piece. Philosophical approaches or generalizations without supporting examples are not considered for publication. Past issues have featured articles on celebrities: an interview with documentary filmmaker Michael Moore, an essay on the films of Quentin Tarantino, a look at the film work of actor Clint Eastwood. The journal also contains essays on other popular culture subjects, of course. One particularly interesting piece examined teenagers and horror films of the 1950s.

Journal of Criminal Justice and Popular Culture

http://www.albany.edu/scj/jcjpc

Frequency of publication: Quarterly

Headquartered at the University of Albany in Albany, New York, this journal features scholarly research and opinion on the relationships among crime, criminal justice, and popular culture. The peer-reviewed journal is written for an academic audience. Although the journal primarily publishes original research articles, it will, from time to time, publish interviews, fiction, photo essays, and the like. Past articles include essays on sex and violence in slasher horror films, the use of torture in television's *24*, and media presentations of identify theft.

Journal of Popular Culture

https://www.msu.edu/~tjpc

Frequency of publication: Six times a year

This journal is the official publication of the Popular Culture Association (PCA) and is considered by many to be the field's premier journal. The peer-reviewed journal is available in print form in about 1,400 libraries worldwide. The PCA believes that the perspectives and experiences of many individuals can enrich the discussion about the role and importance of popular culture in life. Previously published articles include essays on *SpongeBob SquarePants*, *The Man Show*, and the political satire of celebrities Stephen Colbert and Jon Stewart.

Journal of Religion and Popular Culture

http://www.usask.ca/relst/jrpc

Frequency of publication: Three times yearly

This Web-based, peer-reviewed journal is written for an academic audience and features the exploration, analysis, and interpretation of the interrelationships and interactions between religion/religious expression and popular culture. Based in Canada, the journal is international in scope and is open to essays from a variety of religions, nationalities, and cultures. The journal is supported by a grant from the Social Sciences and Humanities Research Council of Canada. Past articles include essays on religion and sexuality in the film *300*, Jesus Christ and Billy the Kid as archetypes of the self, and the Internet matchmaking activities of American Muslims.

Studies in Latin American Popular Culture

http://www.utexas .edu/utpress/journals/jslapc.html

Frequency of publication: Annually

This scholarly journal is interdisciplinary in nature and publishes articles, review essays, and interviews on the diverse aspects of Latin American popular culture. Articles are written in English, Spanish, or Portuguese. The journal defines popular culture as "some aspect of culture which is accepted by or consumed by significant numbers of people." It is especially interested in articles offering new methodological or theoretical approaches, articles exploring the modernization and global impact of Latin American cultural practices, and the social meanings and power images found in popular culture. Past articles include a study on hip hop and black racial identity in Brazil, an essay on Che Guevara as trickster and cultural hero, and a cultural analysis of Brazilian immigration to New Orleans after Hurricane Katrina.

Studies in Popular Culture

http://pcasacas.org/SiPC

Frequency of publication: Biannually

This peer-reviewed journal is an official publication of the Popular Culture Association and the American Culture Association in the South. It is available online and publishes articles dealing with any aspect of American or international popular culture. The emphasis may be either historical or contemporary. Articles in the journal have dealt with subjects from film, literature, radio and television, music, and graphics, among other mediated forms of communication. Celebrities are often the subject of an article or essay. Past articles have included a Freudian analysis of a song by Madonna, and an essay on early radio pioneers.

Selected General-Interest Celebrity Magazines

Details

www.Details.com

Frequency: 10 issues/year

Publisher: Condé Nast Publications

The target audience for this magazine is affluent, career-minded men. Regular features include sections on style and culture, as well as sections with hip names such as "Dossier," "Exit," and "Wiseguy." These sections cover a variety of topics ranging from celebrities and personal relationships to interviews with experienced men who offer life advice.

GQ

www.gq.com

Frequency: Monthly

Publisher: Condé Nast Publications

This magazine's target audience is smart, sharp men. Each issue contains interviews with sports figures as well as photos of some of today's hottest models and actresses. The magazine also provides tips on fine dining, politics, fashion, and grooming. Celebrities are often featured on the magazine's cover.

Interview

www.interviewmagazine.com

Frequency: Monthly

Publisher: Brant Publications

This magazine began as a newsletter in the late 20th century, but has become a cutting-edge publication, particularly in the minds of New York residents. The publication's roots go back to Andy Warhol. It markets itself as "magazine chic at its highest." The magazine utilizes a simple question-and-answer format. However, the individuals selected for interviews are not necessarily the celebrities of today. More likely, those interviewed are the celebrities of the future (in the magazine's judgment). Said to be the ultimate pop culture magazine, *Interview* is not afraid of profanity and nudity. The work of celebrity photographers is often featured in the magazine.

OK!

www.okmagazine .com

Frequency: 51 issues/year

Publisher: Northern and Shell North America

This well-known magazine claims to be the home of celebrity news. Each week, the magazine features stories, photos, and gossip about celebrities from the wonderful world of show business. Celebrities are almost always featured on the cover, with an accompanying detailed story about the individuals inside.

People StyleWatch

www.peoplestylewatch.com

Frequency: 10 issues/year

Publisher: Time Direct Ventures

This magazine is the somewhat lesser-known cousin to *People* magazine. The fashion and beauty information inside the magazine is said to be inspired by celebrities, but not in the typical way. The emphasis in this publication is the real-life, authentic look of the stars, not the look they exhibit at openings and galas. Apparently, the stars do not look all that bad in real life. The magazine claims to pack each issue with must-have products, great deals, and exclusive discounts.

Rolling Stone

www.RollingStone.com

Frequency: 26 issues/year

Publisher: Wenner Media

Rolling Stone is the number one pop culture reference point for millions of young adults. In many ways, the magazine is a cultural icon. In addition to information on music, the magazine regularly covers the broad entertainment field, including movies, television, and technology, as well as national affairs. If it is important, trendy, and worth thinking about, you'll find it in this magazine.

Seventeen

www.seventeen.com

Frequency: Monthly

Publisher: Hearst Magazines

The name of this magazine reflects its target audience. For many young women, the magazine is an important part of their lives. Photos and information on celebrities, fashion, music, movies, and cultural trends are available in each issue. In addition to sections on fashion and beauty, the magazine's other sections include "Love Life," "Your Life," and "Weekend." The magazine claims a readership of 13 million and markets itself as an important part of a young woman's passage into adulthood.

Teen Vogue

www.TeenVogue.com

Frequency: 10 issues/year

Publisher: Condé Nast Publications

This magazine is for teenagers, primarily young females, who care about style, fashion, beauty, health, and entertainment news. The magazine's photographs are high quality. The magazine claims that some readers have been known to purchase two copies of the magazine so they can tear out some of the photos to paste on the walls of their room. Fashion features often include celebrities such as Miley Cyrus or the Jonas Brothers. Celebrities are often featured on the magazine's cover. Celebrities Hayden Panettiere, Ellen Page, and Rihanna are among those on recent covers.

Us Weekly

www.usmagazine.com

Frequency: 52 issues/year

Publisher: Wenner Media

If you are compelled by breaking celebrity news, by Hollywood style, by health and beauty routines, and by nutrition and fitness advice, then you are part of this magazine's target audience. Young educated adults will find a variety of features that not only include the areas just mentioned, but also include news and features about film, television, and music. This magazine features "all things celebrity." Each issue is packed with photos and information. Celebrities almost always appear on the magazine's cover.

Nonprint Resources

Video

American Pop Culture History Films 21-DVD Collection: 1930s, 1940s, 1950s, 1960s, and 1970s Celebrity Pop Culture, American Movie Stars, Famous People and Celebrity Films (2007)

Quality Information Publishers (DVD, time unknown)

This film collection features movies, commercials, interviews, news clips, and other material by and about some of Hollywood's greatest actors and actresses and best-known public celebrities. Marilyn Monroe, Frank Sinatra, Eleanor Roosevelt, Alexander Graham Bell, Paul Newman, Albert Einstein, John Glenn, Richard Nixon, Helen Keller, and Jimmy Stewart are among those whose work is illustrated.

Be a Blogging Celebrity (2009)

BeachViewMedia.com (DVD, 82 minutes)

This video is a "how-to" manual for becoming a celebrity. It suggests setting up your own blog and using it to establish yourself as an expert or a celebrity. The makers of the video seem to believe the only accomplishment you need to become famous is to establish yourself and your "brand" online. Given the nature of online communication and the tendency of online users to be highly gullible, what you write online need not be true. Thus, image trumps reality.

Carl Sagan: A Cosmic Celebrity (2000)

A&E Home Video (VHS, 50 minutes)

This video was an installment in the *Biography* program series on cable television's A&E Network. It traces the life of scientist Carl Sagan with particular emphasis on his accomplishments and his legacy. Some viewers will enjoy the occasional glimpses into his personal life. The material is not overly scientific and is appropriate for all audiences.

Celebrity (1999)

Miramax (DVD, 113 minutes)

There are several films titled *Celebrity*. This particular one is thought by some viewers to be the best of the lot. This may be because it is a Woody Allen movie, or it may be because it stars a number of celebrities: Leonardo DiCaprio, Melanie Griffith, Kenneth Branagh, and Judy Davis, among others. The film is essentially a view of celebrity life. It was shot in black and white and follows life as seen through the eyes of a recently divorced couple. After a divorce, how does one build a new life in a media-saturated, celebrity-driven world? As with many Woody Allen movies, the plot has some complex aspects, but an attentive viewer will be able to piece things together and notice a number of celebrity cameo shots.

Celebrity (1984)

Starmaker (VHS, 106 minutes)

This film also stars several celebrities: Joseph Bottoms, Michael Beck, Tess Harper, and Hal Holbrook, among others. This 1984 film differs from the 1999 one in that this one is an adaptation of a book about a sordid sex crime that claimed the careers of a journalist, a Hollywood superstar, and a fanatical evangelist. Three friends leave their small-town Texas home to find fame and fortune. However, being famous means that the past often comes back to haunt you, as the three ultimately discover.

Celebrity News Reels: Hollywood's Most Infamous Couples and Ugliest Breakups (2005)

Star Rush Media (DVD, 60 minutes)

Calling itself an "unauthorized documentary," this video takes the viewer behind the scenes of the Hollywood dating game. What really goes on with those high-profile celebrity couples?

What happened between Brad and Jennifer, or Ben and J-Lo, or Angelina and Billy Bob? Although the video purports to give the viewer the truth behind the headlines, some viewers will likely feel that some of the information is little more than gossip.

Celebrities: Caught on Camera (2000)

Sling Shot (VHS, 69 minutes)

This tape may be the video equivalent of a supermarket tabloid. The makers of this videotape prowl the places where celebrities might be caught off guard: on the street, at airports, outside health clubs, and the like. The result is a video about celebrities who are not often at their best in these situations. Those caught on tape include Pamela Anderson, Shannon Tweed, Carmen Electra, and Tommy Lee, among others. Most of them are irritated by the camera's intrusion into their private lives: some try to hide their faces; others yell at the camera. Not all viewers have found this video all that interesting because the video's premise—while perhaps somewhat amusing at first—gets old quickly.

Diana: Life through a Lens (2007)

Kultur White Star (DVD, 48 minutes)

Diana, Princess of Wales, was a worldwide celebrity. Her death in 1997 brought an end to a remarkable high-profile life of public service. It was said that more than 2 billion people worldwide watched her televised funeral. This video, however, is not about her death, but about her life. Photographer Jane Fincher accompanied Diana for 17 years, capturing pictures of her in a variety of personal and public situations. Through the photographer's eyes, this video offers an insight into Diana, her adoring public, and the press corps that shadowed her everywhere.

Everybody's Famous (2000)

Miramax (DVD, 97 minutes)

This film won an Academy Award nomination for Best Foreign Language Film in 2000. It is a Belgian comedy that follows a young woman's quest to become a famous singer and her father's often outrageous efforts to help her gain celebrity status. Many viewers found this subtitled movie quite charming.

Ghetto Celebrities (2009)

Phoenix Entertainment (DVD-R, 75 minutes)

High-profile rap artists with roots in the ghetto are featured in this documentary. Jay-Z, Nas, Ja Rule, and others are interviewed about their lives and their work. Some athletes and fashion designers are also interviewed. This video is uncensored and contains adult language. The celebrities are quite willing to say things to a documentary interviewer that they would never say to formal members of the press.

Hip-Hop: Beyond Beats and Rhymes

Media Education Foundation (DVD, 60 minutes)

This film discusses race, gender violence, homophobia, and corporate exploitation in the hip-hop recording industry. Rappers and cultural critics are interviewed with a view toward examining the sometimes destructive male stereotypes often present in hip-hop music. Viewer discretion is advised; this film contains violent and sexual imagery in its unabridged version. An abridged version is available with the nudity and profanity edited out.

Hit Celebrity TV Commercials (2004)

Passport Video (DVD, 95 minutes)

Celebrities have long been used as spokespersons for various products and services. This video provides a fairly comprehensive look at the movie stars, sports figures, and other celebrities, many of them early in their careers, as they appeared in television commercials. Featured celebrities include Marilyn Monroe, O. J. Simpson, Michael Jordan, Cybill Shepard, Dustin Hoffman, and Susan Sarandon, among others.

Hollywood Ghosts and Gravesites (2003)

Delta (DVD, 61 minutes)

Ever wonder where those Hollywood stars are buried? This video provides some of the answers to that question, taking the viewer on a tour of Hollywood gravesites. The crypts, tombstones, or graves of Rudolph Valentino, Harry Houdini, and Marilyn Monroe are located, among others. The video also tours the studio lots and other locations where the stars used to hang out.

Investigative Reports: Celebrity Close Encounters (1991)

A&E Home Video (VHS, 60 minutes)

Journalist Bill Kurtis narrates this look at celebrities who believe in UFOs and alien visits. The video was produced for A&E Network's *Investigative Reports* program series. Celebrities are interviewed in-depth about their beliefs. While this topic may seem bizarre to some, the video presents celebrities' views without bias or judgment. Actor Dennis Weaver, astronaut Gordon Cooper, and film director Robert Wise are among those who believe we are not alone in the universe.

Movie Stars and Celebrities of the 1930s: A 20 DVD Collection (2008)

Quality Information Publishers (DVD, length unknown)

Viewers who love old movies or those who want to see some of the best early movies and their celebrity stars for the first time will enjoy this collection. Some critics feel that performances by many of the stars in the 1930s were the best ever filmed, easily surpassing the work of today's movie celebrities. This collection features the work of Shirley Temple, Béla Lugosi, David Niven, John Payne, Bette Davis, Carole Lombard, and Ginger Rogers, among others.

Playing Unfair: The Media Image of the Female Athlete

Media Education Foundation (DVD, 30 minutes)

Are appearance and sexuality emphasized over athletic excellence in our view of female athletes, some of whom are celebrities? This video explores this question as it looks at how the images created by media impact our understanding of gender and our attitudes toward sports. Sexism, homophobia, and more may be the result of the stories and images we receive from the media. The video suggests that skill and strength should be emphasized when it comes to female athletes.

Prince William and Prince Harry: Prisoners of Celebrity (2005)

Tango Entertainment (DVD, 50 minutes)

Being a member of the British Royal Family automatically makes one a celebrity. Prince William and Prince Harry, sons of Charles and Diana, have been in the celebrity spotlight almost since they were born. This documentary video examines both the positive and negative aspects of having celebrity parents as well as the princes' own search for a meaningful life in a media-saturated, celebrity-mad world.

The Ultimate Vintage Movie Stars Collection: 70 Films Featuring Hollywood's Greatest Actors and Actresses (2008)

Quality Information Publishers (DVD, length unknown)

This collection features films from the early- to mid-20th century. Silent film stars such as Buster Keaton and Stan Laurel are presented as well as the more contemporary John Wayne and Jack Nicholson. From drama to comedy to horror, this collection includes *D.O.A., The Last Time I Saw Paris, Cyrano de Bergerac,* and *Phantom of the Opera.* Superb acting and timeless themes can be found in every featured film.

20th Century with Mike Wallace: Celebrities, Scandal and the Press (no date)

A&E Home Video (VHS, time unknown)

The modern public has almost always been interested in the lives of the rich and famous. Journalism has been more than willing, down through the years, to follow celebrities, particularly when a scandal is involved or when a celebrity's private life is somehow exposed. This video takes a look at how the media handle these stories. Specific cases are examined with a view toward understanding not only how a celebrity-driven story develops but also how following it changes the nature of news.

Video Games

Celebrity Sports Showdown (2008)

Platform: Nintendo Wii

This video game allows people of all ages to compete in a dozen sports events. Marketed as the ultimate party game, you play as your favorite celebrity. Players may select their personas from a list of celebrities that includes Fergie, Nelly Furtado, Mia Hamm, Reggie Bush, and Sugar Ray Leonard, among others. The goal is to become the ultimate celebrity athlete. Games include beach volleyball, badminton, dodgeball, archery, wild water canoeing, and others.

Gotcha: Celebrity Secrets (2010)

Platform: Windows Vista, XP

This game is designed for one player. The player takes on the persona of a celebrity blogger who is desperate to leave a dead-end job for the exciting world of celebrity gossip. By tracking celebrities' activities, you uncover some startling secrets, get tips from anonymous sources, and solve puzzles. A skillful player just might become a famous Hollywood blogger!

MTV's Celebrity Deathmatch **(2003)**

Platform: Windows 98, 2000, XP

Nintendo Wii, PlayStation 2 and 3, XBox

This simple video roughly approximates the animated *MTV Celebrity Deathmatch* program. It gives a player the chance to test a favorite (or least favorite) celebrity's strength in the wrestling ring. Busta Rhymes, Carmen Electra, and Marilyn Manson are some of the featured celebrities. Ringside announcers provide a play-by-play description of the action as well as commentary before and after the match.

Paparazzi! Tales of Tinseltown (1995)

Platform: Windows 95

The object of this video game is to take revealing, candid pictures of two dozen celebrities in Tinseltown. Photos can be sold to various publications, some sleazy tabloids and other well-respected magazines. A 24-hour period is allowed for each play and during that time, a player can go to two different places in an attempt to get the needed photos. There are fewer than 14 periods allowed, so a player must maximize his/her photo opportunities during each 24-hour period. But here's the challenge: not just any photo will do; a player must shoot the "right" photo.

Audio

BVM Quantum Subliminal CD Fame and Celebrity: Become Famous and Be a Celebrity (no date)

Label: Brainwave Mind Voyages

Format: Audio CD

This product is something of an enigma. It is a collection of sounds that, the producers claim, can program your subconscious mind to attract fame and become a celebrity. You can tune your brainwaves to specific frequencies, they say, and thus enable your mind to receive powerful subliminal messages. Some audio tracks feature ocean sounds, and one track is completely silent with no sound at all. While this "subliminal neurotechnology" may be relaxing, there is little evidence that it can help you become a celebrity. The CD may have entertainment value, but its scientific value is questionable.

Celebrities That Helped Shape (2006)

Label: Jerden

Format: Audio CD

Celebrities often serve as role models for some members of the general public. In this and other ways, celebrities often shape our attitudes, beliefs, even our lifestyles. This CD is a collection of speeches, interviews, press conferences, or conversations with celebrities about various aspects of their lives. Elvis Presley holds a 1957 press conference, Mohammed Ali discusses his career as a boxer, Joe DiMaggio remembers his childhood and his heroes, and The Beatles appear at a 1966 press conference. Other celebrities also contribute to this collection whose purpose, it seems, is to provide some insight into the lives of the featured celebrities as well as inspire and motivate others to live productive lives.

NBC Celebrity Christmas (Special Edition) (2001)

Label: NBC

Format: Audio CD

This disk is a collection of Christmas music as performed on an NBC television network holiday special. Most of the performers were, at the time, part of the NBC family of prime time programming. They include Donny and Marie Osmond (from *the Donny and Marie* show), Sean Hayes (from *Will and Grace*), Martin Sheen and Stockard Channing (from *The West Wing*), Alex Kingston (from *ER*), Jane Leeves (from *Frasier*), and Jay Leno (from *The Tonight Show*), among others. The music ranges from the traditional (*Winter Wonderland*) to the sacred (*O Holy Night*). The music is lively. The performances are interesting, good news given the fact that the performers are actors and not professional singers.

Nebraska Celebrities Sing for Sight (2006)

Label: JMR Productions

Format: Audio CD

This CD presents music by celebrities from (or with a connection to) the state of Nebraska. It was produced to raise money to help blind children have a better life. All proceeds from the sale of the CD are donated to the Nebraska Foundation for Visually Impaired Children. Unless you are from Nebraska, or perhaps a nearby state, you will not likely recognize the celebrity performers on this disc: John Beasley, Cory Sanchez, Dick Boyd, State Senator David Landis, among others. Still, the collection has a noble purpose.

Golden Throats: The Great Celebrity Sing Off (1988)

Label: Rhino

Format: Audio CD

Can you imagine *Star Trek*'s Mr. Spock (Leonard Nimoy) singing *Proud Mary*? How about Andy Griffith singing *House of the Rising Sun*? These and other interesting performances appear on this music collection. Some listeners said the celebrities are terrible singers; others said the performances are surprisingly good and enjoyable. At the very least, this disc is good for a laugh. It apparently sold quite well because other collections have been produced, among which are *Golden Throats 2: More Celebrity Rock Oddities* (1991) and *Golden Throats 4: Celebrities Butcher the Beatles* (1997).

Voices of Our Time: Five Decades of Studs Terkel Interviews (2005)

Label: Highbridge Audio

Format: Audio CD

Chicago radio journalist and author Studs Terkel was the premier interviewer of his time. During his career (ca. 1940–1998) he interviewed or conversed with many celebrity authors, actors, and musicians. This collection is drawn from his work and reengineered for modern quality listening. You'll find Terkel talking with Gore Vidal, Woody Allen, Pete Seeger, Dorothy Parker, and Mel Brooks, among others. Just hearing famous voices speak across time makes this collection an important part of celebrity history.

Useful Internet Sites

African American Web Connection

www.aawc.com

This site provides access to profiles of prominent African Americans. Profiles range from better-known celebrities such as poet Maya Angelou and guitarist BB King to lesser-known politicians such as Congresswoman Corrine Brown. Still, the site is fairly comprehensive. A user can also access a variety of information about African Americans including black authors, churches, and publications.

Biography.com

www.biography.com

A variety of information can be found on this site. Biographical information about celebrities (and some not-so-famous people) is available, of course. But the site also delivers news and video features as well as games and information on celebrity birthdays. By accessing the archives, a user can find videos of famous athletes, actors/actresses, and business figures. In other words, there is more to this Web site than just biography.

Buzzle.com

www.buzzle.com

This site specializes in biographies and autobiographies. The bios are short and can be found on artists, authors, actors, scientists, presidents, and other famous people. It is interesting that the site mixes biographies and autobiographies. For example, a user can read a biography of composer Antonio Vivaldi (1648–1741) and then read the autobiography of tennis celebrity Serena Williams. The site also provides news and feature articles on current and past celebrities.

Blog Top Sites

www.blogtopsites.com

This is a directory designed to provide a user with the best blogs available. One can choose from more than 40 categories, ranging from academics to gambling. One of the categories, of course, is celebrity blogs, usually blogs *about* celebrities, not *by* celebrities. The site ranks the number of unique visits each blog receives in a month. Blog owners can register their site with this Web site and gain the attention of a broader audience. In terms of celebrity blogs, a user could, for example, access Celebrity Gossip (http://celebrity.ohfree. net), a site claiming to update information every five minutes with the latest celebrity news, scandals, rumors, and the like worldwide.

Docstoc

www.docstoc.com

This unusual Web site enables a user to find (and share) professional documents. It boasts access to millions of public documents.

A user can select a document category such as business, technology, education, real estate, and so on. Users interested in documents relating to celebrities should find the search box located on the site and type in *celebrities*. The search will result in a list of documents about celebrities. These range from news releases to articles about the paparazzi and celebrity tattoos, among others. Power-Point presentations can occasionally be found on some topics. Most information is free, but access and downloading of some documents may require a payment of some sort.

Internet Movie Database

www.imdb.com

A user might think this site has a single purpose: to provide information about all things related to movies. The site does indeed emphasize movies, celebrity actors and actresses, the latest Hollywood news, how films are doing at the box office, what films will soon be released, and so on, but it also provides a wealth of information about popular television programs. A user can access clips from TV shows as well as movie trailers. It even provides a listing of daily television programs on the major TV networks. It recaps the previous night's television fare and asks a daily poll question.

Laughing Star

www.laughingstar.com

Need a photo of a celebrity? This site is a free celebrity photo database. A user can click on the first letter of a celebrity's last name or select a name from a list of celebrities. Clicking on a name will result in a page showing several thumbnail photos, each of which can be enlarged for a better view. Both male and female celebrities are featured. Celebrities range from Paula Abdul to Renée Zellweger.

LibrarySpot

www.libraryspot.com

This Web site is a free virtual library resource center available to everyone. Its purpose is to break through the overload of information on the Web and focus on the best library and reference sites, particularly those of interest to educators, students, families, and businesses. The sites featured are carefully selected and reviewed by an editorial team. Quality, content, and utility are key considerations. Information is available on a multitude of topics, of course. In terms of celebrities, a user can access information on artists, athletes, musicians, poets, scientists, and so on.

NNDB

www.nndb.com

This site contains more than 35,000 profiles that can be accessed by last name. Although this site presents itself as "tracking the entire world," it does not list everyone. If an individual is the object of permanent public interest, has held certain public offices, or is listed in certain encyclopedias, for example, then the individual is likely profiled. However, just appearing in a film, or being a part of a musical group, or authoring a book, or being married to a celebrity does not usually qualify one for admission to this select group of profiles. Thus, the site appears to have a quite specific, if rather narrow, definition of celebrity (or fame). Still, this site is extremely interesting. It deals with issues of nationality and ethnicity as well as further refining the qualities required for inclusion in its database.

Who's Alive and Who's Dead

www.whosaliveandwhosdead.com

One does not need to be morbidly curious to browse this Web site. Watching movies or hearing someone talk about a celebrity can often result in this question: Is (name) still alive? This is a natural question. This Web site enables a user to find out who is alive and who is dead. One can browse by category (actors and actresses, musical performers, political figures, or athletes and sports figures) or click on the first letter of a celebrity's last name. Birth (and death) dates are given for each celebrity as well as the celebrity's age—current age if alive, or age at death. The site also features special categories such as Living Oscar Winners, Dead Playboy Playmates, and Mouseketeers, Alive and Dead.

Glossary

blog A short form of the word *Weblog*, this term refers to an individual's personal journal or diary, posted online and available for reading and comment by others.

celebration As first used in early English literature, this word referred to a performance or solemn ceremony. In modern times, the word has come to be used for almost any sort of festive gathering.

celebrity A term freely applied by the general public to individuals who are famous or well known. As a concept, however, the term is more complex than usually assumed. A celebrity must meet a number of characteristics beyond being famous or well known. In the 21st century, one of the most important characteristics is regular media exposure; therefore celebrity is fame modernized.

celebrity magazines A term referring to the weekly (and a few monthly) magazines publishing photos and information *about* celebrities. These publications are not sponsored by celebrities but celebrities are the main focus of their content.

celebrity television programs These are 30-minute syndicated television shows *about* celebrities. They often appear in the time period immediately preceding network prime time programming and feature gossip, video, and news about celebrities, most often those in entertainment.

classical civilizations A term used by some historians to denote the contributions made by the early Egyptian, Greek, and Roman cultures. Many of the practices developed by these cultures, such as irrigation techniques and architectural style, are still important and useful in modern life. There is no evidence, however, that any of these accomplishments made the individuals involved celebrities in their time.

collective unconscious First described by psychiatrist Carl Jung, this term refers to a part of the mind containing memories and impulses of which one is not aware. The images and emotions resulting from these memories and impulses are often embodied in one's interest in or attraction to a celebrity or a celebrity's lifestyle.

cultural icon A symbol, an idea, or a concept that is important to people or a culture. An individual may become a cultural icon if the person's work and life illustrate a valued idea or concept. For example, Mother Teresa, a Catholic nun who worked with the poor, the sick, and the dying, could be said to be a cultural icon because of her religious faith and self-sacrifice in the service of others.

demographics A term applied to data relating to human characteristics such as age, gender, income, education, and the like.

famous A word applied to individuals who are prominent and broadly known for their achievements. The word is commonly used by the public as a synonym for *celebrity* and *well known*, although it has a slightly different meaning.

15 minutes of fame A paraphrase of Andy Warhol's well-known statement about how a pervasive and often temperamental media and our desire for recognition will—at some future point—result in everyone in the world being famous for 15 minutes.

global village A term coined by communication scholar Marshall McLuhan that serves as a metaphor or description of the world we live in, one where new technologies link people and events in real time, making us all essentially members of the same human community.

hieroglyphics A term describing early writing in the Egyptian culture (ca. 3100 BCE–200 BCE). Used primarily by priests and religious leaders, the writing consisted not of letters but of pictures and symbols.

media As used in the 21st century, this term means the multitude of ways individuals, groups, organizations, and institutions communicate—in print or electronically—over long distances with others. Media include radio, television, newspapers, magazines, music and sound recordings, film, and the Internet.

new media A term commonly used to describe electronic communication in the 21st century, including computers, iPhones or other cellular devices, the Internet, and so on.

papyrus A plant available in the Nile valley during the Egyptian culture (ca. 3100 BCE–200 BCE). When cut into strips, dried, and pressed together, it became a surface on which one could write.

parchment Popular during the early civilizations, it is the skin of an animal—usually a sheep or a goat—dried and stretched to make a writing surface.

pictograms A word describing pictures made on cave walls by prehistoric peoples. Also, pictures engraved on clay tablets, primarily in Mesopotamia and also in the Egyptian culture (ca. 3100 BCE–200 BCE).

Ponzi scheme An illegal financial-investment plan named for Charles Ponzi, thought to be the inventor. Often called a pyramid-style scam, it involves promising investors large profits, but the promoter keeps their money instead of investing it and pays profits from money collected from new investors. The scam usually collapses when the money from new investors is insufficient to pay promised profits. Almost a dozen businessmen have achieved a sort of criminal celebrity by using this scam to defraud investors.

printing press Invented by Johannes Gutenberg in 1453 from an old wine press, this device used moveable metal type to make impressions on paper. The invention led to a better informed, more literate public and may have been an important factor in some individuals becoming well known.

pseudo-human event A term used by the historian Daniel Boorstin to describe a type of empty celebrity whereby one is famous merely for being well known and not for any accomplishments connected to reality.

social media A term referring to several Web sites where one can post personal information, photos, or videos, and interact with others. Popular sites include Facebook, MySpace, and LinkedIn.

star A term often applied to celebrities in the entertainment field, but rarely applied to celebrities in other fields. For example, a celebrity appearing in a movie is often called a star; however, celebrities in politics, medicine, science, and other fields are not normally considered stars, although they may have significant accomplishments.

taxonomy A word used by scientists and others to describe a classification system whereby objects, animals, plants, even people, are organized and placed into meaningful categories.

technological determinism A theory developed by communication scholar Marshall McLuhan stating that media technology determines how people think, feel, and act. If true, it explains how celebrity is, in large part, a function of media exposure.

The Enlightenment This is the name usually given the historical culture period (ca. 1650 CE–1850 CE) during which civilization made significant advances in science, art, music, and philosophy. There were many famous and well-known people in this era, but communication during the time was oral, written, or printed and was not widespread enough to qualify the famous or well known as celebrities.

twitter A small-scale communication service available to Internet users and usually accessible by cell phone enabling an individual to post a message of 140 characters or fewer and have the message sent to or read by one's "followers."

Index

About the Author

Larry Z. Leslie, Ph.D., is Associate Professor Emeritus in the School of Mass Communications at the University of South Florida, Tampa, where he still teaches an occasional course. He holds a bachelor's degree in English from Eastern Illinois University (1966), a master's in English from Austin Peay State University (1972), and a Ph.D. in Communications from the University of Tennessee (1986). He has been a high school teacher in Illinois, a community college teacher in Kentucky and South Carolina, and a disc jockey, news reporter, and program director at radio stations in Illinois and Tennessee. His areas of expertise include media ethics, communication research methods, public opinion, and postmodern culture.

The recipient of numerous teaching awards, he has published a dozen journal articles and has written two books, *Mass Communication Ethics: Decision Making in Postmodern Culture* (Second edition, 2004, Pearson/Allyn & Bacon) and *Communication Research Methods in Postmodern Culture: A Revisionist Approach* (2010, Pearson).